D0948117

Poland

WORLD BIBLIOGRAPHICAL SERIES

General Editors:
Robert G. Neville (Executive Editor)
John J. Horton

Robert A. Myers   Ian Wallace
Hans H. Wellisch   Ralph Lee Woodward, Jr.

John J. Horton is Deputy Librarian of the University of Bradford and currently Chairman of its Academic Board of Studies in Social Sciences. He has maintained a longstanding interest in the discipline of area studies and its associated bibliographical problems, with special reference to European Studies. In particular he has published in the field of Icelandic and of Yugoslav studies, including the two relevant volumes in the World Bibliographical Series.

Robert A. Myers is Associate Professor of Anthropology in the Division of Social Sciences and Director of Study Abroad Programs at Alfred University, Alfred, New York. He has studied post-colonial island nations of the Caribbean and has spent two years in Nigeria on a Fulbright Lectureship. His interests include international public health, historical anthropology and developing societies. In addition to *Amerindians of the Lesser Antilles: a bibliography* (1981), *A Resource Guide to Dominica, 1493-1986* (1987) and numerous articles, he has compiled the World Bibliographical Series volumes on *Dominica* (1987), *Nigeria* (1989) and *Ghana* (1991).

Ian Wallace is Professor of German at the University of Bath. A graduate of Oxford in French and German, he also studied in Tübingen, Heidelberg and Lausanne before taking teaching posts at universities in the USA, Scotland and England. He specializes in contemporary German affairs, especially literature and culture, on which he has published numerous articles and books. In 1979 he founded the journal *GDR Monitor*, which he continues to edit under its new title *German Monitor*.

Hans H. Wellisch is Professor emeritus at the College of Library and Information Services, University of Maryland. He was President of the American Society of Indexers and was a member of the International Federation for Documentation. He is the author of numerous articles and several books on indexing and abstracting, and has published *The Conversion of Scripts, Indexing and Abstracting: an International Bibliography* and *Indexing from A to Z*. He also contributes frequently to *Journal of the American Society for Information Science, The Indexer* and other professional journals.

Ralph Lee Woodward, Jr. is Director of Graduate Studies at Tulane University, New Orleans, where he has been Professor of History since 1970. He is the author of *Central America, a Nation Divided*, 2nd ed. (1985), as well as several monographs and more than sixty scholarly articles on modern Latin America. He has also compiled volumes in the World Bibliographical Series on *Belize* (1980), *Nicaragua* (1983), and *El Salvador* (1988). Dr. Woodward edited the Central American section of the *Research Guide to Central America and the Caribbean* (1985) and is currently editor of the Central American history section of the *Handbook of Latin American Studies*.

VOLUME 32

Poland

Revised Edition

George Sanford and Adriana Gozdecka-Sanford

Compilers

CLIO PRESS

OXFORD, ENGLAND · SANTA BARBARA, CALIFORNIA
DENVER, COLORADO

British Library Cataloguing in Publication Data

Poland. – (World bibliographical series; v.32)
I. Sanford, George   II. Gozdecka-Sanford, Adriana
III. Series
016.9438

ISBN 1–85109–180–7

Clio Press Ltd.,
55 St. Thomas' Street,
Oxford OX1 1JG, England.

ABC-CLIO,
130 Cremona Drive,
Santa Barbara,
CA 93116, USA.

Designed by Bernard Crossland.
Typeset by Columns Design and Production Services Ltd, Reading, England.
Printed and bound in Great Britain by
Bookcraft (Bath) Ltd., Midsomer Norton

THE WORLD BIBLIOGRAPHICAL SERIES

This series, which is principally designed for the English speaker, will eventually cover every country (and many of the world's principal regions), each in a separate volume comprising annotated entries on works dealing with its history, geography, economy and politics; and with its people, their culture, customs, religion and social organization. Attention will also be paid to current living conditions – housing, education, newspapers, clothing, etc.– that are all too often ignored in standard bibliographies; and to those particular aspects relevant to individual countries. Each volume seeks to achieve, by use of careful selectivity and critical assessment of the literature, an expression of the country and an appreciation of its nature and national aspirations, to guide the reader towards an understanding of its importance. The keynote of the series is to provide, in a uniform format, an interpretation of each country that will express its culture, its place in the world, and the qualities and background that make it unique. The views expressed in individual volumes, however, are not necessarily those of the publisher.

VOLUMES IN THE SERIES

1 *Yugoslavia*, John J. Horton
2 *Lebanon*, C. H. Bleaney
3 *Lesotho*, Shelagh M. Willet and David Ambrose
4 *Rhodesia/Zimbabwe*, Oliver B. Pollack and Karen Pollack
5 *Saudi Arabia*, Frank A. Clements
6 *USSR*, Anthony Thompson
7 *South Africa*, Reuben Musiker
8 *Malawi*, Robert B. Boeder
9 *Guatemala*, Woodman B. Franklin
10 *Pakistan*, David Taylor
11 *Uganda*, Robert L. Collison
12 *Malaysia*, Ian Brown and Rajeswary Ampalavanar
13 *France*, Frances Chambers
14 *Panama*, Eleanor DeSelms Langstaff
15 *Hungary*, Thomas Kabdebo
16 *USA*, Sheila R. Herstein and Naomi Robbins
17 *Greece*, Richard Clogg and Mary Jo Clogg
18 *New Zealand*, R. F. Grover
19 *Algeria*, Richard I. Lawless
20 *Sri Lanka*, Vijaya Samaraweera
21 *Belize*, Ralph Lee Woodward, Jr.
23 *Luxembourg*, Carlo Hury and Jul Christophory
24 *Swaziland*, Balam Nyeko

25 *Kenya*, Robert L. Collison
26 *India*, Brijen K. Gupta and Datta S. Kharbas
27 *Turkey*, Merel Güçlü
28 *Cyprus*, P. M. Kitromilides and M. L. Evriviades
29 *Oman*, Frank A. Clements
31 *Finland*, J. E. O. Screen
32 *Poland*, Rev. Ed. George Sanford and Adriana Gozdecka-Sanford
33 *Tunisia*, Allan M. Findlay, Anne M. Findlay and Richard I. Lawless
34 *Scotland*, Eric G. Grant
35 *China*, Peter Cheng
36 *Qatar*, P. T. H. Unwin
37 *Iceland*, John J. Horton
38 *Nepal*, John Whelpton
39 *Haiti*, Frances Chambers
40 *Sudan*, M. W. Daly
41 *Vatican City State*, Michael J. Walsh
42 *Iraq*, A. J. Abdulrahman
43 *United Arab Emirates*, Frank A. Clements
44 *Nicaragua*, Ralph Lee Woodward, Jr.
45 *Jamaica*, K. E. Ingram
46 *Australia*, I. Kepars
47 *Morocco*, Anne M. Findlay, Allan M. Findlay and Richard I. Lawless

48 *Mexico*, Naomi Robbins
49 *Bahrain*, P. T. H. Unwin
50 *The Yemens*, G. Rex Smith
51 *Zambia*, Anne M. Bliss and J. A. Rigg
52 *Puerto Rico*, Elena E. Cevallos
53 *Namibia*, Stanley Schoeman and Elna Schoeman
54 *Tanzania*, Colin Darch
55 *Jordan*, Ian J. Seccombe
56 *Kuwait*, Frank A. Clements
57 *Brazil*, Solena V. Bryant
58 *Israel*, Esther M. Snyder (preliminary compilation E. Kreiner)
59 *Romania*, Andrea Deletant and Dennis Deletant
60 *Spain*, Graham J. Shields
61 *Atlantic Ocean*, H. G. R. King
62 *Canada*, Ernest Ingles
63 *Cameroon*, Mark W. DeLancey and Peter J. Schraeder
64 *Malta*, John Richard Thackrah
65 *Thailand*, Michael Watts
66 *Austria*, Denys Salt with the assistance of Arthur Farrand Radley
67 *Norway*, Leland B. Sather
68 *Czechoslovakia*, David Short
69 *Irish Republic*, Michael Owen Shannon
70 *Pacific Basin and Oceania*, Gerald W. Fry and Rufino Mauricio
71 *Portugal*, P. T. H. Unwin
72 *West Germany*, Donald S. Detwiler and Ilse E. Detwiler
73 *Syria*, Ian J. Seccombe
74 *Trinidad and Tobago*, Frances Chambers
76 *Barbados*, Robert B. Potter and Graham M. S. Dann
77 *East Germany*, Ian Wallace
78 *Mozambique*, Colin Darch
79 *Libya*, Richard I. Lawless
80 *Sweden*, Leland B. Sather and Alan Swanson
81 *Iran*, Reza Navabpour
82 *Dominica*, Robert A. Myers
83 *Denmark*, Kenneth E. Miller
84 *Paraguay*, R. Andrew Nickson
85 *Indian Ocean*, Julia J. Gotthold with the assistance of Donald W. Gotthold
86 *Egypt*, Ragai, N. Makar
87 *Gibraltar*, Graham J. Shields
88 *The Netherlands*, Peter King and Michael Wintle
89 *Bolivia*, Gertrude M. Yeager
90 *Papua New Guinea*, Fraiser McConnell
91 *The Gambia*, David P. Gamble
92 *Somalia*, Mark W. DeLancey, Sheila L. Elliott, December Green, Kenneth J. Menkhaus, Mohammad Haji Moqtar, Peter J. Schraeder
93 *Brunei*, Sylvia C. Engelen Krausse, Gerald H. Krausse
94 *Albania*, William B. Bland
95 *Singapore*, Stella R. Quah, Jon S. T. Quah
96 *Guyana*, Frances Chambers
97 *Chile*, Harold Blakemore
98 *El Salvador*, Ralph Lee Woodward, Jr.
99 *The Arctic*, H.G.R. King
100 *Nigeria*, Robert A. Myers
101 *Ecuador*, David Corkhill
102 *Uruguay*, Henry Finch with the assistance of Alicia Casas de Barrán
103 *Japan*, Frank Joseph Shulman
104 *Belgium*, R.C. Riley
105 *Macau*, Richard Louis Edmonds
106 *Philippines*, Jim Richardson
107 *Bulgaria*, Richard J. Crampton
108 *The Bahamas*, Paul G. Boultbee
109 *Peru*, John Robert Fisher
110 *Venezuela*, D. A. G. Waddell
111 *Dominican Republic*, Kai Schoenhals
112 *Colombia*, Robert H. Davis
113 *Taiwan*, Wei-chin Lee
114 *Switzerland*, Heinz K. Meier and Regula A. Meier
115 *Hong Kong*, Ian Scott
116 *Bhutan*, Ramesh C. Dogra
117 *Suriname*, Rosemarijn Hoefte
118 *Djibouti*, Peter J. Schraeder
119 *Grenada*, Kai Schoenhals
120 *Monaco*, Grace L. Hudson
121 *Guinea-Bissau*, Rosemary Galli
122 *Wales*, Gwilym Huws and D. Hywel E. Roberts
123 *Cape Verde*, Caroline S. Shaw
124 *Ghana*, Robert A. Myers
125 *Greenland*, Kenneth E. Miller

126 *Costa Rica*, Charles L. Stansifer
127 *Siberia*, David N. Collins
128 *Tibet*, John Pinfold
129 *Northern Ireland*, Michael Owen Shannon
130 *Argentina*, Alan Biggins
132 *Burma*, Patricia M. Herbert
133 *Laos*, Helen Cordell
134 *Montserrat*, Riva Berleant-Schiller
135 *Afghanistan*, Schuyler Jones
136 *Equatorial Guinea*, Randall Fegley
137 *Turks and Caicos Islands*, Paul G. Boultbee
138 *Virgin Islands*, Verna Penn Moll
139 *Honduras*, Pamela F. Howard-Reguindin
140 *Mauritius*, Pramila Ramgulam Bennett

141 *Mauritania*, Simonetta Calderini, Delia Cortese, James L. A. Webb, Jr.
142 *Timor*, Ian Rowland
143 *St. Vincent and the Grenadines*, Robert B. Potter
144 *Texas*, James Marten
145 *Burundi*, Morna Daniels
146 *Hawai'i*, Nancy J. Morris, Love Dean
147 *Vietnam*, David Marr, Kristine Alilunas-Rodgers
148 *Sierra Leone*, Margaret Binns, J. Anthony Binns
149 *Gabon*, David Gardinier
150 *Botswana*, John A. Wiseman
151 *Angola*, Richard Black

To Alexa

Contents

INTRODUCTION xv

NOTE ON TRANSLITERATION xxi

LIST OF ABBREVIATIONS xxiii

THE COUNTRY AND ITS PEOPLE 1

GEOGRAPHY 5
    General   5
    Historical and political geography   6
    Economic geography   8
    Maps and cartography   8

TOURISM AND TRAVEL 10
    General guidebooks and travellers' accounts   10
    City guides   12
        Częstochowa   12
        Gdańsk   12
        Kórnik   13
        Kraków   13
        Poznań   14
        Szczecin   14
        Warsaw   14
        Wrocław   15

FLORA AND FAUNA 16

PREHISTORY AND ARCHAEOLOGY 18

HISTORY (pre-1980) 20
    Poland within Eastern Europe   20
    General histories of Poland   22
    Medieval and early modern history (pre-1795)   24
    Modern history (1795-1918)   27
    Interwar history   30

Contents

Second World War 33
    General 33
    German administration 34
    Jews 37
    Polish Underground, Government-in-Exile and
        forces in the West 43
    Soviet aspects 46
    Communist Poland (pre-1980) 48
    Regional history 50

ETHNIC MINORITIES 51
    Germans 51
    Gypsies 51
    Jews 52
    Ukrainians 56

POLONIA (POLES ABROAD) 57
    General 57
    Canada 58
    United States 59
    Australia 63
    Great Britain 63
    New Zealand 65
    USSR 65

LANGUAGE 66
    Texts 66
    Dictionaries 67

RELIGION 70
    Church history 70
    Roman Catholicism 70
    Pope John Paul II 74
    Maximilian (Rajmund) Kolbe 76
    Jerzy Popiełuszko 76
    National Catholic Church 77
    Protestant churches 77
    Orthodox and Greek Catholic churches 78

SOCIETY 79
    Social groups and conditions 79
    Social and ethical issues 83

SOCIAL SERVICES, HEALTH AND WELFARE 84

POLITICS 86

LAW, INSTITUTIONS AND ADMINISTRATION 101

Contents

SOLIDARITY AND POLAND IN THE 1980s 105

POST-COMMUNIST POLAND (1989-) 120

FOREIGN RELATIONS 125
  General 125
  Polish-British 129
  Polish-Czechoslovak 131
  Polish-French 131
  Polish-German 132
  Polish-Haitian 133
  Polish-Indian 133
  Polish-Lithuanian 134
  Polish-Pakistani 135
  Polish-Russian and Soviet 135
  Polish-Swedish 138
  Polish-Ukrainian 138
  Polish-United States 139

ECONOMY AND ECONOMIC HISTORY 141

FINANCE, BANKING AND STATISTICS 148

TRADE 151

INDUSTRY 153

AGRICULTURE, FORESTRY AND FISHING 155

TRANSPORT 158

EMPLOYMENT AND LABOUR 159

ENVIRONMENT 161

EDUCATION, UNIVERSITIES AND LEARNING 162

LITERATURE 167
  Literary history and criticism 167
  Individual writers 170
  English translations 171

THE ARTS 179
  History of art 179
  Architecture 181

PERFORMING ARTS 184
  Music 184
  Theatre 187
  Cinema 188
  Ballet 189

Contents

FOLKLORE, CUISINE, FOLK-ART AND CUSTOMS 190
    Folklore and folk-art   190
    Cuisine   191
    Genealogy and honours   192
    Customs   193
    Philately   193

SPORT 194

LIBRARIES, ARCHIVES AND MUSEUMS 195

BOOKS AND BOOK TRADE 197

NEWSPAPERS AND JOURNALS 199

PROFESSIONAL PERIODICALS 203

ENCYCLOPAEDIAS AND DIRECTORIES 208

BIBLIOGRAPHIES 211

INDEX OF AUTHORS, TITLES AND SUBJECTS 217

MAP OF POLAND 251

Introduction

The Poles claim that few peoples have been more moulded by their geography and their history than they have. Their state is located in the centre of Europe with open western and eastern frontiers with their German and Russian neighbours on the Great European Plain. The Carpathian hills on their southern frontier while offering protection have, however, also prevented them from forming a larger West Slav super-state with the Czechs and Slovaks which might have provided a stronger and more secure counterpoise to the former. Poles attribute their resilient national characteristics, and the almost spiritual-messianistic quality of their nationalism, which has assured their national survival as well as a whole series of other responses, including Roman Catholicism, to such basic factors. Yet the old stereotype, although still very strong, has been altered fundamentally by postwar developments. Poland has been transformed from a largely rural-agricultural backward society into one that is urban-industrial, highly educated and socially stratified and mobile. With a population of 38 million it now has all the potential for advanced modernity and much that is original, drawn from its unique past, to offer.

In the early 1980s Poland challenged communist rule, with the emergence of free trade unions and Solidarity. The intervention of the military and the repression of martial law in 1982-83 extended the life of the communist *regime*; but the ruling elites failed to use this breathing space to resolve the country's acute political, social and economic problems. They were, therefore, in a much weakened and very divided state by the time Gorbachevism permitted genuine communist reform and Round Table negotiations designed to incorporate the opposition, led by Wałęsa's Civic Committee, within a revised and mixed system. The process of 'Negotiated Revolution' thus led to the peaceful, gradual and wholly constitutional abdication of the communist elites led by General Wojciech Jaruzelski and Interior Minister Czesław Kiszczak at the end of the decade.

Introduction

Poland is now building a democratic system within the framework of its old constitutional and political values. Some of the consequences in terms of a fragmented multi-party system, disputes concerning the parliamentary or presidential forms of government, a peculiar balance between individualist and authoritarian values in its political culture and social impatience with the costs of modernization, especially marketization, will no doubt, strike outsiders as odd, even troubling; but the responses, while specifically related to the gravity of current problems, are also deeply rooted in folk traditions and memories of past experiences.

Polish society was deprived of its state during the nineteenth century partitions. It underwent processes of massive social alienation during the Nazi occupation of the Second World War and, at least, during the Stalinist period when the communists attempted to build a totalitarian system. Although this enterprise was largely abandoned, and social conditions and the degree of political authoritarianism eased after 'October' 1956, the feeling of psychological stress and other types of abnormality continued until the 1989 revolution. On the other hand one should remember that the interwar period of national independence also produced a shift, but in the opposite direction, from an extreme of multi-party democracy with short-lived coalition governments (1919-26) to another of authoritarian rule by Piłsudski and his successors.

Poland's traditions, reflecting its diverse historical experience, have been both very mixed and very intense. One should, therefore mention the historical memories of Poland's Great Power status in late medieval and early modern times linked with the degeneration of Gentry Democracy and the Elective Monarchy of the latter post-1572 Commonwealth period. Such traditions also naturally assume new and evolving forms which makes it difficult to assess the balance between continuity and change and their effect on contemporary behaviour. At one extreme, commentators, both domestic and external, argue that the present can almost wholly be explained in terms of Poland's historical experience. They point not only to the above-mentioned factors but also to the other potent symbols of Poland as the defender of Western civilization against the Turkish, Mongol, Tartar or Bolshevik hordes. The Romantic school, since the Napoleonic Legions and insurrections of 1830 and 1863, went further in viewing Poland as a suffering Christ amongst nations constantly holding the torch both for its liberty and independence and for that of others. Its protagonists in literature were Mickiewicz, Słowacki and Krasiński, Chopin in music, and politicians who, like Piłsudksi, thought that Poland could only survive by playing an important role in international politics. The other, more realist, point of view argued that the survival of the nation and its elites necessitated temporary accommodation with dominant powers in order to ensure the country's fullest development. The heroes in this tradition are Count Czartoryski and Marquis Wielopolski who attempted to gain autonomy for Poland under Russian rule, the 'Organic Work' socioeconomic development, school in the late nineteenth century and Roman Dmowski, who despite his ideological prejudices against the Left coldly saw the need for a Russian alliance against German imperialism. Postwar, Gomułka, Gierek and Jaruzelski redefined the methods and structures of communist rule in Poland in a way that ensured Polish distinctiveness, and eventually social autonomy, within the parameters of Soviet overlordship. Such an emphasis on history and traditions largely explains the importance of symbolism in Polish life, as for example in Pope John Paul's pilgrimages to his homeland. It may be argued, however, that while some underlying structural regularities continue to recur other cycles have come to an end and only survive as the husks of symbols and folk traditions.

Finally, and above all, although the Poles say that they have always been part of European civilization in cultural terms, the collapse of communism and of the USSR now enables them to work for their practical 'return to Europe' in political and economic terms of association, and eventually membership, of the EEC. The re-unification of Germany holds potential threats ranging from, at best, loose economic and cultural subordination to potentially much worse scenarios in one generation's time for Poland; but the Poles' historical dilemma of being ground between two stronger and hostile neighbours has been transformed fundamentally. Hence the importance of the re-emergence of traditional regional links with the Hungarians, Czechs and Slovaks and bilateral relationships with such neighbours as the Lithuanians and the Ukrainians which had been largely suppressed during the period of Soviet hegemony. Overall Poland's prospects for assuring its security and development within the new European framework have never been more favourable. The specifics of its domestic political and socio-economic development, will, as in the past, undoubtedly cause outsiders concern and impatience for another generation. The editors hope, however, that the material in this bibliography will act as a guide to increasing the knowledgeable and sympathetic understanding which the Poles need if they are to build constructively on their past virtues while coming to terms with the pressing challenges of the present.

The bibliography
This guide is a successor to, and, in one respect, is designed to build on the first edition compiled by Richard C. Lewański. It was

published in 1984 although the bulk of the entries did not go much beyond the beginning of the decade. The current volume has retained roughly a quarter of the works contained therein; these can be regarded either as classics or documentary sources or publications which are well-established and still of major utility in their field. The comments on their significance in the annotations have been changed in most cases.

The main aim has been to produce a guide to the burgeoning English language literature, which has been published since 1980 largely as a response to global perceptions of the significance of Polish events since then. The vast bulk of the references are to generally available books and articles although there are a few to other sources such as university and research institute papers or conference proceedings. Much of the material has been in the historical, social science and economic areas; hence the heavy representation of these fields in this volume and this also concerns Poland's foreign policy and her crucial role in the international arena. But with the moves towards Europe, democracy and the market there is already the beginnings of a trend away from 'high politics' towards coverage of more normal, everyday and sectoral aspects. The significance of Poland's vibrant, intellectual, cultural and literary life also remains of unabating interest as do the activities of Polish communities abroad (*Polonia*).

The overwhelming bulk of the items are in English. A very small number of Polish or French entries have been included either because they fill a gap or because they are significant works which have not been translated into English. The criterion for selection has been the item's direct relevance or significance for Polish affairs; given the vast and continually growing bulk of the material we have had to interpret it in a more limiting way than in some previous usage on such aspects as Joseph Conrad and Isaac Bashevis Singer or national minority publications not appearing in English, for example.

We have produced occasional references to other relevant items within some of the annotations. The index is, however, designed as the basic reference-guide and should be utilized as such.

The reader should also note that the period following the replacement of communism in 1989 was one of exceptional fluidity especially as far as Polish newspapers were concerned. That section, therefore, represents at best a provisional assessment of the most significant publications at the time of going to press. The problem, and the generalization applies across the board, of the balance between continuity and change has always been, and continues to be, a complicated matter in Poland.

The editors hope that their publication will provide a comprehensive general guide to all aspects of Poland conveying a broad brush picture for general readers as well as one which will enable them to satisfy queries or interests of a general, tourist or cultural type. Students and scholars will be able to use it as a research tool for their more specialized purposes, as the annotations have a judgemental quality and provide a useful commentary on the state of the literature as well as a guide to it. For the same reason the bibliography is designed to assist government officials, politicians, businessmen and others with an interest in Polish affairs.

Acknowledgements
The authors wish to acknowledge their gratitude to the following individuals and institutions for their invaluable assistance in the production of this bibliography; Ursula Phillips and the Library of the School of Slavonic Studies, University of London; Dr Zdzisław Jagodziński and the Polish Library, London; the staff of the Biblioteka Narodowa, Warsaw, for their courtesy and facilities and in particular for the use of a computer terminal on publications in English in Poland during the 1980s; the staff and libraries of Warsaw University, the Marie Curie-Skłodowska University in Lublin, the Adam Mickiewicz University in Poznań, the University of Bristol and the Alexander Baykov Library in the Centre for Soviet and East European Studies of the University of Birmingham.

G.S.
A.G.-S.

Note on transliteration

Some of the English forms, like Cassubia or Cuyavia, shown on the map are, in practice, rarely used. It is impossible to be entirely consistent, using either wholly Polish or Anglicized transliterations, as certain of the latter forms like Warsaw, Greater and Lesser Poland, Upper Silesia, Vistula or Pomerania have clearly gained predominance in English usage. The authors, therefore, follow this in the text but otherwise generally use the Polish form. Some cases remain unclear, and even controversial, however, such as Kraków; the Polish form raises no particular difficulty as there is no simplifying linguistic benefit in using 'Cracow' but a number of historical-traditional sentiments have created a bandwagon in favour of the latter. The reader will note that this tendency is resisted very sternly in this volume although the anglicized form has had to be used where it appears in a title!

Another difficulty raised by this vexatious problem is that some authors with Polish names, resident in Western countries, have long dropped the accents on their names while others have asked their publishers to retain them. We have tried to follow author's preferences as far as possible, even though it may occasionally cause some inconsistency. One should also note that compromise latinized forms also creep in, such as Stanislaus for Stanisław, especially in America.

List of abbreviations

GUS	Główny Urząd Statystyczny: Main Statistical Office
KOR	Komitet Obrony Robotników: Workers Defence Committee
KAW	Krajowa Agencja Wydawnicza: National Publishing Agency
KiW	Książka i Wiedza Publishing House
KPN	Konfederacja Polski Niepodległej: Confederation for an Independent Poland
MON	Ministerstwo Obrony Narodowej: Ministry of National Defence
PAN	Polska Akademia Nauk: Polish Academy of Sciences
PAP	Polska Agencja Prasowa: Polish Press Agency
PPWK	Państwowe Przedsiębiorstwo Wydawnictw Kartograficznych: State Cartographic Publishing House
PR	Polska Rzeczpospolita: Polish Republic
PRL	Polska Rzeczpospolita Ludowa: Polish People's Republic
PWE	Państwowe Wydawnictwo Ekonomiczne: State Economic Publishing House
PWM	Polskie Wydawnictwo Muzyczne: Polish Musical Publishing House
PWN	Państwowe Wydawnictwo Naukowe: State Publishing House
PWRiL	Państwowe Wydawnictwo Rolnicze i Leśne: State Agricultural and Forestry Publishing House
PZPR	Polska Zjednoczona Partia Robotnicza: Polish United Workers Party
UJ	Uniwersytet Jagielloński: Jagiellonian University, Kraków
UW	Uniwersytet Warszawski: Warsaw University
WL	Wydawnictwo Literackie: Literary Publishing House

xxiii

The Country and Its People

1 **The struggles for Poland.**
Neal Ascherson. London: Michael Joseph, 1987. 242p.
An attractively illustrated and glossy companion book to a much praised British television series. A useful introduction for the general reader to Poland's history and how it affected her mid-1980s situation. The book gives only slight coverage to the Solidarity and normalization experiences but contains clear vignettes of the Second World War and the postwar, Stalinist, Gomułka and Gierek eras. These are set against the broad background of the nineteenth century independence struggles, the interwar period and the broad themes emerging from a millenium of Polish history.

2 **We live in Poland.**
Donna Bailey, Anna Sproule. Basingstoke, England: Macmillan, 1989. 32p.
Coloured illustrations of aspects of life in Poland with very basic explanatory commentary for a children's readership.

3 **The real Poland; an anthology of self-perception.**
Alfred Bloch. New York: Continuum Publishing, 1982. 201p.
A series of translated excerpts from the writings of various Polish intellectual and political figures diagnosing the difficulties and complexities of the Polish condition.

1

4 **Poland in Christian civilization.**
Edited by Jerzy Braun. London: Veritas Foundation, 1985. 633p. bibliog.

A very useful Reader made up translations of thirty-two Polish passages which discuss key aspects of Poland's specifically Christian, and largely Catholic, contribution to European civilization.

5 **Poland for beginners.**
Olgierd Budrewicz, translated by Edward Rothert. Warsaw: Interpress, 1980. 3rd ed. 179p. Miami, Florida: American Institute of Polish Culture, 1985. 216p.

Widely praised as a lucid, precise and well-presented introduction to the country's varied features. Budrewicz was a prominent journalist with a particularly witty and entertaining style. The book remains useful despite today's vastly different political and social context.

6 **A panorama of Polish history.**
Edited by Hanna Cierlińska. Warsaw: Interpress, 1982. 175p.

This is an introductory overview of Polish history aimed at a popular readership giving the view of the liberal communist establishment in its final stage. Stefan Kuczyński presents the history of the Polish coat of arms, flag and national anthem. Tadeusz Lalik, Henryk Rutkowski, Jerzy Skowronek, Andrzej Ajnenkiel and Jerzy Topolski cover the main periods of Poland's history in very broad terms.

7 **Poland in world civilization.**
Roman Dyboski, edited by Ludwik Krzyzanowski. New York: J. M. Barrett, 1950. 285p. maps. bibliog.

An overview of Poland's history and intellectual and cultural development up to the Second World War. Carried out in the grand manner by a celebrated scholar it emphasizes traditional Polish values but in a balanced way. It can still be read with profit as a description of the pre-communist past which some Poles aspire to return to.

8 **Polish civilization. Essays and studies.**
Edited by Mieczysław Giergielewicz. New York: New York University Press, 1979. 318p.

A collection of fifteen essays by distinguished writers on topics varying from Copernicus, Mickiewicz, and medieval Polish towns to Polish peasant rituals and folk customs.

9 **Poland.**
Carol Greene. Chicago: Children's Press, 1983. 126p. maps.

This book is intended largely for children. Greene provides a clear general introduction, illustrated in colour, which discusses both the land and people of Poland.

10 **An outline history of Polish culture.**
Edited by Bolesław Klimaszewski.   Warsaw: Interpress – Jagiellonian
University, 1984. 383p. bibliog.
Contains largely historical sections by academics from the Jagiellonian University in
Kraków on all aspects of Poland's intellectual and cultural development. A useful
introduction at the middlebrow to academic level.

11 **Portrait of Poland.**
Edited Jan Krok-Pazkowski, preface by Czesław Miłosz.   London:
Thames & Hudson, 1982. 172p. maps.
The rich and diverse aspects of Poland, both urban and rural, are presented very
powerfully in Bruno Barbey's magnificent coloured illustrations. Useful textual
comment is provided by Polish writers and foreign observers.

12 **Poland.**
William P. Lineberry.   New York: H. W. Wilson, 1984. 169p. bibliog.
A popular discussion of the background to the 1980 Polish Crisis. The author considers
the emergence and life of Solidarity as well as its suppression under martial law, and
discusses Western reactions to the international repercussions of the Polish Question.

13 **Poland. A country study.**
Edited by Harold D. Nelson.   Washington, DC: US Government
Printing Office, 1983. (Country Studies/Area Handbook Program).
483p. maps. bibliog.
An American University handbook which covers all aspects of Poland's political,
economic and social systems as well as cultural and military aspects.

14 **For your freedom and ours: Polish progressive spirit from the fourteenth
century to the present.**
Krystyna M. Olszer.   New York: F. Unger, 1981. 371p.
A collection of speeches, manifestos and documents up till the Solidarity period,
aimed at popularizing Poland's democratic heritage and values to an American
readership. A revised version of Manfred Kridl, *For your Freedom and Ours* (F.
Unger, 1943. 359p.).

15 **Poland. Land of freedom fighters.**
Christine Pfeiffer.   Minneapolis, Minnesota: Dillon Press, 1984. 175p.
bibliog.
A children's guide to Poland covering such aspects as history, food, education and
recreational activity. It emphasizes the Polish struggle for liberty throughout its
history.

16 **The tradition of Polish ideals. Essays in history and literature.**
Edited by Władysław Józef Stankiewicz. London: Orbis Books,
1983. 288p.

A background study of Poland centred around the idea that a nation's history is best
understood in the light of its ideals and traditions. The essays in this volume, by
various writers, deal with poetry, music, Poland's great men, national identity,
tolerance, the gentry and the Warsaw Uprising.

17 **The Poles.**
Stewart Steven. London: Collins; New York: Macmillan; London:
Collins-Harvill, 1982. 427p. bibliog.

An extremely lively, readable and deeply-informed account of 1980-81 Poland by a
well known British journalist. Based on a wide range of first hand contacts with both
influential and ordinary Poles and an intimate knowledge and sensitive feel for Polish
realities.

18 **A history of Polish culture.**
Bogdan Suchodolski, translated by Edward Czerwiński. Warsaw:
Interpress, 1986. 2nd rev. ed. 255p.

Poland's foremost authority on the subject presents a historical overview of the
development of Polish culture. His very clear synthesis identifies the major factors,
trends and personalities which have shaped it. The value of the work is enhanced by
411 useful illustrations.

19 **Heritage: the foundations of Polish culture**
Translated by Marta Zaborska. Toronto: Polish-Canadian Women's
Federation in Canada, 1981. 96p. maps.

A basic description of the main features of Polish culture stressing its Christian, Latin
and native aspects.

20 **Panorama of Polish history.**
Janusz Żarnowski. Warsaw: Interpress, 1984. 231p.

A publicist essay designed to reinforce the 'realist' view of Polish history immediately
after martial law. The author identifies major episodes in Poland's past which he
considers have given rise to widely believed 'myths'.

Geography

General

21   **Poland. Landscape and architecture.**
Irena Kostrowicka, Jerzy Kostrowicki.   Warsaw: Arkady, 1980. 334p.
A beautiful album showing Poland's architecture and landscape in the context of its
national environment and how it has been socio-economically transformed. After a
comprehensive historical introduction six further chapters deal with: Poland's major
geographical regions; the Carpathian mountains and sub-Carparthian upland; the
central plains; the Sudetan mountains and Silesia; the Greater Poland plateau; the
Masurian lowlands; the seaboard lowlands. Includes 497 illustrations, some in colour,
and coloured maps.

22   **Human geography in Eastern Europe and the Soviet Union.**
Ludwik Mazurkiewicz, foreword by R. J. Johnson.   London: Belhaven
Press, 1992. 163p. bibliog.
Written by a Polish specialist in the Polish Academy of Sciences, this is a largely
introductory overview to the historical development of the discipline in Eastern
Europe, covering geography in pre-socialist Eastern Europe and Russia and the
post-war development of economic, regional and social geography approaches.

23   **Eastern Europe: a geography of Comecon countries.**
Roy E. H. Mellor.   New York: Columbia University Press, 1975. 358p.
maps. bibliog.
Mellor covers the historical, political, economic and physical geography of the region
in its entirety as well as the geography of the individual East European countries. He
deals separately with Comecon, Soviet influence, economic development, urban-rural
populations, migration and the impact of socialism upon everyday life.

24 **National Geographic.**
Washington, DC: National Geographic Society 1888- .
Previously called the *National Geographic Magazine*, this is a popular and respected glossy illustrated journal. The following articles, in chronological order, have been published postwar about Poland: Delia and Ferdinand Kuhn, 'Poland opens her doors' no. 3 (1958) p. 354-98; Peter T. White, 'Springtime of hope in Poland' no. 4 (1972) p. 465-501; Yva Momatiuk and John Eastcott, 'Poland's mountain peoples' no. 1 (1981) p. 104-29. Tad Szulc, 'Poland: the hope that never dies' no. 1 (January 1988), p. 80-121.

25 **Eastern Europe.**
Norman J. G. Pounds. London: Longman; Chicago: Aldine, 1969. 932p. maps. bibliog.
A fine introduction to the physical, demographic, economic and transport geography of Eastern Europe. Valuable for its coverage of historical and environmental geography, it demonstrates the lack of uniformity and cohesiveness among the East European countries even though they were, at the time, living through the Soviet model of rapid industrialization and socio-economic change.

Historical and political geography

26 **The Oder-Neisse line. A re-appraisal under international law.**
Philip A. Buhler. New York: Columbia University Press, 1990. 154p. (East European Monographs no. 277). bibliog.
A committed Germany-first argument that the Oder-Neisse territories, which had been part of Poland since the ending of the Second World War, still legally remain part of Germany despite the postwar Yalta and Potsdam agreements and the 1970 treaties. Buhler considers that it would be 'just' for these territories to return to Germany and for Germans to resettle there. All Poles should be transferred back to Poland 'humanely'; Buhler's publication coincides with German re-unification but he fails to acknowledge the potential resurgence of old fears of German aggression and *revanchism* among her neighbours.

27 **The Oder-Neisse boundary and Poland's modernization: the socio-economic and political impact.**
Z. Anthony Kruszewski. New York: Praeger, 1972. 245p.
The book's argument is that the westward shift of her boundaries after the Second World War was, on the whole, beneficial to Poland. It claims that the movement favoured industrialization, socio-economic modernization and the social and political integration of the Recovered Territories.

Geography. Historical and political geography

28 **Polish arguments. Poland on the Odra, Lusatian Nysa and Baltic.**
Edmund Męclewski, translated by Lech Petrowicz. Warsaw:
Interpress, 1987. 53p.
This is a publicist presentation of the Polish case for its rights to the territories
mentioned in the title. The author was a Sejm Deputy during the communist period, a
well-known journalist and founding chairman of the Association for the Development
of the Western Territories.

29 **Political geography and the world.**
Stanisław Otok. *Political Geography Quarterly*, vol. 4, no. 1 (October
1985), p. 321-7.
The article reports that a new organizational framework was established by the
creation of a department of socio-political geography at Warsaw University. This
concentrated its research on the organization of political space and its determinants,
paying particular attention to Polish emigrants abroad and Poland's place in political
space.

30 **Germany's Eastern neighbours: problems relating to the Oder-Neisse and
the Czech frontier regions.**
Elizabeth Wiskemann. London: Oxford University Press, 1964. 309p.
maps. bibliog.
An outline history of Poland's Northwestern territories and of the frontier with
Germany established in 1919 and modified after the Second World War. Wiskemann
examines the Polish-German territorial dispute, the resettlement of the Germans
expelled from Poland, the economic importance of Pomerania, Silesia, Warmia and
Masuria to both Poland and Germany, and the problems of the inhabitants of the
border areas ruled successively by Germany and Poland.

31 **Border of Europe: a study of the Polish Eastern provinces.**
Adam Żółtowski. London: Hollis & Carter, 1950. 348p. map. bibliog.
An examination which provides useful historical and demographical material, even
today, to the territories occupied by the USSR in September 1939 on the basis of the
secret appendix to the Ribbentrop-Molotov Pact and later formally annexed by her.
These eastern borderlands (*kresy*) had been inhabited by a mixed Polish-Ukrainian-
Belorussian-Jewish population for centuries. The Polish element was largely deported
into the USSR during the Second World War and repatriated mainly to Poland's newly
Recovered Territories in the west at its end.

Economic geography

32 **Planning in Eastern Europe.**
Edited by Andrew H. Dawson. London: Croom Helm, 1987. 348p. maps.

The book examines spatial economic planning in communist Eastern Europe on a country by country basis. Dawson himself contributes the chapter on Poland (p. 195-228) in which he pays particular attention to regional, demographic and environmental factors.

33 **Wieliczka. Seven centuries of Polish salt.**
Marian Hanik, translated by Rafał Kiepuszewski, Wojciech Worstynowicz. Warsaw: Interpress, 1988. 74p

A coloured illustrated work on the history and development of the Wieliczka salt mine near Kraków which was worked from medieval until recent times. It has now become an important tourist attraction especially for its museum and underground chapel. Also of interest is the section on Wieliczka in *National Geographic*, 'Salt the essence of life', (September 1977), p. 381-401.

34 **Urban ecology in planning.**
Piotr Zaremba. Wrocław, Poland: Ossolineum, 1986. 283p.

An academic discussion of the way the urban environment affects planning in Poland.

Maps and cartography

35 **Atlas historyczny Polski** (Historical atlas of Poland)
Władysław Czapliński, Tadeusz Ładogórski. Warsaw: PPKW, 1979. 4th ed. 54p maps + 55p text.

The main emphasis is on political history, territorial changes and the evolution of the state frontiers. There is also substantial coverage of economic, social and cultural aspects.

36 **Poland. A historical atlas.**
Iwo Cyprian Pogonowski. New York: Hippocrene Books, 1987. 321p. bibliog.

Poland's history over 2,000 years is covered in about 200 maps, genealogical tables, charts, diagrams and graphs, together with explanatory commentaries. This constitutes an encyclopedic guide rather than a historical atlas in the strict sense of the term. It is not particularly rigorous or scholarly but a popular readership will find it both useful and informative.

37   **Road atlas of Poland.**
Warsaw: Państwowe Przedsiębiorstwo Wydawnictw Kartograficznych,
1980. rev. ed. maps.
The standard road atlas which is revised and re-issued periodically by the official
cartographic publishing house. The atlas contains detailed maps catering to the needs
of tourists travelling around Poland by car.

Tourism and Travel

General guidebooks and travellers' accounts

38 **The Białowieża Forest.**
Edward Badyda, Krzysztof Wolfram, translated by Wiktor Bukato.
Warsaw: Sport i Turystyka, 1987. 32p.
An illustrated guide (with two coloured maps) to one of the few major primeval forest areas left in Europe. It is situated in Białystok province on what was the pre-1991 Soviet frontier.

39 **Poland invites you.**
Translated by Zbigniew Chyliński. Warsaw: Interpress, 1986. 32p.
This is a translation of a very basic information guide to Poland originally published in Polish.

40 **Travels with my sketchbook: a journey through Russia, Poland, Hungary and Czechoslovakia.**
Nicholas Garland. London: Harrap, 1987. 22p.
A cartoonist for the London *Daily Telegraph* records his impressions, drawn from his visit to Eastern Europe, and particularly to Poland in October 1981 (p. 95-125). Extremely light and pleasant reading, with a number of Garland's extemporaneous drawings of the sights and personalities which he encountered.

Tourism and Travel. General guidebooks and travellers' accounts

41 **Insider's guide to Poland.**
Alexander Jordan, foreword by Jerzy Kosiński. New York:
Hippocrene Books, 1990. rev. ed. 220p.
An explanatory guide to diverse aspects of Polish life ranging from everyday activities
such as shopping and currency, to tourism (accommodation, cycling, youth-hostels)
and to more unusual ventures such as parachuting or buying a castle! Two other
readable general guides, which concentrate on the historical, cultural and regional
background are: Marc E. Heine, *Poland.* New York: Hippocrene, 1987. 182p; and Jill
Stephenson, Alfred Bloch, *Hippocrene companion guide to Poland.* New York:
Hippocrene, 1991. 175p.

42 **Let's go to Poland.**
Keith Lye. London: Franklyn Watts, 1984. 32p.
An extremely basic and preliminary introduction, this guide consists of coloured
photographs, each with historical, geographic or associated information.

43 **Gothic house in Nowy Sącz.**
Maria Teresa Maszczak, translated by Małgorzata Walczak. Nowy
Sącz, Poland: The District Museum, 1991. 26p.
This is a popular guide to a major tourist attraction in Nowy Sącz, in Poland's southern
mountain ranges. The Gothic Castle, which was blown up by the Nazis at the end of
the Second World War has been partially rebuilt.

44 **Let's visit Poland.**
Julian Popescu. London: Burke, 1984. 96p. maps.
Popescu's book provides illustrations and very basic introductory information on
Poland for children.

45 **Poland. The rough guide.**
Mark Salter, Gordon McLachlan. London: Harrap-Columbus, 1991.
383p. (Rough Guide Series).
Salter and McLachlan provide a wide range of information about accommodation,
restaurants, transport and the Polish way of fixing things required for getting around,
and suggest the best ways of seeing the country as cheaply and comprehensively as
possible. There is similar coverage of Poland's cities and regions in David Stanley's
Eastern Europe on a shoestring. (Hawthorn, Victoria, Australia: Lonely Planet
Publications, 1989. 665p. Polish section p. 138-218).

46 **Poland.**
Tim Sharman. London: Columbus Books, 1988. 351p. (Travelscape
Series).
Sharman's excellent guide considers the cities and regions of Poland individually in
seventeen chapters. The book contains appendices on basic Polish pronunciation, a list
of the monarchs of Poland and a historical chronology.

47 **Polish cities. Travels in Cracow and the South, Gdańsk, Malbork and Warsaw.**
Philip Ward. Cambridge, England: Oleander Press, 1988. 202p.
A perceptive and informative guide to the cities and regions mentioned in the title. The author provides a mixture of historical and geographical background, tourist information and personal insight and experience.

48 **Poland. A tourist guidebook.**
Edited by Marlena Wilczek, translated by Ryszard Wawrocki. Warsaw: Central Committee of Physical Culture and Tourism, 1987. 47p.
This official guide provides a short and very basic preliminary introductory overview to the nation's attractions and amenities for visitors.

49 **A Polish-American's guide to Poland.**
Tadeusz Wojnowski. Warsaw: Interpress, 1989. 190p.
A general guidebook to the country aimed at Polish-Americans and their special interests.

City guides

Częstochowa

50 **Jasna Góra. A companion guide.**
Zbigniew Bania, Jan Golonka, Stanisław Kobelius, translated by Bogna Piotrowska. Warsaw: Interpress, 1986. 123p.
An illustrated, popular guide to the Jasna Góra monastery in Częstochowa which houses the shrine of the celebrated Black Madonna.

Gdańsk

51 **Gdańsk. City sights.**
Andrzej Januszajtis. Gdańsk, Poland: National Tourist Information Centre, 1986.
This is an official publication of a coloured tourist map of Gdańsk. The map is particularly useful as a guide to the architecture of the city centre.

Kórnik

52 **The Castle of Kórnik.**
Barbara Dolczewska, translated by Jędrzej Polak. Kórnik, Poland:
Kornik Library, 1991. 32p.
An illustrated brochure-guide to the history, architecture and current interior
decoration of Kórnik Castle together with its magnificent park. It was the Działyński
family residence until 1880, and then that of Count Władysław Zamoyski.

Kraków

53 **An illustrated guide to Kraków.**
Jan Adamczewski, translated by Bogna Piotrowska. Warsaw:
Interpress, 1989. 197p. maps.
The best English-language Polish guide to Kraków and its environs, this handbook
contains comprehensive information and useful maps.

54 **The Wawel castle.**
Antoni Franaszek, translated by Krystyna Macharek. Warsaw:
Omnipress, 1991. 24p.
Franaszek provides a basic tourist guide to the history and contents of the Wawel
Castle in Kraków. This ancient seat of the Polish monarchs was converted into a
museum in 1918, and is most noted for its celebrated collection of Jagiellonian
tapestries, magnificent state-rooms and armoury.

55 **Seven days in Cracow i.e. a practical and slightly ironical guide for those
who have come here for the first time.**
Bolesław Klimaszewski, translated by Lucjan Błuszcz. Kraków:
Centre of Tourist Information, 1991. 127p.
This is an amusing and eccentric guide for strangers to the city. Klimaszewski had also
produced *How to live and study in this city. Cracow* (Kraków: Centralny Ośrodek
Informacji Turystyczne UJ, 1986. 41p.) for foreign students at the Jagiellonian
University.

56 **Cracow – a treasury of Polish art and culture.**
Michał Różek, translated by Doris Ronowicz. Warsaw: Interpress,
1988. 163p.
A popular, heavily illustrated, introduction to the artistic and cultural treasures to be
found in Kraków.

57 **Cracow Cathedral on Wawel. Guide-book for visitors.**
Michał Różek, translated by Małgorzata Komornicka. Kraków:
Wydawnictwo Kurii Metropolitalnej, 1984. 2nd ed. 84p.
A straightforward illustrated guide to the Wawel Castle intended for the general
reader.

13

Tourism and Travel. City guides

Poznań

58 **Poznań. Guide to amenities.**
Edited by Walenty Trudnowski. Poznań, Poland: Pospress, 1988. 52p.
A general information guide to Poznań. The major regional and historical capital of
Greater Poland (Wielkopolska) on the River Warta, the city of Poznań has a
population of about 600,000 (1987). It is noted for the architecture of the city centre,
the university named after Adam Mickiewicz and for varied and developed industrial
plants and an annual trade fair.

59 **Poznań.**
Jerzy Unierżyński. Poznań, Poland: Wydawnictwo Poznańskie, 1980.
23p.
This guide provides a general introduction to the city, illustrated with forty-eight black-
and-white and coloured plates.

Szczecin

60 **Szczecin. Yesterday, today and tomorrow.**
Henryk Mąka, translated by Susan Brice Wojciechowski. Warsaw:
Interpress, 1979. 179p.
Mąka describes the port of Szczecin at the mouth of the River Oder as it was in the
late 1970s. Set against the background of its disputed history on the Polish-German
borderlands, the work naturally emphasizes the extent to which the city has become
wholly Polonized, whilst serving as an important political and economic bridge to
Germany, since it was returned to Poland at the end of the Second World War.

Warsaw

61 **Warsaw. A concise guide.**
Wiesław Głębocki, Karol Morawski, translated by Marek Cegiala.
Warsaw: Krajowa Agencja Wydawnicza, 1987. 100p.
This is a useful general guide to the city and its suburbs with illustrations.

62 **Łazienki and Belweder.**
Krzysztof Jabłoński, Marek Kwiatkowski, translated by Doris
Ronowicz. Warsaw: Arkady, 1986. 39p.
A richly illustrated guide to the Belvedere Palace in central Warsaw, which is used as
the Presidential residence. The guide also covers the Łazienki Park which adjoins the
Palace.

14

63 **The book of Warsaw palaces.**
Tadeusz S. Jaroszewski, translated by Stanisław Tarnowski. Warsaw: Interpress, 1985. 168p.

Jaroszewski offers a general illustrated guide to the major aristocratic residences of historical and architectural interest in Warsaw. A more detailed account of the Royal Castle destroyed during the Second World War which was rebuilt in the 1970s, is provided by Jerzy Lilejko, *A companion guide to the Royal Castle in Warsaw.* (Warsaw: Interpress, 1980. 249p.). *The Royal Way*, also by Lilejko (Warsaw: Krajowa Agencja Wydawnicza, 1981. 78p.) is also informative for those interested in Poland's stately homes.

64 **Warsaw as it was. Original city maps before 1939 and in 1945.**
Edited and introduced by Jerzy Kasprzyczak, translated by Krzysztof Samplawski. Warsaw: Dalfa G, [n.d.]. 20p.

The maps of Warsaw in 1939 and 1945 are supplemented with an alphabetical list of street names. The 1945 map also contains an inventory of the destruction caused by the Germans during the war.

65 **A guide to Warsaw and its environs.**
Janina Rutkowska. Warsaw: Sport i Turystyka, 1981. rev. ed. 350p. map.

The guide offers a basic acount of the history and growth of the city. It provides a number of interesting tourist itineraries to major historical monuments and palaces, and useful information is supplied concerning transport, street-layouts, restaurants and hotels. The author also suggests excursions to nearby points of interest like Chopin's birthplace at Żelazowa Wola, the Kampinos Forest and the Jabłonna Palace.

66 **The Old Town and the Royal Castle in Warsaw.**
Jan Zachwatowicz (et al), translated by Jerzy A. Bałdyga. Warsaw: Interpress, 1983. 62p.

An attractive, illustrated guide, this book contains sections on; the Old Town and the Royal Castle, by Zachwatowicz; the reconstruction of the Old Town, by Piotr Biegański; the history of the Royal Castle, by Stanisław Lorentz; and the reconstruction of the Royal Castle, by Aleksander Gieysztor.

Wrocław

67 **Wrocław, Lower Silesia. Poland.**
Ryszard Chanas, Janusz Czerwiński, translated by J. Milencki. Warsaw: Polish Tourist Information Centre, 1988. 16p.

This illustrated guide to Wrocław is of interest because it seeks to describe the city in its context within Lower Silesia.

Flora and Fauna

68 **Structure of the fauna of Warsaw and the urban pressure on animal communities.**
Edited by Wojciech Czechowski, Bohdan Pisarski for the PAN Institute of Zoology. Wrocław, Poland: Ossolineum, 1986. 500p.
The authors have collected together a series of academic studies on how the native fauna has reacted to the growing expansion of the Warsaw conurbation.

69 **The Tardigrada of Poland.**
Hieronim Dastych. Warsaw: Państwowe Wydawnictwo Naukowe, 1988. 255p. bibliog.
A technical monograph on this species of moss-inhabiting fauna in Poland.

70 **Polish amber.**
Janina Grabowska, translated by Emma Harris. Warsaw: Interpress, 1983. 39p.
A comprehensive guide to the history of Polish amber (fossilized tree resin), amply illustrated with numerous colour plates.

71 **European bison. Bison Bonasus bonasus (Linnaeus 1758) in Wielkopolska.**
Ryszard Graczyk. Poznań, Poland: Annals of the Agricultural University in Poznań, Scientific Dissertations volume 173, 1987. 35p. bibliog.
This small volume reports on the successful re-introduction in 1980 of eight bison into a region of Greater Poland from which they had disappeared in the 13th or 14th century. See also W. A. Lasocki, *The saga of an (sic) European bison.* (London: Wiesław Antoni, 1982. 39p.).

72 **Beekeeping in Poland.**
Edited by Henryk Ostach, translated by Lech Petrowicz. Warsaw: Wydawnictwo Spółdzielcze, 1987. 46p. map.

This resumé of apiaries in Poland was issued on the occasion of the thirty-first International Beekeeping Congress APIMONDIA, held in Warsaw in 1987.

73 **Atlas of plant parasitic nematodes of Poland.**
A. Szczygiel. Dundee, Scotland: Scottish Crop Research Institute, 1985. 32p. (European plant parasite nematode survey).

Szczygiel identifies the territorial distribution in Poland of this type of parasitic eelworm which attacks crops such as potatoes.

Prehistory and Archaeology

74 **The earliest Polish farmers; results of recent research.**
Peter I. Bogucki. *Polish Review*, vol. 31, nos. 2-3 (1986), p. 113-26.
Bogucki presents a readable discussion of the main trends of recent archaeological studies in Poland. The article's main theme is to trace the development of food production and its progression from the periods of Linear Pottery to that of the Funnel Beaker, approximately between five and seven millennia ago on the territory of present day Poland.

75 **Prehistoric contacts of Kujavian communities with other European peoples.**
Edited by Aleksandra Cofta-Broniewska. Warsaw: Wydawnictwo UW, 1989. 291p. bibliog.
A joint Warsaw and Jagiellonian University research symposium on the inter-regional and wider European links with the Kujavy region, located between Bydgoszcz and Włocławek, during the Mesolithic period.

76 **Mesolithic in Poland. A new approach.**
Stefan Karol Kozłowski. Warsaw: Polish Research Programme RP – III – 35, 1986. 246p.
A detailed academic monograph covering the Mesolithic period from the eighth to the end of the fourth century BC in Poland. This is an improved version of the author's 1971 study taking new research findings into account.

77 The Neolithic settlement of Southern Poland.
Janusz Kruk. Oxford: BAR, 1980. 129p. (British Archeological
Reports International Series 93). bibliog.
This is a translation of a research report, first published in Poland in 1973 by
Ossolineum. The investigation aimed to reconstruct the patterns of settlement in the
loess uplands of Southern Poland between the fifth and third millennia BC. Another
report in the same series which may be of interest is Peter I. Bogucki, *Early Neolithic
subsistence and settlement in the Polish Lowlands* (BAR, 1982. International Series no
150).

78 Early Neolithic settlement and society at Olszanica.
Sarunas Milisauskas. Ann Arbor, Michigan: The Regents of the
University of Michigan, 1986. 319p. (Memoirs of the Museum of
Anthropology, University of Michigan no 19). bibliog.
An extremely detailed and well-illustrated site report presenting the results of early
Neolithic excavations carried out at the Linear Pottery culture settlement of Olszanica
close to Kraków from 1967 to 1973.

79 Unconventional archeology: new approaches and goals in Polish
archeology.
Edited by Romuald Schild. Wrocław, Poland: Ossolineum, 1980.
233p.
The contributors discuss new archaeological techniques and approaches to the
problems of assessing the prehistoric socio-economic development of the Oder and
Vistula basins on the evidence of early settlements and remains.

History (pre-1980)

Poland within Eastern Europe

80 **Eastern Europe and communist rule.**
   James F. Brown.   Durham, North Carolina: Duke University Press,
   1988. 562p. bibliog.

A highly thematic analysis of the development of communist Eastern Europe which concentrates on the 1970s as a follow up to Brown's, *The New Eastern Europe* (New York: Praeger, 1966). This is coupled with introductory *apercus* of the eight individual East European countries in separate chapters. The coverage on Poland (p. 158-99) concentrates heavily on the Gierek period.

81 **The origins of backwardness in Eastern Europe. Economics and politics from the Middle Ages until the early twentieth century.**
   Edited by Daniel Chirot.   Berkeley, California: University of California Press, 1989. 260p.

This symposium on the broad historical reasons for East Europe's backward economic development contains Polish material and discussion throughout. Jacek Kochanowicz contributes a chapter specifically on 'The Polish economy and the evolution of dependency' (p. 92-130).

82 **The Slavs in European history and civilization.**
   Francis Dvornik.   New Brunswick: Rutgers University Press, 1962.
   688p. maps. bibliog.

A classic work on the Slav countries, written by a Czech scholar. It is impressively informative in its coverage of Slav history and civilization from the 13th to 17th centuries. The work is a continuation of an earlier book by the same author: *The Slavs, their early history and civilization* (Boston: American Academy, 1956). Almost all the chapters deal extensively with Poland, Polish relations with Bohemia and with other neighbouring countries, the Jagiellonian Commonwealth, social developments, religious reformation and the growing threat of Muscovy.

83 **Class struggles in Eastern Europe 1945-83.**
Chris Harman. London: Pluto Press, 1983. 2nd ed. 339p.
A popular political history of communist Eastern Europe prior to 1981, written from a British critical marxist (International Socialist) point of view. It glorifies workers' revolts against the Stalinist bureaucracies especially in Poland in 1956, 1970 and 1980.

84 **Independent Eastern Europe: a history.**
Carlile A. Macartney, Alan Warwick Palmer. New York: St. Martin's Press: London: Macmillan, 1967. 499p. bibliog.
A classic work of reference, this book provides the most thorough and reliable history of the area, from Finland to Greece. The authors stress the extent to which the 'external' German and Russian Great Powers influenced the foreign policies, and even the internal structures, of the smaller states within this region.

85 **Eastern Europe 1968-84.**
Olga A. Narkiewicz. London: Croom Helm, 1986. 273p. bibliog.
Narkiewicz concentrates on the effects of economic downturn and the interplay between domestic and bloc-wide factors in this study of post-1968 Eastern Europe. She sketches in the leadership and elite developments but eschews detailed blow by blow political history in favour of thematic analysis. The examination of the burgeoning literature on the 1980-81 crisis is one of the book's highlights.

86 **Return to diversity. A political history of East Central Europe since World War II.**
Joseph Rothschild. Oxford, New York: Oxford University Press, 1989. 257p. bibliog.
A readable survey of Eastern Europe's postwar history which emphasizes the region's return to national and cultural diversity after the full-blooded Stalinization and Sovietization of the late 1940s and early 1950s. A much revised and updated version of the author's *Communist Eastern Europe*, (New York: Walker, 1964. 168p.).

87 **Eastern Europe in the postwar world.**
Thomas W. Simons. Basingstoke, England: Macmillan, 1991. 246p.
Simon's well-structured political history provides coverage of the main communist period, balanced by sufficient attention to the interwar and Second World War experiences. Simons, an American diplomat with postings in Eastern Europe including Warsaw, and a direct academic specialization in the area produces a workmanlike and generally sound overview for an undergraduate and general readership.

88 **The socialist regimes of East Central Europe. Their establishment and consolidation, 1944-67.**
Jerzy Tomaszewski, translated by Jolanta Krauze. London: Routledge, 1989. 352p. bibliog.
Written by a well-known Polish economic historian, this is a heavily descriptive political history valuable to Western readers because it introduces an additional dimension of East European material and viewpoints.

89 **The making and breaking of Eastern Europe.**
Zbigniew A. B. Zeman. London: Chatto & Windus, 1991. 364p. (First published as *Pursued by a bear. The making of Eastern Europe.* 1989).
A stimulating analysis of the historical factors which led to the progressive drawing apart of Eastern Europe and Western Europe in the century before 1989. About two thirds of the book is devoted to examining pre-communist Eastern Europe, mainly from the turning point of the 1917 Bolshevik Revolution onwards. Zeman identifies what he terms 'the autonomous aspects of its recent past'; these gave the region the original characteristics which survived and outlasted the communist experience. Zeman believes that the individuality of Eastern Europe will continue to hinder the region's full re-integration with Western Europe even after the collapse of communism and the USSR.

General histories of Poland

90 **Poland.**
Vaclav L. Benes, Norman G. Pounds. New York: Praeger, 1970. 416p. maps.
This comprehensive and perceptive overview of Polish history covers wider aspects such as economic, social and constitutional development, cultural heritage and political aspirations. Historical, economic, demographic and political maps are included and are a useful supplement to the text.

91 **The meaning and uses of Polish history.**
Adam Bromke. New York: Columbia University Press, 1987. 244p. (East European Monographs no. 212).
Bromke reviews the special role of the study of history in the first part of this book and re-examines his thesis on the cyclical swings between political idealism and realism first set out in *Poland's politics* (see item no. 370). The second part of the book consists of his selection of writings on Polish political thought which illustrate the major themes of nationalism, Roman Catholicism and the idealist-realist conflict. The main excerpts are from Andrzej Walicki, Aleksander Hall, Jan Szczepański, Roman Dmowski and Stanisław Stomma.

92 **A history of Poland: God's playground.**
Norman Davies. New York: Columbia University Press, 2 vols. maps.
bibliog.

This comprehensive history in two volumes (*The Origins to 1795* and *1795 to the Present*) aroused much controversy when first published, but is now firmly established as the most widely read general history of Poland. It has been praised for its deep historical insights and freedom from national bias, and criticized for its idiosyncratic, thematic, and non-chronological presentation. The latter, combined with Davies' witty phraseology is, however, the essential distinctive feature of an outstanding work which combines wide academic and popular appeal. Readers may wish to refer to the review by John J. Kulczycki in *East European Politics and Societies*, vol. 1, no. 3 (Fall 1987), p. 456-73.

93 **Heart of Europe. A short history of Poland.**
Norman Davies. Oxford: Oxford University Press, 1984. 511p. bibliog.

This volume is essentially a summary of Davies' larger work, *A history of Poland: God's playground* (q.v.). It is equally thematic in approach and designed to explain Poland's present in terms of her past. Readers may be interested by the very critical review of this work by Stanisław Bóbr-Tylingo in *Polish Review*, vol. 30, no 3 (1985), p. 277-82.

94 **Poland in the twentieth century.**
Marian Kamil Dziewanowski. New York: Columbia University Press, 1977. 309p. bibliog.

A readable account of Poland's modern history which brings out its most distinctive characteristics. Dziewanowski presents a balanced overview in successive chapters on the pre-independence, interwar, Second World War, Stalinist, Gomułka and Gierek periods. He also attempts to elucidate the historical roots and dynamics of the Polish paradox in his introduction and conclusion.

95 **History of Poland.**
Aleksander Gieysztor, Stefan Kieniewicz, Emanuel Rostworowski, Janusz Tazbir, Henryk Wereszycki, translated by Krystyna Cękalska (et al). Warsaw: Państwowe Wydawnictwo Naukowe, 2nd ed revised by George Sakwa, 1979. 668p. maps. bibliog.

This excellent volume is the work of a team of prominent native Polish historians. Intended mainly for foreign readers it has established itself successfully as a valuable introduction, providing a good blend of political history and socio-economic and cultural background.

96 **A history of Poland.**
Oskar Halecki, with additional material by Antony Polonsky. London: Routledge & Kegan Paul, 1983. rev. ed. 441p. maps.

Halecki attempts to combine his ardently patriotic, conservative and deeply Catholic views with high-quality scholarship. His committed interpretation of Poland's history appeals compellingly to adherents. Polonsky updated the 1978 edition of this much published and widely read history by adding two final chapters which smoothed down some of its more Polonocentric aspects.

97 **The Cambridge history of Poland.**
   Edited by William Fiddian Reddaway. Cambridge, England: Cambridge University Press. 2 vols (I *From the Origins to Sobieski*, 1941. II *From Augustus II to Piłsudski*, 1950.). maps. bibliog. Reprinted, New York: Octogon, 1971.

Some of Poland's best-known pre-war historians, such as Władysław Konopczyński, Paweł Skwarczyński, Marian Kukiel and Marceli Handelsman, contributed specialist chapters on all aspects of Poland's history prior to 1935. This is still respected as an authoritative work despite its age, and subsequent advances in historical knowledge.

98 **An outline history of Poland.**
   Jerzy Topolski, translated by Olgierd Wojtaszewicz. Warsaw: Interpress, 1985. 315p. maps. bibliog.

Topolski is a well-known academic from Poznań University specializing in early modern economic history and the methodology of history. His overview has been praised for its broad and comprehensive approach but criticized for his self-censorship of many aspects concerning Russia and the postwar communist period.

99 **The Polish way. A thousand-year history of the Poles and their culture.**
   Adam Zamoyski. London: John Murray, 1987. 422p. bibliog.

Zamoyski overviews the entire one thousand years of Poland's statehood, in this attractive illustrated volume. He balances the outline of political history with good coverage of intellectual and cultural developments. The work is purely derivative but is quite elegant in style although it has a particularly unclear looking bibliography. It is useful as a popular explanation of the connection between Poland's historical achievements and failures and their relevance to contemporary problems.

Medieval and early modern history (pre-1795)

100 **Polish armies, 1569-1696.**
   Richard Brzezinski. London: Osprey, 2 vols, 1987-88. (Men-at-Arms series nos 184 & 188).

A generously illustrated guide (with some of the plates in colour) to the organization, strategy, uniforms and medals of Polish armies in the sixteenth and seventeenth centuries.

101 **The Union of Lublin in the Golden Age.**
Harry E. Dembiński. New York: Columbia University Press, 1982.
380p. (East European Monographs no. 116). bibliog.
The author examines how the Union of Lublin, establishing the Commonwealth of
Poland and Lithuania, was arrived at in 1569. Dembiński discusses its historical
consequences and whether it can be regarded as a successful case of early federalism.

102 **A Republic of nobles. Studies in Polish history to 1864.**
Edited and translated by Jacek K. Fedorowicz, co-editors Maria
Bogucka, Henryk Samsonowicz. Cambridge, England: Cambridge
University Press, 1982. 293p.
Thirteen distinguished Polish academics (including Bronisław Geremek, Antoni
Mączak, Janusz Tazbir and Jerzy Topolski) contribute chapters on aspects of the
history of the Polish Commonwealth from early modern times up till 1864.

103 **The Polish nobility in the Middle Ages.**
Edited by Antoni Gąsiorowski, translated by Aleksandra Rodzińska-
Chojnowska. Wrocław, Poland: Ossolineum, 1984. 298p. (PAN
Komitet Nauk Historycznych no. 5).
Contains nine essays by a group of experts on the development of the Polish medieval
nobility.

104 **Boleslaus the Bold, called also the Bountiful, and the Bishop Stanislaus.
The story of a conflict.**
Tadeusz Grudziński. Warsaw: Interpress, 1985. 255p. bibliog.
Grudziński discusses the dispute between King Bolesław (1040-81) and the Bishop of
Kraków, later canonized as Saint Stanisław (1039-79), which ended in the Bishop's
execution for alleged treason. The study provides the historical background to one of
the most famous episodes in Polish history, which has many parallels with the case of
England's Thomas à Beckett.

105 **Piast Poland.**
Paweł Jasienica, translated by Alexander Jordan. New York:
Hippocrene Books, 1985. 266p.
A history of the Piast dynasty which ruled from the tenth to the fourteenth century,
written by a major Polish postwar historian in a popular style for a wide readership.

106 **The Commonwealth of both nations (Poland and Lithuania). The silver
age.**
Paweł Jasienica, translated by Alexander Jordan. New York:
Hippocrene Books, 1987. Miami, Florida: American Institute of Polish
Culture. 338p.
An English translation of a classic popular-historical work covering the decline of the
Polish-Lithuanian Commonwealth, starting with the adoption of the Elective
Monarchy in 1572, to the military defeats suffered by the Vasa dynasty in the first half
of the sixteenth century.

107 **The first partition of Poland.**
Herbert Harold Kaplan. New York: Columbia University Press, 1962.
215p. bibliog.
An impressively researched and balanced presentation of the circumstances leading up
to the First Partition of Poland in 1772. The interaction between internal attempts to
renew the country and external schemes to destroy it is examined in detail.

108 **The second partition of Poland: a study in diplomatic history.**
Robert Howard Lord. Cambridge, Massachusetts: Harvard
University Press, 1915. 586p. bibliog. Reprinted, New York: AMS
Press, 1969. 596p.
A historiographical classic which deals exhaustively both with its central topic and with
Poland's partitions in general.

109 **Liberty's folly. The Polish-Lithuanian Commonwealth in the eighteenth
century 1697-1795.**
Jerzy Tadeusz Lukowski. London: Routledge, 1991. 316p.
Based extensively on post-war Polish historiography as well as on Polish sources this is
now an established study of the decline and fall of the Commonwealth.

110 **East-Central Europe in transition from the fourteenth to the seventeenth
centuries.**
Edited by Antoni Mączak, Henryk Samsonowicz, Peter Burke.
Cambridge, England: Cambridge University Press, 1985. In association
with Editions de la Maison des Sciences de l'Homme. 207p. (Studies in
Modern Capitalism).
Twelve studies on the general transition from feudalism to capitalism in East-Central
Europe (defined as Poland, Bohemia and Hungary) in the late medieval to early
modern period. Written by Polish and Hungarian historians.

111 **The formation of the Polish state; the period of ducal rule, 963-1194.**
Tadeusz Manteuffel, translated by Andrew Górski. Detroit: Wayne
State University Press, 1985. 171p. maps. bibliog.
A translation of a history, first published in Poland in 1976, on the origins and
foundations of early Piast rule. Manteuffel is the leading Polish specialist in the field.

112 **The Tsars, Russia, Poland and the Ukraine, 1462-1725.**
Martyn Rady. London: Hodder & Stoughton, 1990. 190p. bibliog.
(Access to history series).
A concise introduction for students to the principal events and developments from
1462-1725 in Muscovy, the Polish Commonwealth and the Western Steppes. The
principal emphasis is on the expansion of Muscovy westwards from the time of Ivan the
Terrible to the consolidation of the process by Peter the Great.

113 The Enlightenment and the birth of modern nationhood: Polish political thought from Noble Republicanism to Tadeusz Kościuszko.
Andrzej Walicki, translated by Emma Harris. Notre Dame, Indiana: University of Notre Dame Press, 1989. 152p.
A revisionist essay by a well-known Polish scholar which attempts to identify the specific features of Polish romantic nationalism and its form of nation-building in the age of the Enlightenment. Walicki also makes a spirited case for the importance of Kościuszko's political thought which he claims has been neglected in modern times.

Modern history (1795-1918)

114 Prussian Poland in the German Empire 1871-1900.
Richard Blanke. Boulder, Colorado: Columbia University Press, 1981. 268p. bibliog. (East European Monographs no. 86).
A study of the Polish community in the Prussian Partition and of the evolution of Prussia's Polish policy. The monograph emphasizes the growth of nationalism on both sides, describing the conflicts which ensued on various different levels.

115 Realism in Polish politics: Warsaw Positivism and national survival in nineteenth century Poland.
Stanisław A. Blejwas. New Haven, Connecticut: Yale Concilium on International and Area Studies, 1984. 312p. bibliog.
An in-depth examination of the growth of the values of political realism and Organic Work in the various parts of partitioned Poland after the failure of the 1864 uprising. Organic Work has been defined as a rejection of armed insurrection in favour of ensuring the survival and strengthening of the Polish national community through economic, social and cultural activity. Blejwas shows how this trend interacted with the rise of socialist ideas from the 1880s onwards.

116 Polish national liberation struggles and the genesis of the modern nation. Collected papers.
Emmanuel Halicz, translated from the Polish by Roger Clarke.
Odense, Denmark: Odense University Press, 1982. 197p.
A Polish historian publishes his writings on various aspects of the Polish struggle for national liberation between 1794 and 1863. Part I discusses the role of leaders such as Kościuszko, Bem and Traugutt, part II, military aspects and part III, the international context. An earlier work by Halicz, *Partisan warfare in 19th century Poland; the development of a concept* (Odense: Odense University Press, 1975. 220p.) is also useful.

117 **Germans, Poles and Jews. The nationality conflict in the Prussian East, 1772-1914.**
William W. Hagen.   Chicago: University of Chicago Press, 1980. 406p. bibliog.

Hagen argues that the Prussian elite's struggle to Germanize the Prussian Partition of Poland from Bismarck onwards was linked organically to the conflict with domestic democratic and socialist opponents of the Hohenzollern Empire. Hagen's linkage argument may be controversial but it is well documented here. The study concentrates primarily on Poznań province, and the Polish nationalist movement's resistance to German autocratic imperialism and de-Polonization.

118 **Independence or incorporation? The idea of Poland's national self-determination and independence within Russian and Soviet socialism from the 1870s to the 1920s.**
Jyrki Iivonen.   Helsinki: Finnish Institute of International Affairs, 1990. 334p.

This is the text of a Helsinki University dissertation on the above clash between national independence or incorporation within the partitioning power, in the ideas and practice of the Russian and early Soviet socialist movements.

119 **Polish publicists and Prussian politics. The Polish press in Poznań during the Neu Kurs of Chancellor Leo von Caprivi. 1890-94.**
Ted Kamiński.   Stuttgart, West Germany: Steiner, 1988. 286p. bibliog.

Originally begun as a Hamburg University doctoral dissertation in 1986 this is a balanced and well-documented study of Prussia's Polish policy in the 1890s. Based very heavily on official Prussian sources and the Polish language press in Poznań it provides an excellent picture of political life and opinion in the province.

120 **School strikes in Prussian Poland 1901-1907: the struggle over bilingual education.**
John J. Kulczycki.   New York: Columbia University Press, 1981. 279p. maps. bibliog. (East European Monographs no. 82).

A fine and detailed academic study of Polish resistance to Prussian efforts to impose German as the sole language of instruction in all the schools in the partitioned territory under their control.

121 **Polish politics and the revolution of November 1830.**
Robert F. Leslie.   London: Athlone Press; New York: De Graff, 1956. 306p. maps. bibliog. Reprinted, Westport, Connecticut: Greenwood Press.

A thorough and measured academic study based mainly on Polish sources. Leslie argues that the nationalist November Uprising in Russian Poland represented the last challenge to Russia by pre-partition nobility-ruled Poland. The peasant problem represented the decisive factor in the country's future.

122 Reform and insurrection in Russian Poland 1856-65.
Robert F. Leslie. London: Athlone Press, 1963. 284p. bibliog.
Reprinted, Westport, Connecticut: Greenwood Press, 1970.
This important, if controversial, work suggests that the January 1863 Insurrection, the
last uprising of the Romantic period, was the first modern revolution, even though its
basic aim was the restoration of the pre-partition regime in Poland.

123 The history of Poland since 1863.
Edited by Robert F. Leslie. London: Cambridge University Press,
1980. 528p. maps.
The editor, together with Antony Polonsky, Jan Ciechanowski and Zbigniew
Pełczyński, span the major periods of Poland's recent history including the pre-
Solidarity communist period. The book strikes the right balance between politico-
ideological, socio-economic and cultural-intellectual history, and examines the communist governmental structure thoroughly. Although dated somewhat by the most
recent changes the book was, for a while, regarded as the most authoritative and most
up to date overall study of the last century of Poland's development.

124 Napoleon's campaign in Poland 1806-7.
Francis Loraine Petre. London: Greenhill, 1989. 354p.
Although first published in 1901 this book is still relevant, as is evidenced by its
reprinting on numerous occasions. France's defeat of Austria and Prussia, two
partitioning powers, raised Polish hopes of independence. Napoleon's exclusive
concern for his own and French grandeur, however, caused him to disappoint the Poles
who had joined his cause.

**125 The imperfect autocrat. Grand Duke Constantine Pavlovitch and the
Polish Kingdom.**
Angela T. Pienkos. New York: Columbia University Press, 1987.
186p. bibliog. (East European Monographs no. 217).
A study of the life and career of Grand Duke Constantine Pavlovitch (1779-1831). It
centres on his role as *de facto* Russian viceroy in the Congress Kingdom of Poland
from 1814 up till the 1830 Uprising. Pienkos argues that Constantine did not have
sufficient personal and political ability to prevent the erosion of his earlier policy of
autonomy once Nicholas I had become Czar in 1825. To that extent he is partly
responsible for the breakdown of Polish-Russian relations and the Uprising.

**126 Romantic nationalism and Liberalism. Joachim Lelewel and the Polish
national idea.**
Joan S. Skurnowicz. New York: Columbia University Press, 1981.
224p. bibliog. (East European Monographs no. 83).
A biography of Joachim Lelewel (1786-1861) the celebrated progressive leader of the
democratic wing of the Great Emigration. Skurnowicz also examines the methodology
and scholarship of his influential historical writing. See also her 'Lelewel in Polish
historiography in People's Poland', *Polish Review*, vol. 36, no. 3 (1991), p. 269-82.

127 **Marie Walewska: Napoleon's great love.**
Christine Sutherland. London: Weidenfeld & Nicholson, 1979: Robin
Clark, 1986. 256p. bibliog.

A popularly written, but well-documented biography of the life of Marie Walewska
(1786-1817), and the personal and political background to her famous romance with
Napoleon Bonaparte.

128 **The Kulturkampf in Prussian Poland.**
Lech Trzeciakowski, translated by Katarzyna Krętkowska. New
York: Columbia University Press, 1990. 223p. (East European
Monographs no. 283).

Translation of a work, first published in Poland in 1970, by a leading specialist on
Polish-German relations in the nineteenth century. The study concentrates on the
course of the Church-State conflict in Prussian Poland and considers that conflict in the
wider historical context of the Prussian policy of attempted Germanization during the
1870s and 1880s and Polish society's response to it.

129 **Philosophy and romantic nationalism. The case of Poland.**
Andrzej Walicki. London: Clarendon Press, 1982. 415p. bibliog.

A study of the various philosophical strands in Polish Romantic Nationalism between
1830-50 as well as of Marx and Engels' view on the Polish Question. For an
examination of how the latter developed see Walicki's *Stanisław Brzozowski and the
Polish beginnings of 'Western Marxism'* (Oxford: Clarendon Press, 1989. 349p.
bibliog.).

130 **The lands of partitioned Poland 1795-1918.**
Piotr Stefan Wandycz. Seattle, Washington: University of
Washington Press, 1975. 431p. maps. bibliog.

A scholarly, although not particularly specialist, general history. It analyses Poland's
history under foreign occupation, emphasizing the importance of culture in national
survival.

Interwar history

131 **Poland: key to Europe.**
Raymond Leslie Buell. New York: Knopf, 1939. 3rd ed. 406p. map.

A classic which still deserves to be read because of its informative and sympathetic
evocation of Poland's problems in the years preceding the outbreak of the Second
World War. Buell examines the significance of Poland's place in Europe, her relations
with Germany and the historical background to the regaining of her independence in
1918. The bulk of the book combines depth of knowledge with a lucid literary style in
discussing interwar Poland's political system and her economic, agricultural, national
minority and foreign policy problems.

132 **White eagle, red star: the Polish-Soviet war 1919-20.**
Norman Davies. New York: St. Martin's Press, 1972. London:
Macdonald, 1974. 318p and 332p. maps. London: Orbis Books, 1983.
New York: Hippocrene Books, 1985. 2nd ed. 308p.

A pioneer work in English detailing the whole course of the Polish-Soviet war, which
considers political and military aspects as well as the role of major figures such as
Piłsudski, Tukhachevsky, Petlura and Żeligowski. The book shows how the conflict
affected the development of Soviet foreign policy and the movement away from the
theory of World Revolution towards that of Socialism in One Country.

133 **Piłsudski. A life for Poland.**
Wacław Jędrzejewicz, preface by Wanda Piłsudski, introduced by
Zbigniew Brzezinski. New York: Hippocrene Books, 1982. 385p.
bibliog.

A clear and comprehensive, although somewhat uncritical study by a close supporter of
Piłsudski. Despite the more up-to-date documentation provided in this work,
Reddaway's 1939 biography is still the most highly regarded work on the subject.

134 **From Versailles to Locarno. Keys to Polish foreign policy, 1919-25.**
Tytus Komarnicki, Anna M. Cienciała. Lawrence, Kansas: University
Press of Kansas, 1984. 384p. bibliog.

Professor Cienciała from Kansas University has edited and completed a manuscript
by the noted Polish diplomat and international historian, which continues his political
history, *Rebirth of the Polish Republic* into the early 1920s.

135 **Rebirth of the Polish Republic: a study in the diplomatic history of
Europe 1914-20.**
Tytus Komarnicki. London: Heinemann, 1957. 776p. maps. bibliog.

An important and exhaustively documented study of Poland's resurgence after the
First World War by a former Polish diplomat, international lawyer and university
professor. Great attention is devoted to the Versailles Peace Conference and the
problem of Poland's eastern boundaries but there is less coverage of the Silesian,
Cieszyn and Wilno issues. Komarnicki also deals at length with Piłsudski's plans for a
confederation of independent East European states stretching from the Baltic to the
Black seas (*międzymorze*). Although such ideas have always had a bad press in
English-speaking countries as 'Polish imperialism' the basic issues re-emerged in a
modern form with the breakup of Russian control of both Eastern Europe and the
USSR in 1989-91. For an excellent and more recent volume which covers the domestic
as well as the external dimension see Paul Latawski (editor), *The Reconstruction of
Poland, 1914-23* (Basingstoke, England: Macmillan, 1991. 217p.).

136 **General Weygand and the battle of the Vistula, 1920.**
Zdzisław Musialik, edited by Antoni Bohdanowicz. London: Józef
Piłsudski Institute of Research, 1987. 146p.

A clerical specialist examines the controversy over whether the French General
Maxime Weygand or the Poles themselves worked out the strategic war-plan for the
battle of the Vistula which defeated the Russians in the Russo-Polish War of 1920.
Unsurprisingly, the major credit here is given to Piłsudski and his associates such as
Chief of Staff, Tadeusz Rozwadowski.

137 **Politics in independent Poland 1921-39: the crisis of constitutional
government.**
Antony Polonsky. Oxford: Clarendon Press, 1972. 572p. maps.
bibliog.

A clear, comprehensive and very well-researched history of the interwar period in
Poland's history which dominated the field for almost two decades. Polonsky produces
a critical, although academically balanced, interpretation of the transition from
democratic parliamentarianism to Piłsudski's dictatorial regime. He also examines the
struggle over the direction taken by his successors and the evolution of the country's
foreign policy.

138 **Poland between the wars 1918-45.**
Edited by Timothy Wiles. Bloomington, Indiana: Indiana University
Polish Studies Centre, 1989. 319p.

The volume contains twenty-three essays by noted Polish and Western historians on
varied aspects of Poland's interwar politics and culture. The papers were first presented
at a conference held in 1985 at Indiana University's Polish Studies Centre.

139 **The battle for the Marchlands.**
Adam Zamoyski. New York: Columbia University Press, 1981. 218p.
maps. bibliog. (East European Monographs no. 88).

A study of the military course of events in the Russo-Polish War of 1920. It seeks to
explain why the Soviet troops were routed before Warsaw.

140 **November 1918.**
Janusz Żarnowski, translated by Jan Sęk. Warsaw: Interpress, 1984.
231p.

A publicist examination of how Poland regained her independence in 1918 set against a
wider discussion of alleged 'myths' concerning interwar Poland's successes and failures.

Second World War

General

141 **The war Hitler won; the fall of Poland, September 1939.**
Nicholas Bethell. New York: Holt, 1973. 472p. maps. bibliog.
A popular and readable, although academically superficial, account of the first six
weeks of the war. The author discusses the German and the Soviet invasions and the
fall of Poland. He is critical of British and French incompetence and their failure to
fulfill their treaty obligations.

142 **Poland 1939-47.**
John Coutouvidis, Jaime Reynolds. Leicester, England: Leicester
University Press, 1986. 393p. (Politics of Liberation Series). bibliog.
A historical study which was much praised for its authoritative academic coverage of
the interplay between the domestic and the external aspects of the Polish Question
during, and immediately after, the Second World War. Coutouvidis covers the 1939-44
wartime experience and Reynolds the 1944-47 period of liberation from Nazism and
the establishment of communist rule in Poland.

143 **Poland in the Second World War.**
Józef Garliński. Basingstoke, England: Macmillan, 1987. 2nd ed.
387p. bibliog.
A heavily descriptive political history of both Poland's role and the Polish Question
during the Second World War. Garliński, who participated in the events which he
describes and who was for many years the chairman of the London based Association
of Polish Writers, is ideally placed to present the Polish *emigré* viewpoint: but he does
so in a fair and balanced, if excessively factual way, as in his earlier books on the
Polish Underground and in *Fighting Auschwitz*.

144 **Great Britain, the Soviet Union and the Polish Government-in-Exile,
1939-45.**
George Kacevitch. The Hague: Martinus Nijhoff, 1979. 255p. bibliog.
A thorough study of the Polish Government-in-Exile's dilemmas regarding Soviet
demands and British pressure to accept them. Central issues such as the role of the
Polish armed forces in the West, the breaking-off of Polish-Soviet relations after the
revelation of the Katyń massacre and Allied decisions on Poland's frontiers are
discussed in depth.

145 **The last European war. September 1939-December 1941.**
John Lukacs. Garden City, New York: Doubleday, 1976. 562p.
The German-Polish War of September 1939, which quickly escalated into a European
and world conflict, is described in detail. Coverage is provided of the diplomatic
background including British appeasement. The author stresses the significance of
France's military failure to assist her Polish ally; this assured Germany of the
immobility on her Western Front which enabled her to go ahead unhindered with her
blitzkrieg strategy. A later study which provides less detailed coverage of the
September campaign but which situates its origins and the first phase of the Second

World War in its global setting is William Carr, *Poland to Pearl Harbour* (London: Edward Arnold, 1985. 183p.).

146 **The Polish Campaign 1939**
Steven Zaloga, Victor Madej. New York: Hippocrene Books, 1985. 185p.

A crisp, general overview of Poland's military resistance to German and Soviet aggression in September 1939. The authors, without going into much academic depth, make it clear why Poland was isolated and had to fight without the assistance of her Western allies. Although the Poles were defeated in a war of manoeuvre, starting off from unsuitable military positions dictated by previous diplomatic arrangements, by significantly better equipped and prepared German forces, they nevertheless inflicted very heavy losses on their enemy.

German administration

147 **Bełżec, Sobibór, Treblinka: the Operation Reinhardt death camps.**
Yitzhak Arad. Bloomington, Indiana: Indiana University Press, 1987. bibliog.

A detailed academic study of the three major death camps designed to implement the 'Operation Reinhardt' policy of exterminating the Jews in the Nazi occupied General-Gouvernement of Poland.

148 **KL Auschwitz seen by the SS – Hoss, Broad, Kremer.**
Edited by Jadwiga Bezwińska, Danuta Czech, translated by Constantine Fitzgibbon, Krystyna Michalik. New York: Howard Fertig, 1984. 331p.

Selections from documents written by three SS-men who ran the Auschwitz concentration camp (Hoss's memoirs, Kremer's diary and a personal account by Broad).

149 **Mauthausen. The history of a death camp.**
Evelyn Le Chêne. Bath, England: Chivers, 1987. 302p. (A New Portway Book). Reprint of London: Methuen, 1971.

Written by the wife of a French SOE agent who was imprisoned in the Mauthausen camp, near Linz, Austria, from 1943 to May 1945. Le Chêne details the camp's development, organization and personnel and estimates the number of prisoners held and executed there at various times with exemplary clarity.

150 **Majdanek.**
Edited and introduced by Edward Dziadosz, translated by Lech Petrowicz. Lublin, Poland: Krajowa Agencja Wydawnicza, 1985. 2nd ed. 192p.

Parallel texts in Polish, English, French, German and Russian accompany the photographs of the major death camp in Lublin. The first edition was published in Warsaw by Interpress in 1980 and re-issued in 1986.

151   The Kraków Ghetto and the Płaszów camp remembered.
Malvina Graf, foreword by George M. Krein.   Tallahassee, Florida:
Florida State University Press, 1989. 183p.

The recollections of a survivor of the Kraków Ghetto and the nearby Płaszów
concentration camp which emphasizes the elements of personal terror and gratuitous
individual cruelty by the prison guards.

152   Polish society under German occupation: the General Gouvernement,
1939-44.
Jan Tomasz Gross.   Princeton, New Jersey: Princeton University
Press, 1979. 343p. bibliog.

Gross examines German policy and behaviour and Polish social responses during the
occupation period. The Polish underground state and guerrilla resistance emerged
because of unbridled and total Nazi brutality and the German refusal to even consider
floating intermediate organizations which might collaborate with them.

153   Nightmare memoir: four years as a prisoner of the Nazis.
Claude J. Letulle.   Baton Rouge, Louisiana: Louisiana State
University Press, 1987. 132p.

The personal account of a drafted French student's experience as a POW, some of it in
camps in Poland, during the Second World War.

154   Forgotten Holocaust. The Poles under German occupation, 1939-44.
Richard C. Lukas.   Lexington, Kentucky: University Press of
Kentucky, 1986. 300p. bibliog.

Lukas, an American academic specialist on Poland's Second World War experience,
documents his case that as many Polish Gentiles as Polish Jews died as a result of the
Nazi's genocidal occupation. The former were therefore 'co-victims' in a Holocaust
which has largely been forgotten by Western public opinion. Lukas is strictly academic
and objective in terms of tone, presentation and sound documentation, in his attempt
to redress the historical imbalance. He touches on numerous sensitive controversies
but this can be regarded as one of the best expressions of the moderate and balanced
Polish view.

155   Out of the inferno. Poles remember the Holocaust.
Edited by Richard C. Lukas.   Lexington, Kentucky: University Press
of Kentucky, 1989. 201p.

A major collection of personal accounts by Poles of what life was like under vicious
Nazi occupation during the Second World War. The author, in his introduction,
demolishes the alleged connection between Polish anti-Semitism and the Nazi
building of their death camps in Poland. He also produces a valuable corrective view
on the issue of Polish-Jewish relations in this period.

156 **Birkenau. The camp of death.**
Marco Nahon, translated from the French by Jacqueline Havaux
Bowers. Tuscaloosa, Alabama: University of Alabama Press, 1990.
149p. (Judaic Studies series). bibliog.).
The memoirs of a Greek Jew's experiences at Birkenau-Auschwitz and Dachau and of
the medical 'experiments' carried out by the infamous Dr Joseph Mengele. For an
illustrated introduction to the subject aimed at a general readership see *Auschwitz.
Nazi extermination camp*. Foreword by Józef Buszko, translated by Ian M. Taylor,
Lech Petrowicz (Warsaw: Interpress, 1985. 204p. bibliog.).

157 **Values and violence in Auschwitz: a sociological analysis.**
Anna Pawełczyńska, translated by Catherine Leach. Berkeley,
California: University of California Press, 1980. 170p.
A sociological study of the moral bonds and the social communities formed by the
inmates of Auschwitz in order to give themselves the inner strength to continue under
hideous and hopeless conditions.

158 **No time-limit for these crimes!**
Czesław Pilichowski. Warsaw: Interpress, 1980. 180p.
A publicist study of German war-crimes against the Polish population during the
Second World War. It deals with reprisals, deportations and both labour and
extermination camps and opposes any statute of limitations for the perpetrators of such
atrocities. Written by the Chairman of the Main Committee for Investigating Hitlerite
War-Crimes in Poland from 1965-85; in the West he was generally perceived as being
closely associated with the Partisan propaganda drives of the late 1960s.

159 **And I am afraid of my dreams.**
Wanda Półtawska, translated by Mary Craig. London: Hodder &
Stoughton, 1987. 191p.
The personal reminiscences of a Polish POW held in the Ravensbruck concentration
camp north of Berlin. The largest Nazi camp for women, it was infamous for its
pseudo-medical 'experiments' on its inmates. It is estimated that 17,000 of the 30,000
Polish women (out of a total of 132,000) imprisoned there perished. The category of
concentration camp literature, which overlaps with that on the Holocaust in the next
section, is enormous. A far from exhaustive list of items not covered in full in this
bibliography would include the following; Jack Eisner, *The Survivor* (London: Sphere,
1980. 263p.). Fania Fenelon, *Playing for time* (London: Sphere, 1980. 253p.). Thomas
Geve, *Youth in Chains* (Jerusalem: Rubin Mass, 1981. 261p.). Eugene Heimler,
Concentration Camp (1979). Wiesław Kielar, *Annus Mundi. 1,500 days in Auschwitz-
Birkenau*, (New York: Times Books, 1980. 312p.). Isabella Leitner, *Fragments of
Isabella. A memoir of Auschwitz* (London: New English Library, 1980. 83p.). Nyiszli
Miklos, *Auschwitz. A doctor's eye-witness account* (London: Mayflower, 1978. 158p.).
Pietro Mirchuk, *In the German mills of death, 1941-45* (Washington: Survivors of the
Holocaust, 1976. 225p.). Filip Muller, *Auschwitz inferno. The testimony of a
Sonderkomando* (London: Routledge & Kegan Paul, 1979. 180p.). Ellio Romano, *A
generation of wrath* (London; Severn House, 1984. 288p.).

160   **Stutthof. A historical guide.**
Tadeusz Skutnik.   Warsaw: Krajowa Agencja Wydawnicza, 1980. 42p.
A Nazi concentration camp for civilians situated in Elbląg province, Stutthof had a particularly high mortality rate; about 85,000 of the 110,000 prisoners (most of them Polish) died there.

161   **Polish children during the Second World War.**
Zofia Tokarz.   Warsaw: Interpress, 1986. 13p.
A short pamphlet on the subject of German war-crimes against Polish children during World War Two.

Jews

162   **The Łódź Ghetto; inside a community under siege.**
Edited by Alan Adelson, Robert Lapides.   New York: Viking, 1989.
526p. bibliog.
A compilation of photographs, some in colour, and extracts from diaries, notebooks, documents and other sources. It was inspired and developed out of Dobroszycki's, *Chronicle of the Łódź Ghetto* (see item no. 171).

163   **Documents on the Holocaust; selected sources on the destruction of the Jews of Germany and Austria, Poland and the Soviet Union.**
Edited by Yitzhak Arad, Yisrael Gutman, Abraham Margoliot.
Jerusalem: Yad Vashem, 1981. 504p. bibliog.
The editors aimed to produce a comprehensive collection of 213 documents, for both students and laymen, interested in the history of the Holocaust. The section on Poland (documents 73-168), introduced by Gutman, illustrates German policy towards the Jews, the organization and activities of Jewish councils and underground resistance movements, Polish attitudes towards the Jews and the brutality of the concentration and extermination camps.

164   **The Warsaw ghetto: a Christian's testimony.**
Władysław Bartoszewski, translated by G. Cappellari.   New York:
Harper & Row, 1988. London: Lamp Press, 1989. 117p.
The ex-chairman of the Warsaw PEN-club, and a prominent historian of contemporary Polish-Jewish relations with numerous well-known publications on the subject, Bartoszewski discusses Polish assistance to Jews during the Second World War in order to help them survive Nazi occupation and extermination policies.

165   **Winter in the morning: a young girl's life in the Warsaw Ghetto and beyond.**
Janina Bauman.   London: Virago Press, 1986. 195p.
An account, based on her diary but written some four decades later, by a survivor of the Warsaw Ghetto and the concentration camps. Also of interest are *Children of the Ghetto* by Sheva Glas-Wiener (translated by Sheila Young Fitzroy, Victoria: Globe Press, 1983) which recalls a childhood spent in a camp near Łódź, and also *Return to*

Auschwitz. The remarkable story of a girl who survived the Holocaust, by Kitty Hart (London: Panther; New York: Atheneum, 1983. 240p.).

166 **The last Jew from Węgrow. The memoirs of a survivor of the step-by-step genocide in Poland.**
Shraga Feivel Bielawski, edited by Louis W. Liebowitch. New York: Praeger, 1991. 165p.
The recollections of a Holocaust survivor living in a small town fifty miles outside Warsaw. Bielawski details the systematic destruction of the Jewish community living there by the Nazis.

167 **Auschwitz chronicle, 1939-45. From the archives of the Auschwitz memorial and the German Federal archives.**
Danuta Czech, foreword by Walter Laqueur. London: I. B. Tauris, 1990. 855p. bibliog.
A complete chronological record based on the surviving camp documents of the development of the Auschwitz death camp and its annexes throughout the whole period of its existence. It includes the most comprehensive listing of the numbers of victims.

168 **A square of sky; and a touch of earth.**
Janina David. New York: W. W. Norton, 1964. 221p.;
Harmondsworth, England: Penguin, 1981. 349p.
A personal account by a Jewish survivor of the Warsaw Ghetto. The sequel was *A touch of earth. A wartime childhood* (New York: Orion Press, 1969. 207p.).

169 **The Holocaust and the historians.**
Lucy S. Dawidowicz. Cambridge, Massachusetts: Harvard University Press, 1981. 187p.
An outstanding specialist explores the literature on the subject to determine how the Holocaust has been treated by historians at different times, and in a wide range of countries. Chapter five, on 'Polish historical revisionism', makes some useful points about the return to integral nationalism by the Stalinists and the Partisans; but her overall interpretation of the balance of factors in the coverage of the Polish-Jewish relationship is somewhat controversial, especially as she down-plays the significance of the gradual evolution of post-1970 Polish historiography.

170 **Jews in Eastern Poland and the USSR, 1939-46.**
Edited by Norman Davies, Antony Polonsky. Basingstoke, England: Macmillan, 1991. 326p.
A joint publication, sponsored by the School of Slavonic Studies, London University, and the Institute for Polish-Jewish Studies, Oxford, recording a conference held in Jerusalem in February 1988. The editors introduce the subject, and of the thirteen chapters by specialists those of most general interest may be Ryszard Terlecki's examination of the Jewish issue in the Polish Army in the USSR and the Middle East, and Włodzimierz Rozenbaum's discussion of the role of postwar communists in the USSR before their return to postwar Poland.

171 **The chronicle of the Łódź Ghetto.**
Edited by Lucjan Dobroszycki, translated by Richard Lourie (et al).
New Haven: Yale University Press, 1984. 551p.
This English edition contains about a quarter of the bulletins, written in Polish and German, by a variety of individuals in the ghetto's archive office between 12 January 1941 and 30 July 1944. They serve as a chronicle of the life and activities of the Jewish community in the Łódź ghetto which is estimated to have numbered about 240,000 at peak. The bulk of the final population of 68,561 were deported to Auschwitz-Birkenau immediately after the final entry.

172 **In the shadow of Auschwitz. The Polish Government-in-Exile and the Jews.**
David Engel. Charlotte, North Carolina: University of North Carolina Press, 1987. 338p. bibliog.
A detailed, but reasonably balanced examination given the controversial nature of the subject of the thinking and policy of the Polish Government-in-Exile towards the Jewish Question during the first half of the Second World War. Engel presents the moderate Jewish viewpoint accepting that there was not an automatic continuity between the legacy of alleged interwar Polish anti-semitism and the wartime Holocaust. Nevertheless the Government's guidelines on the issue favoured the interests of ethnic Poles rather more than those of Jewish Poles and handled the issue tactically to further its central interests. On the other hand Jewish obduracy was as much responsible as Polish irascibility for the official misunderstandings and splits which led to the failure to gain Allied assistance against Nazi preparations for the Holocaust and later for its victims.

173 **Atlas of the Holocaust.**
Martin Gilbert. New York: Holt, Rinehart & Winston, 1981. 368p.
Oxford: Pergamon, 1988. 256p. bibliog.
Contains 316 maps which provide an indispensible guide to the location and functioning of the Nazi extermination camps and units in Poland and elsewhere during the Second World War. It also contains exhaustive, but clearly presented, information on deportation routes, the size of the Jewish communities and the number of Jewish survivors.

174 **Auschwitz and the allies.**
Martin Gilbert. Feltham, England: Hamlyn, 1983. London: Mandarin, 1991. 368p. bibliog.
Gilbert examines the controversial question of the reasons why the Western Allies were so slow to respond to the Nazi extermination of the Jews during the Second World War.

175 **The Warsaw Ghetto: a photographic record, 1941-44.**
Edited by Joe J. Heydecker, foreword by Heinrich Boll. London: I. B. Tauris, 1990. 96p.
A collection of original photographs concentrating on snapshots of individuals. These are designed to convey a sense of personal experience of what life was like in the Warsaw Ghetto. A similar compendium edited by Ulrich Keller, covering a wide range

of ghetto life and administration is *The Warsaw Ghetto in photographs. 206 views made in 1941.* (New York: Dover, London, England: Constable, 1984. 131p.).

176 **The Jews and the Poles in World War II.**
    Stefan Korboński. New York: Hippocrene Books, 1989. 136p.
    bibliog.
Stefan Korboński was a noted leader of the Polish Underground movement. This book, written at the very end of his life, sought to present the case against the 'groundless, unfair and slanderous' charges by some that the Poles must share the responsibility for not preventing the Nazi slaughter of the Jews during the Second World War. For the contrary Jewish argument see *Unequal Victims. Poles and Jews during the Second World War.* by Yisrael Gutman, Shmuel Krakowski, translated by Ted Gorelick, Witold Jedlicki, (New York: Holocaust Library, 1986. 399p. bibliog.).

177 **Ghetto diary.**
    Janusz Korczak (pseud. Henryk Goldszmit), translated by Edwin P.
    Kulawiec. New York: Holocaust Library; Washington, DC:
    University Press of America, 1978. 127p.
The memoirs of the celebrated Jewish doctor and philanthropist (1878-1942) who ran the childrens' home and orphanage in the Warsaw Ghetto and who chose to go to his death with his wards at Treblinka. See also Maria Falkowska, *A chronology of the life, activities and work of Janusz Korczak*, translated by Edwin P. Kulawiec. (New York: Kościuszko Foundation, 1980. 50p.). Korczak's book of adventure stories for children, written in 1923, was first published in English as *King Matt the First*, translated by Richard Lourie, introduced by Bruno Bettelheim (New York: Farrar, Straus & Giroux, 1986. 332p.); also see *Little King Matty and the desert island*, translated by Adam Cząsak. (London: Joanna Pinewood Enterprises, 1990. 432p.).

178 **The war of the doomed; Jewish armed resistance in Poland, 1942-44.**
    Shmuel Krakowski, translated from the Hebrew by Orah Blaustein.
    New York: Holmes Meir, 1984. 340p. bibliog.
A detailed exposition of the case for the significance of Jewish armed resistance in Poland during the Second World War. The Warsaw Ghetto Uprising has been heavily chronicled so this study concentrates on other ghettoes and regions, the camps and partisan organizations. Written by a prominent scholar from Tel Aviv University the study is based on a wide range of primary sources and interviews with numerous participants.

179 **Survival in Auschwitz and the re-awakening; two memoirs.**
    Primo Levi, translated from the Italian by Stuart Woolf. New York:
    Summit Books, 1986. 397p.
A celebrated postwar Italian writer sets out the reminiscences of his deportation and stay in Auschwitz in 1944, and his roundabout return to Italy via the USSR.

180   A cup of tears; a diary of the Warsaw Ghetto.
      Abraham Lewin, translated by Christopher Hutton, edited by Antony
      Polonsky.   Oxford: Basil Blackwell, Institute for Polish-Jewish
      Studies, 1988. London: Fontana, 1990. 310p.
Lewin was a pro-Zionist teacher in a school for Jewish girls in inter-war Warsaw.
Polonsky's edition contains Lewin's diary of events in the Warsaw Ghetto from March
1942 until 16 January 1943 when Lewin is presumed to have perished in a series of
major deportations to the death camps. A major original source on this tragic episode.

181   The King of Children. A biography of Janusz Korczak.
      Betty Jean Lifton.   New York: Farrar, Strauss & Giroux, 1987.
      London: Chatto & Windus, 1988. 464p.
An authoritative biography of the life and work of the Jewish child psychologist and
philanthropist. His work in saving Jewish children in the Warsaw Ghetto orphanage,
for which he is best remembered, is covered in part four. His life inspired a famous
film by Andrzej Wajda entitled simply *Korczak*. See also Adina Blady-Szwajger,
translated by Jasja Darowska, Danusia Stok. *I remember nothing more. The Warsaw
children's hospital and the Jewish Resistance* (London: Collins Harvill, 1990. 184p.
bibliog.).

182   The Holocaust in history.
      Michael R. Marrus.   Hanover, New Hampshire: University Press of
      New England, 1987. London: Weidenfeld & Nicholson, 1988. 267p.
      bibliog.
Widely regarded as one of the most outstanding attempts to place a broad range of
issues concerning the Holocaust in a balanced historical perspective. Marrus deals with
the role of Germany's allies, collaborators and vanquished states, the Holocaust's
victims and Jewish resistance, public opinion and bystanders and whether more Jews
could have been saved at the end of the Second World War.

183   I shall live. Surviving against all odds, 1939-45.
      Henry Orenstein, foreword by Claude Lanzmann.   New York:
      Beaufort Book Publishers, 1987. Oxford: Oxford University Press,
      1988. 288p.
The well-written memoirs of a Jewish survivor of the Second World War Holocaust
from Hrubieszów in Eastern Poland. Orenstein lived through Soviet and German
occupation and somehow came through the horror of the Budzyn, Płaszów,
Majdanek, Ravensbruck and Sachsenhausen camps. Another similar account of a
Jewish student's quest for survival in Nazi occupied Eastern Poland is Oscar Pinkus'
The house of ashes. (London: I. B. Tauris, 1991. 282p.).

184   Witness. Life in occupied Kraków.
      Miriam Peleg-Mariańska, Mordechai Peleg, translated by Teresa
      Prout.   London: Routledge, 1991. 187p.
A memoir by a husband and wife who survived the Second World War on false papers
as 'Aryans'. This is an account of their experiences whilst working for the Council for
Providing Assistance to Jews (Żegota) in Nazi occupied Kraków.

185 **My brother's keeper? Recent Polish debates on the Holocaust.**
Edited by Antony Polonsky. London: Routledge, 1990. 242p.

A symposium of sixteen intellectually hard and truthful contributions by Polish and Jewish historians and publicists to the long-running debate about their own and Polish reactions to the Nazi exermination of the Jews on Polish territory during the Second World War. The debate was renewed by Jan Błoński's controversial article, 'The poor Poles look at the ghetto' in *Tygodnik Powszechny* in January 1978.

186 **Escape from Sobibór. The heroic story of the Jews who escaped from a Nazi death camp.**
Richard L. Raschke. Boston, Massachusetts: Houghton, Mifflin, 1982. 389p. London: Sphere, 1984. 433p. bibliog.

Based on the recollections of survivors, this is an account of the most successful revolt and escape by Jews during the Second World War, from the Sobibór death camp near Chełm in Eastern Poland.

187 **Polish-Jewish relations during the Second World War.**
Emanuel Ringleblum, introduction by Joseph Kermisch. New York: Fertig, 1976. 330p. First published, Jerusalem: Yad Vashem, 1974.

Ringleblum's work is now established as one of the most academically convincing studies of the complex relationship between the Jewish and the Polish communities in Poland during the Second World War.

188 **The survivor in us all. A memoir of the Holocaust.**
Erna F. Rubinstein. Hamden, Connecticut: Archon Books, 1983. 185p.

A Jewish Second World War survivor recounts her experiences. Similar accounts are: by Helen Kotlar, *We lived in a grave* (New York: Shengold Publishers, 1980. 124p); and by Rachela & Sam Walshaw, *From out of the firestorm: a memoir of the Holocaust* (New York: Shapolsky Publishers, 1991. 154p.).

189 **A private war; surviving in Poland on false papers, 1941-45.**
Bruno Shatyn, translated by Oscar Swan, foreword by Norman Davies. Detroit: Wayne State University Press, 1985. 285p.

An interesting account of how a Polish Jew survived the Nazi occupation by living as an Aryan on false papers.

190 **When light pierced the darkness. Christian rescue of Jews in Nazi occupied Poland.**
Nechama Tec. Oxford: Oxford University Press, 1986. 262p. bibliog.

An objective and systematic academic study, based on interviews and a broad range of sources. The author is a sociologist, herself a Jewish survivor who pretended to be an Aryan Pole during the German occupation. Tec attempts to identify Jewish survivors and Polish rescuers, and to understand their motivations and behaviour. This is a vividly written and impeccably documented work.

Polish Underground, Government-in-Exile and forces in the West.

191 The Warsaw Rising of 1944.

Jan Ciechanowski. Cambridge, England: Cambridge University Press, 1974. 332p. bibliog.

The major academic study in English of the Warsaw Rising of August-September 1944 organized by the Polish Home Army (AK). Ciechanowski analyses the background, as well as the course of the Rising and its military and diplomatic repercussions. His argument concerning the consequences of the Home Army leadership's attempts to ensure that the liberation of Warsaw should not lead to the installation of a Soviet controlled administration remains valid. The study now needs to be supplemented by subsequent Polish analyses of Soviet reactions and decisions.

192 The civilian population and the Warsaw uprising.

Joanna K. Hanson. Cambridge, England: Cambridge University Press, 1982. 345p. bibliog.

This excellent academic, although very readable study considers how the uprising in Summer 1944 against the Germans affected the civilian population of Warsaw. Hanson argues that, although the uprising initially generated universal enthusiasm, the memory of its suppression and of the total destruction of Warsaw contributed to the postwar spirit of realism in the political compromises designed to prevent the repetition of similar human tragedies.

193 Dying we live. The personal chronicle of a young freedom-fighter in Warsaw, 1939-45.

Julian E. Kulski. New York: Holt, Rinehart & Winston, 1979. 304p. maps.

Personal reminiscences of the author's experiences, from August 1939 onwards, as a young resistance fighter in German occupied Warsaw during the Second World War.

194 Poland's secret envoy, 1939-45.

George Lerski (pseud. 'Jur'). New York: Bicentennial Publishing, 1988. 278p.

First published in London in 1984 as well as by the Polish underground press. Lerski was sent as a personal courier by Sikorski and the London Government-in-Exile to its representatives in occupied Poland. He later became secretary to Prime Minister Tomasz Arciszewski which meant that he continued to meet many of Poland's most prominent democratic politicians during the Second World War.

195 Polish contribution to the ultimate allied victory in the Second World
War.
Tadeusz Modelski. Worthing, England: The author, 1988. 211p.
2nd ed. 278p.

A prewar Polish Government official and retired *emigré* Sussex farmer, the author has
attempted an assessment of Poland's contribution, political and military, to the
ultimate Allied victory in the Second World War. A large part of the original 1986
publication (p. 15-107) was a historical chronology: unfortunately the analysis is
disjointed and rather unsuccessful.

196 Courier from Warsaw.
Jan Nowak. Detroit: Wayne State University Press; London: Collins,
1982. 477p.

The important wartime experiences of a courier who maintained high level contact
between the Polish Home and External Resistance movements are recounted in this
volume. He was in Warsaw during the uprising of Summer 1944 but managed to escape
to England at its end.

197 Polish Resistance movement in Poland and abroad, 1939-45.
Edited by Stanisław Okęcki, translated by Bohdan Ambroziewicz,
Halina Dzierżanowska, Jerzy Tomaszczyk. Warsaw: Państwowe
Wydawnictwo Naukowe, 1987. 453p.

Contains chapters by Polish specialists on the activities of the Polish Resistance
movements during the Second World War in Poland, France, Soviet territories,
Czechoslovakia and in the Scandinavian, Mediterranean and Low Country regions as
well as in the Reich itself. The authors argue that the Polish resistance in all areas was
both legitimate and legal given the character of Nazi war-aims and methods.

198 Airlift to Poland; the rising of 1944.
Neil Orpen. London: Foulsham, 1984. 184p. bibliog.

A retired South African military participant examines the problems involved in
mounting the Allied airlift from Brindisi to support the Warsaw Uprising of Summer
1944. The Polish, South African and British aircrews who carried out 186 sorties
suffered almost seventeen per cent losses. They were not always able to parachute
their supplies into insurgent held sectors of the city because of a range of technical and
climatic difficulties and Soviet lack of co-operation which weakened the Allies' political
will to continue.

199 The Polish white book: official documents concerning Polish-German
and Polish-Soviet relations, 1933-39.
Polish Ministry of Foreign Affairs. London: The author. 1940. 222p.

An official collection of documents published by the Government-in-Exile in London
designed to demonstrate that Poland was wholly the victim of unprovoked German and
Soviet aggression in September 1939.

200　Józef Retinger. Memoirs of an eminence grise.
　　Edited by John Pomian.　Brighton, England: Harvester Press;
　　London: Chatto & Windus, 1972. 265p.
Retinger was a close confidant of Sikorski's who entrusted him with many delicate
missions during the Second World War so this constitutes an important primary source
on Polish resistance politics.

201　The man in the middle; a story of the Polish Resistance, 1940-44.
　　Witold Sagajłło.　London: Leo Cooper & Secker & Warburg, 1984.
　　220p.
A popularly written account of the life and experiences of Sagajłło, who was born in
White Russia, became a sailor in the Polish navy, and eventually, during the Second
World War, sailed in the British navy. The book naturally concentrates on his
resistance experiences in German occupied Poland, and his escape from Soviet
controlled Poland at its end.

202　Freely I served.
　　Stanisław Sosabowski.　Nashville, Tennessee: Battery, 1982. 203p.
　　(reprint of Parachute general. London: William Kimber, 1961. 159p.
　　maps).
The author narrates his experience as commanding officer of the Polish Autonomous
Parachute Brigade. He participated very bravely in the combined British-led Arnhem
operation in Eastern Holland in September 1944 which ended in disaster through no
fault of the Poles.

203　Sikorski. Soldier and statesman. A collection of essays.
　　Edited by Keith Sword, introduction by Frank Roberts.　London:
　　Orbis Books, 1990. 224p.
A useful symposium on Sikorski's life and career. The contributions by Wapiński on
his early career, Garlicki on his relations with Piłsudski, Polonsky on his post-1928
opposition activities and Szudek on his military capacities confirm that Sikorski was a
capable, although generally inferior, rival to Piłsudski. Ciechanowski, Coutouvidis
and Sir Frank Roberts demonstrate how Sikorski's performance as Poland's wartime
leader, until his tragic death in July 1943 in the faulty Liberator bomber off Gibraltar,
indicates that he probably would not have coped with Russo-Polish relations and the
Yalta Settlement any better than his successors.

204　The Polish army, 1939-45.
　　Steven J. Zaloga.　London: Osprey Publishing, 1982. 40p. (Men-at-
　　Arms Series no. 117).
A beautifully edited and illustrated large format series. Zaloga's text was criticized for
some mistakes but the concise overview, dealing with a narrower topic, by Krzysztof
Barbarski in the same series met with greater acclaim (Polish Armour, 1939-45.
London: Osprey Publishing, 1982. 40p.). Barbarski covers armoured and support-
vehicles, including weapons systems, organizational units, uniforms, insignia and
markings.

205 **Nothing but honour. The story of the Warsaw uprising, 1944.**
Janusz Kazimierz Zawodny. London: Macmillan; Stanford,
California: Hoover Institution Press, 1978. 328p. bibliog.

A meticulously researched examination of the sixty-three day-long uprising by Polish
Underground and civilian forces against the German occupiers of Warsaw in the
summer of 1944. Zawodny presents the Polish view of the clash between Polish and
Soviet aims which led to the Soviet failure to provide assistance to the insurgents, and
to the tragedy of the city's total destruction.

Soviet aspects

206 **Revolution from abroad. The Soviet conquest of Poland's Western
Ukraine and Western Belorussia**
Jan Tomasz Gross. Princeton, New Jersey: Princeton University
Press, 1988. 334p. bibliog.

An academic analysis, based on original interview material from participants, of the
sociological impact involved in the building of a totalitarian political system in the
Eastern Territories occupied by the Red Army from 17 September 1939 onwards.

207 **War through children's eyes. The Soviet occupation of Poland and the
deportations, 1939-41.**
Edited by Irena Grudzińska-Gross, Jan Tomasz Gross, translated by
Ronald Strom, Dan Rivers. Stanford, California: Hoover Institution
Press, 1981. 260p. bibliog.

The volume is made up of 120 children's essays, lodged in the Hoover Institution,
describing the experience of Soviet invasion and occupation in what had been interwar
Poland's Eastern Provinces.

208 **A boy in the Gulag.**
Jerzy Kmiecik. New York: Quartet Books, 1983. 238p. map.

Gulag memoirs of a sixteen-year-old Polish boy who fled from German invasion in
1939 into Soviet imprisonment. He was eventually repatriated with other Poles out of
the USSR in 1942.

209 **The road to Katyń. A soldier's story.**
Salomon W. Slowes, edited by Władysław T. Bartoszewski,
translated by Naftali Greenwood. Oxford: Basil Blackwell – Institute
of Jewish Studies, 1992. 234p.

One of the 448 survivors from the three camps (in his case Kozielsk), which housed the
15,000 Polish reserve army officers before their slaughter by the NKVD at 'Katyń'
analyses the question against the background of his own experiences. In fact only the
Kozielsk inmates were murdered in the Katyń woods while those from the other two
camps were killed in locales which only began to be traced down in the early 1990s.

210 **The Soviet takeover of the Polish Eastern Provinces, 1939-41.**
Edited by Keith Sword. London: Macmillan – SSEES, 1991. 318p.
bibliog.

The papers cover the Soviet occcupation of interwar Poland's eastern territories and the fate of its mixed population up till the German invasion of Summer 1941. John Erickson, Tomasz Strzembosz and Jerzy Węgierski deal with the military aspects of Polish resistance to the Soviet invasion from 17 September 1939 onwards, Jan Gross discusses the fate of captured POWs and Zbigniew Siemaszko examines Stalin's mass deportations from the region. David Marples and Mikolaj Iwanow demonstrate that, contrary to Soviet propaganda, Ukrainians and Belorussians suffered as severely as the Poles as the result of incorporation in the USSR.

211 **My century. The Odyssey of a Polish intellectual.**
Aleksander Wat, edited and translated by Richard Lourie, foreword by
Czesław Miłosz. New York: W. W. Norton, 1988. 407p.

This is a translation of Miłosz' 1977 Polish-language edition of his tape-recorded conversations with Wat on his life as an interwar *avant-garde* communist fellow-traveller and on his wide-ranging experience of Soviet prisons and exile from Lwów to Alma Ata during the Second World War. For Wat's small corpus of almost forgotten poetry, see *With the skin. Selected poems.* Aleksander Wat, edited and translated by Czesław Miłosz, Leonard Nathan (Harmondsworth, England: Penguin, 1991. 111p. [Penguin International Poets]. Reprint, New York: Eco, 1969).

212 **The dark side of the moon.**
Zoe Zajdlerowa, edited by John Coutouvidis, Tom Lane. London:
Harvester Wheatsheaf, 1989. 182p. bibliog.

A re-issue of a much published postwar memoir which highlighted the fate of over one million Poles deported to the USSR and their Gulag experience during the Second World War, (London: Faber, 1946; New York: C. Scribner, 1947. 299p.). The new edition is tightly edited and introduced by two British academics who place the subject in its historical context and bring the issue of rehabilitation up to date in an Afterword. Amongst other personal reminiscences of Polish deportees into the USSR are; Józef Czapski, *The Inhuman Land* (London: Polish Cultural Foundation, 1987. 356p. reprint of New York: Sheed & Ward and London: Chatto & Windus, both 1951). John Geller, *Through darkness to dawn* (London: Veritas Foundation, 1989. 121p.). Janka Goldberger, *Stalin's little guest* (London: J. Lunzer, 1988. 190p.). Anna Kant, Norbert Kant, translated by Barbara O'Driscoll, *Extermination. Killing Poles in Stalin's Russia* (London; Unicorn, 1991. 241p.). Zdzisława Krystyna Kawecka, *Journey without a ticket. To England through Siberia* (Nottingham: Author's publication, 1990. 3rd ed. 196p.). Barbara Porajska, *From the steppes to the savanah* (London: Hodder & Staughton, 1990. 144p.). Danuta Teczarowska, *Deportation into the unknown* (Braughton: Merlin Books, 1985. 178p.).

213 **Death in the forest; the story of the Katyń massacre.**
Janusz Kazimierz Zawodny. Notre Dame, Indiana: Notre Dame
University Press, 1962. 235p. bibliog.

Zawodny's examination was an authoritative demonstration that the Katyń murders were carried out in 1940 when the USSR controlled the territory and not in 1941 after the German invasion as it claimed. The conclusion is also an implicit criticism of the immoral refusal of Western elites and public opinion to accept this basic truth until well after the Cold War started.

Communist Poland (pre-1980)

214 **Flashpoint Poland.**
George Blazynski. New York: Pergamon, 1979. 416p. bibliog.

A detailed and valuable, although somewhat turgidly written, political history of the Gierek era by a BBC journalist of Polish origins. Edward Gierek's term as PZPR First Secretary from 1970 to 1980 was marked by the contrast between its initial dynamic social and cultural development and eventual political and economic collapse. The book is somewhat incomplete as it was published just before the 1980 outburst; its strengths are, however, that it conveys a genuine picture of the optimism and achievements of the early 1970s in Part I. It also brings out in Part II the ambiguous character of the factors which then gathered force in building up towards the 1980 crisis.

215 **Poland; bridge for the abyss.**
Richard Hiscocks. London: Oxford University Press, 1963. 359p. maps. bibliog.

An interpretation of political, economic, social and intellectual developments in Poland from 1944 up till the early years of the Gomułka *regime*. Its excellent sources and elegant literary style means that it is still one of the most readable accounts of this period of communist Poland especially on 'October' and its consequences.

216 **Countdown. The Polish upheavals of 1956, 1968, 1970, 1980. . .**
Jakub Karpiński, translated by Olga Amsterdamska, Gene Moore. New York: Karz-Cohl, 1982. 214p.

A readable, although basic, chronologically organized political history, which covers postwar Poland's crisis-ridden development up to 1977.

217 **Prelude to Solidarity. Poland and the politics of the Gierek regime.**
Keith John Lepak. New York: Columbia University Press, 1988. 271p. bibliog.

Lepak's crisper and academically stronger study now replaces Blazynski's earlier history as the most authoritative examination of the Gierek period. The contradictions caused in every field by Gierek's attempts to modernize while maintaining a rationalized and technocratic form of communist hegemonic rule over an increasingly educated, differentiated and dynamic society are analysed fairly and soundly. The central thesis that Gierek's failure to manage the stress and strains generated by his development policy, his halfway house between autocracy and pluralism as well as his disastrous economic mistakes and tolerance of elite corrruption caused the intense political and social crisis of 1980 and the near-collapse of communist rule seems well founded.

218   **Red eagle. The army in politics, 1944-88.**
Andrew A. Michta.   Stanford, California: Hoover Institution Press,
1990. 270p. bibliog.
A historical overview of civil-military relations in communist Poland. Michta concludes
that the party and the military mainly worked together in their common concern of
defending the communist system.

219   **The beginnings of communist rule in Poland.**
Edited by Antony Polonsky, Bolesław Drukier.   London: Routledge
& Kegan Paul, 1980. 464p.
A detailed account covering the period from the establishment of the National Council
for the Homeland (KRN) in Lublin to the enlargement of the Provisional Government
by the inclusion of some non-communist politicians. The editors' work is based on
documents which had just become available. A list of pseudonyms and biographical
data is included.

220   **Background to crisis; policy and politics in Gierek's Poland.**
Edited by Maurice D. Simon, Roger E. Kanet.   Boulder, Colorado:
Westview Press, 1981. 418p.
This volume is the result of a major symposium. Thirteen American specialists
overview the aspects of the Gierek period which led up to the 1980 crisis.

221   **Poland 1944-62; the Sovietization of a captive people.**
Richard Felix Staar.   Baton Rouge, Louisiana: Louisiana State
University Press, 1962. Reprinted, Westview, Connecticut: Greenwood
Press, 1975. 320p. bibliog.
The author, a well-known Kremlinologist, sets out to prove the thesis of the title. Staar
presents informative and exceptionally heavily documented material of a traditional
social science character especially on communist elite composition, turnover and
dynamics. Despite the ideologically motivated trappings of an erstwhile Marines
professor of politics this remains a basic work on the Stalinist period in Poland.

222   **The independent satellite. Society and politics in Poland since 1945.**
Hansjakob Stehle.   New York: Praeger, 1965. 361p. bibliog.
Has weathered time as one of the most readable examinations of the first half of
communist rule in Poland. Stehle, a West German journalist, combines academic
thoroughness with exceptional insight and a vivid rendering of personal experience. He
covers the original features of the communist party and the Roman Catholic Church,
the 'Polish Way' and the issues of Polish security and the division of Germany and
Europe.

223   **Poland in perspective.**
Konrad Syrop.   London: R. Hale, 1982. 255p. maps.
A revised version of the author's *Poland. between the hammer and the anvil* (London:
R. Hale, 1968. 200p.) up-dated till the declaration of martial law.

224 **Spring in October. The story of the Polish revolution, 1956.**
Konrad Syrop. London: Weidenfeld & Nicholson, 1957. 207p.

This is high grade academic journalism, but still remains one of the best introductory accounts of the Polish 'October' of 1956. It does, however, need to be supplemented by the voluminous subsequent Polish language material on the subject. A useful summary is included, with long passages of direct translation, of Gomułka's crucial speech to the Eighth Plenum of the Polish United Workers' Party on 20 October 1956 (p. 98-110).

225 **Poland. Socialist state, rebellious nation.**
Ray Taras. Boulder, Colorado: Westview Press, 1986. 200p.

A pithy and highly interpretative essay. Taras' main theme is the historically conditioned split between the socialist state and the rebellious national community in Poland which produced the six great postwar confrontations before communism came to an end. Successive chapters review the historical background, the politics of the communist period, Poland's international situation and her postwar economic, cultural and social development admirably for a student and general readership.

226 **Oni. Stalin's Polish puppets.**
Teresa Torańska, translated by Agnieszka Kołakowska. London: Collins Harvill; New York: Harper & Row, 1987. 384p.

These interviews, carried out by an opposition journalist, with veteran survivors who had played important roles in the Stalinist period (Edward Ochab, Roman Werfel, Jakub Berman, Julia Minc and the somewhat contrasting figure of Stefan Staszewski) were widely and very effectively used as political propaganda by Solidarity and its Western supporters. It is, however, an interesting historical record and can now be read more dispassionately as an evocative source of information.

Regional history

227 **History of Gdańsk.**
Edmund Cieślak, Czesław Biernat, translated by Bożena Blaim, George M. Hyde. Gdańsk: Wydawnictwo Morskie, 1988. 547p.

A splendidly illustrated and authoritative history of Gdańsk from its foundation in the middle of the tenth century up till the present. The chapters on the city during the Second World War and the communist period are relatively skimpy (p. 461-525).

228 **Warsaw between the World Wars. Profile of the capital city in a developing land.**
Edward Wynot. New York: Columbia University Press, 1983. 375p. (East European Monographs no. 129). bibliog.

A history of interwar Warsaw which became the capital city of the newly independent state with all the centralized administrative and cultural prestige that accompanied it. Wynot covers Warsaw's economic, cultural, municipal and political life in extensive detail.

Ethnic Minorities

Germans

229 **To lose a war: memories of a German girl.**
Regina Maria Shelton.   Carbondale, Illinois: Southern Illinois
University Press, 1982. 228p.
The author reminisces about her Second World War experiences as a German girl
(born 1927) in Upper Silesia. Shelton had to leave at its end on the approach of the
Red Army and emigrated to the USA. This is a very personal account and contains few
insights either on Polish-German relations or the fate of the German expellees from
Poland.

230 **Gdańsk: national identity in the Polish-German borderlands.**
Carl Tighe.   London: Pluto, 1990. 314p. maps.
A leftwing polemic which takes Gdańsk as the focus of Polish-German national
antagonisms. It attempts to explain them in terms of the impact of industrialization and
capitalism on the formation of national identities and struggles in East-Central Europe.

Gypsies

231 **The gypsies in Poland. History and customs.**
Jerzy Ficowski, translated by Eileen Healey.   Warsaw: Interpress,
1989. 303p.
A lavishly illustrated work, partly in colour, presenting the history, social and cultural
customs, lifestyles and community organizations of the gypsies since they first appeared
in Poland in the fifteenth century. Ficowski's commentary gives due weight to the Nazi

extermination of most Polish gypsies during the Second World War. The book is less enlightening on postwar Stalinist attempts to integrate the remaining 20,000 odd gypsies into the workforce, for example at Nowa Huta, and about contemporary aspects of the gypsy problem including current Polish social attitudes.

Jews

232 The Jews in Poland.
Edited by Chimen Abramsky, Maciej Jachimczyk, Antony Polonsky. Oxford: Basil Blackwell, 1986. 264p. maps.

Contains seventeen papers which emerged from an international conference on Polish-Jewish studies held in Oxford in September 1984. According to the editors the essays describe 'the establishment, flourishing and destruction of one of the most important Jewish communities in the world'. The volume covers the whole historical period from Gieysztor's discussion of the beginning of Jewish settlement in the Polish lands to Łukasz Hirszowicz' analysis of the Jewish issue in postwar communist politics.

233 The scapegoats: the exodus of the remnants of Polish Jewry.
Józef Banas, translated by Tadeusz Szafar, edited by Lionel Kochan. London: Weidenfeld & Nicholson, 1979. 221p.

Banas, an engineer of Jewish origins who left Poland in 1969, presents a dispassionate and intellectually convincing analysis of the broad range of factors which produced the 'Anti-Zionist' campaign of 1967-68 and the March 1968 suppression of students and radicals in Poland. He is particularly enlightening on the rise of Mieczysław Moczar's national communist 'Partisan' faction and the mechanisms of power-struggle within the Polish communist party. This led to the tactical scapegoating of party members of Jewish origins, many of whom emigrated, as a cover for the broader suppression of all reformists.

234 The Jews in Warsaw. A history.
Edited by Władysław T. Bartoszewski, Antony Polonsky. Oxford: Basil Blackwell in association with the Institute for Polish-Jewish Studies, 1991. 392p.

A comprehensive and cohesive collection of 15 papers, most of which were originally published in *Polin* by some of the best specialists in the field. The volume gives a full account of the history of the Jewish community in Warsaw from the time it was first allowed to settle there in the late eighteenth century to its destruction during the Second World War.

235 A dream of belonging. My years in postwar Poland.
Janina Bauman. London: Virago Press, 1988. 202p.

An interesting and extremely well-written account, by the wife of the well-known revisionist-marxist sociologist Zygmunt Bauman. The latter was forced to leave Poland as a result of the Anti-Zionist purge of the late 1960s and since 1971 has been a Professor at Leeds University in Britain. The book concentrates on bringing out the complex web of personal identity problems in the postwar Polish-Jewish experience for the general reader by interweaving the past and the present as well as the personal and national-political dimensions. The author made a successful career in the film industry and was also a 'believing' socialist within the communist party. However, she gives away few 'insider's' hints in passing and leaves many questions unanswered.

236 **Journey to Poland.**
Alfred Döblin, translated by Joachim Neugroschel, edited by Heinz Graber. London: I. B. Tauris, 1991. 274p.

Alfred Döblin (1878-1957) was a Jewish doctor and novelist who lived in Germany but whose parents originated from Polish teritories. The above, recounting his personal quest for his family roots, was first published in 1925 (Berlin, S. Fischer Verlag). It gives a vivid picture of the Jewish communities in interwar Poland.

237 **The emancipation of the Jews in Poland, 1780-1870.**
Artur Eisenbach, introduced by Antony Polonsky. Oxford: Basil Blackwell, 1991. 640p. (Jewish Society and Culture).

An authoritative examination of the process of the legal emancipation of Jews in nineteenth century Poland written by the former Director of the Jewish Historical Institute in Warsaw.

238 **Polish Jewry. History and culture.**
Marian Fuks, Zygmunt Hoffman, Maurycy Horn, Jerzy Tomaszewski, translated by Bogna Piotrowska, Lech Petrowicz. Warsaw: Interpress, 1982. 196p.

An interesting and richly illustrated introduction to various aspects of the life of the Jewish community which was destroyed by the Nazis during the Second World War. The authors cover such aspects as art, education, customs, printing, theatre, music, the press and literature. The text also presents the historical background, the Nazi occupation period and subsqent postwar Jewish cultural development.

239 **Jewish privileges in the Polish Commonwealth. Charters of rights in the sixteenth to eighteenth centuries. Critical edition of original Latin and Polish documents with English introduction and notes.**
Edited by Jacob Goldberg. Jerusalem: Israel Academy of Sciences and Humanities, 1985. 477p. maps.

A most comprehensive and scrupulously annotated collection of documents on the subject set out in the title.

240 **The Jews of Poland between Two World Wars.**
Edited by Yisrael Gutman, Ezra Mendelson, Jehuda Reinharz, Chone Shmeruk. Hanover, New Hampshire: The University Press of New England, 1989. 574p.

Based on the proceedings of an international conference held at the Tauber Institute at Brandeis University; a comprehensive symposium of twenty-seven previously unpublished papers which provides a many-sided examination of the complex history of Polish Jewry during the interwar period.

241 **The Jews in Polish culture.**
Aleksander Hertz, translated by Richard Lourie, edited by Lucjan Dobroszycki. Evanston, Illinois: Northwestern University Press, 1992. 266p.
Hertz was an interwar sociologist who contributed to the Paris *Kultura* after the Second World War. This study, first published in Paris in the mid-1960s, discusses whether the Jews constituted a separate caste in interwar Poland. It also seeks to examine the mechanisms and the different layers of cultural interpenetration between Jews and Poles.

242 **The Jews in a Polish private town. The case of Opatów in the eighteenth century.**
Gershon David Hundert. Baltimore: Johns Hopkins University Press, 1992. 241p. bibliog.
A detailed academic case-study of a local Jewish community in the Kielce region of Little Poland. Designed to illustrate 'how central Jews were in the urban history' of eighteenth century Poland.

243 **Jewish-Polish co-existence.**
Edited by George J. Lerski, Halina T. Lerski. New York: Greenwood, 1986. 230p. (Bibliographies and Indexes in World History Series no. 5).
A comprehensive compilation of 2,778 entries divided into thirty-four chapters but without annotations or cross-references. The book was criticized for too many careless mistakes and for concentrating on the Jewish contribution to Polish history, neglecting the balance of Polish-Jewish relations over time.

244 **The Jewish community in Poland. Historical essays.**
Isaac Lewin. New York: Philosophical Library, 1985. 247p. map. bibliog.
A wide-reaching history of what the author claims is a thousand years of the Jewish presence in Poland.

245 **Social and political history of the Jews in Poland.**
Joseph Marcus. Berlin: Mouton, 1983. 569p. bibliog.
The most comprehensive study of the subject covering both social and political aspects.

246 **Memoirs of a Jewish revolutionary.**
Hersch Mendel, translated by Robert Michaels. London: Pluto, 1988. 366p.
Memoirs of a Jewish revolutionary socialist who was born in Poland in 1893. Mendel ran the gamut of all varieties of Jewish, Polish and Russian socialism ending up as a Trotskyist and then a Zionist. The volume was first published in Hebrew (1959) and German (1979).

247 **The Jews of East-Central Europe between the wars.**
Ezra Mendelson. Bloomington, Indiana: Indiana University Press,
1983. bibliog.
Examines the internal development as well as the relationship with the host community
in interwar Hungary, Czechoslovakia, Romania and the Baltic States. The section on
Poland (p. 10-128) is the most detailed and comprehensive. Mendelson presents
balanced comparative conclusions on this important chapter in Modern European
Jewish history before the Holocaust.

248 **Zionism in Poland: the formative years 1915-26.**
Ezra Mendelson. New Haven, Connecticut: Yale University Press,
1981. 373p. maps. bibliog.
A detailed academic study of the development of Zionism in Poland from the regaining
of national independence to Piłsudski's *coup d'état*.

249 **Remnants. The last Jews of Poland.**
Małgorzata Niezabitowska, photos by Tomasz Tomaszewski. New
York: Friendly Press, 1986. 272p.
A well-known Polish journalist, who became the press-spokesperson in Mazowiecki's
government, carried out an exhaustive investigation to produce this comprehensive
presentation, based on colour photos and accompanying explanatory text, of the
remaining 10,000 or so strong Jewish community in Poland. See *National Geographic*
(April 1986), p. 362-89 for a review and a selection.

250 **Shtetl Jews under Soviet rule: Eastern Poland on the eve of the
Holocaust.**
Ben-Cion Pinchuk. Oxford: Basil Blackwell, 1990. 186p. (Jewish
Society and Culture Series). map. bibliog.
A history of the small-town Jews in the territories in the eastern part of Poland
annexed by the USSR in September 1939 up to the German invasion in Summer 1941.
Written by a history professor at Haifa University.

251 **Preserving traces of Jewish culture in Poland for the living and the dead.**
Edited and introduced by Radosław Piszczek, translated by Lech
Petrowicz. Warsaw: Krajowa Agencja Wydawnicza, 1988. 86p.
This pamphlet was commissioned by the Nissenbaum Foundation to popularize the
aims set out in the title.

252 **The generation. The rise and fall of the Jewish communists of Poland.**
Jaff Schatz. Berkeley, California: University of California Press,
1991. 408p. bibliog. (Society and Culture in East-Central Europe).
Written by a Jewish academic at Lund University, Sweden. The study is based on a
comprehensive range of sources as well as interviews with forty-three surviving ex-
communists of Jewish origins. It traces out the story of 'the generation' of Polish
Jewish communists through the extremes of original messianistic commitment to final
expulsion from the party (and often from the country), in 1967-68.

Ukrainians

253 **Galician villagers and the Ukrainian national movement in the nineteenth century.**
John-Paul Himka. Basingstoke, England: Macmillan in association with the Canadian Institute of Ukrainian Studies, University of Alberta, 1988. 358p. maps. bibliog.

A detailed study of the emergence of Ukrainian national consciousness within the mixed-nationality rural population of Austrian Galicia between 1772-1914. The main emphasis is on 1867-1900 when the Ukrainian national movement blossomed, primarily in Eastern Galicia. The author regards this region as a Piedmont for the Ukrainian peoples controlled by Russia until 1991 as well as for Transcarpathian Ruthenia.

254 **The Ukrainian national movement in Galicia, 1815-49.**
Jan Kozik, edited and introduced by Lawrence D. Orton. Edmonton, Alberta: Canadian Institute of Ukrainian Studies, University of Alberta, 1986. 498p.

This volume represents the amalgamation and translation of two heavily researched studies on the subject by a major specialist, first published in Poland in 1973 and 1975. This an important examination of the rise of Ukrainian national consciousness. It explains its collision with Polish nationalism and why all the pro-Polish orientations within it were largely squeezed out.

255 **Between Poland and the Ukraine: the dilemma of Adam Kysil, 1600-53.**
Frank E. Sysyn. Cambridge, Massachusetts: Harvard Ukrainian Research Institute, 1985. 406p.

An extensive academic study of the career of a Ruthenian nobleman of Orthodox religion who served the Polish Commonwealth as a soldier, Royal Secretary, Sejm representative and Senator. His failed attempts to persuade the dominant Catholics to grant political and religious autonomy to their confederates on the eastern borderlands is used to explain why the Polish multi-ethnic state decayed in the seventeeth century and why Poland lost the Ukraine.

Polonia (Poles Abroad)

General

256 **Writing home: immigrants in Brazil and the United States, 1890-91.**
Witold Kula, Nina Assodobraj Kula, Marcin Kula, edited and translated by Josephine Wtulich. New York: Columbia University Press, 1986. 698p. (East European Monographs no. 210).
Annotated translation of a collection of letters (first published in Poland in 1973) written by immigrants, mainly to the USA and Brazil, during 1890-91. The editor, in a substantial introduction, presents a theory of cultural pluralism and survival drawn from Weber, Dilthey and Znaniecki.

257 **The Polish peasant in Europe and America.**
Florian Znaniecki, William Isaac Thomas. Chicago: University of Chicago Press, 1918-1920. 5 vols. new rev. ed, New York: Dover, 1958. 2,205p.
One of the world's sociological classics which marked the beginning of a truly experimental method of research in the subject. Its original contribution to the understanding of Polish *emigré* society in the United States is now largely of historical interest but the work's profound influence on sociology as a discipline still remains. The authors made an innovative attempt to combine theoretical analysis of social factors with subjective experience. See *A commemorative book in honour of Florian Znaniecki on the centenary of his birth. Papers and communiqués presented to the international scientific symposium, 3-4 December 1982 at the Adam Mickiewicz University in Poznań.* Edited by Zygmunt Dulczewski (Poznań: Wydawnictwo UAM, 1986. 335p. (Sociology series no. 15). bibliog.).

258 Soldiers and peasants, together with various documents relating to the economic and political migrations from Poland since the Third Partition. Jerzy Zubrzycki. School of Slavonic Studies – Orbis Books, 1988. 167p. (Second M. B. Grabowski Memorial Lecture).

Zubrzycki studies the historical phenomenum of Polish emigration since the 1770s to a wide range of countries, like the USA, Brazil, Australia, France and the United Kingdom, examining the movement within the context of a broad sociological theory of emigration. In Poland's case it assumed both a political and an economic form. The 'soldiers' formed military groupings abroad in friendly countries with the ultimate aim of restoring their country's independence. Although most Polonia communities, postwar, were largely made up of 'peasants' the distinction is indistinguishable in the sociology of Polish immigration.

Canada

259 The maple leaf and the white eagle. Canadian-Polish relations, 1918-78. Aloysius Balawajder. New York; Columbia University Press, 1980. 300p. (East European Monographs no. 66). bibliog.

An academic examination of the development of the Polish community in Canada and how it has affected Canadian-Polish relations. The author stresses the community's democratic aspirations and the political, trade and cultural detente which was fostered during the Gierek period.

260 Heritage and the future. Essays on Poles in Canada. Edited by Benedykt Heydenkorn. Toronto: Canadian Polish Research Institute Studies, 1988. 234p. (Canadian Polish Research Institute Studies no. 20).

A commemorative symposium to mark the thirtieth anniversary of the Canadian-Polish Research Institute. Papers include Tadeusz Brzezinski's memoirs of forty years amongst the Polish Canadians and contributions on the Poles and the Multicultural History Society of Ontario, Polish archival collections in Canada and specifically in Ontario and the University of Toronto as well as an analysis of the 1986 population census. Other works by Heydenkorn are; *The organizational structure of the Polish-Canadian community* (Toronto: Canadian-Polish Research Institute, 1979. 224p. Studies of the Canadian-Polish Research Institute no. 15); and *Memoirs of Polish immigrants in Canada* (Toronto: Canadian-Polish Research Institute, 1979. 323p. Studies of the Canadian-Polish Research Institute no. 16).

United States

261 **The Poles in Oklahoma.**
Richard M. Bernard. Norman, Oklahoma: University of Oklahoma
Press, 1980. 90p. maps. bibliog.
A study of the small Polish community in Oklahoma from the time of the state's entry
into the Union in 1907 up till 1976.

262 **Pastor of the Poles. Polish-American essays.**
Stanislaus A. Blejwas, Mieczysław B. Biskupski. New Britain,
Connecticut: Central Connecticut State College, 1982. 223p.
A *Festschrift* by the authors on various aspects of the life of the American *Polonia* in
honour of Monsignor John P. Wodarski.

263 **Polish Americans 1854-1939.**
Andrzej Brożek, translated by Wojciech Worstynowicz. Warsaw:
Interpress, 1985. 274p. bibliog.
An examination, based on Polish sources and historiography, of the basic issues
concerning the Polish community in the USA prior to the Second World War.
Contains biographical pen-portraits of the most notable Polish-Americans during this
time.

264 **Last of the Titans; Monsignor-Colonel Alphonse A. Skoniecki of
Massachusetts.**
Daniel S. Buczek. Sterling Heights, Michigan: The Society of Christ
in America, 1986. 231p.
The biography of a remarkably strong-minded Polish priest, born in Płock (1894-
1975), is used by the author to interpret the Polish-American religious and social
experience in the twentieth century. Skoniecki achieved a prominent position in the
American *Polonia* especially as a spokesman for Polish independence and territorial
integrity during the Second World War. He was also a very capable fund-raiser, pastor
and religious organizer but his work as a social activist often brought him into conflict
with the ecclesiastical authorities.

265 **And my children did not know me; a history of the Polish-Americans.**
John J. Bukowczyk. Bloomington, Indiana: Indiana University Press,
1987. 190p.
A readable academic study which focuses on both the history of nineteenth century
Polish immigration into the USA and contemporary social attitudes and transforma-
tions. Bukowczyk digests the existing material and presents the current state of
knowledge very expertly; some of his conclusions, for example his emphasis on the
recent breakdown of ethnic Polish links in favour of more class based ones, are,
however, controversial.

Polonia (Poles Abroad). United States

266 A history of the Polish-Americans in Pittsfield, Massachusetts, 1862-
1945.
Florence W. Clowes. Webster, Massachusetts: Economy Press, 1981.
144p. bibliog.
This study reviews a century of the cultural and economic life of this Polish community
in a town in West Massachusetts.

267 America through Polish eyes. An anthology.
Edited by Bogdan Grzeloński, translated by Edward Czerwiński.
Warsaw: Interpress, 1988. 302p.
The anthology contains twenty extracts from the journals or memoirs of mainly
intellectual Poles, who either visited or settled, in America between the end of the
eighteenth century and 1914. The most notable names are Julian Ursyn Niemcewicz,
Henryk Sienkiewicz, Helena Modjeska and Ignacy Paderewski.

268 To New York, Chicago and San Francisco. Polish-American
biographies.
Bohdan Grzeloński, translated by Emma Harris. Warsaw: Interpress,
1986. 204p. maps. bibliog.
This is a collection of biographical pen-portraits of the most prominent Polish-
Americans from the time of the Civil War to the present. This was a successor to his
Poles in the United States of America, 1776-1865 (Warsaw: Interpress, 1976. 240p.).

269 Polish past in America.
Mieczysław Haiman. Chicago: Polish Roman Catholic Union, 1939.
178p. maps. Reprinted, Chicago: Polish Museum of America, 1974.
Although not as rigorously scholarly as subsequent work, Haiman's seminal
examination of Polish-American relations laid the foundations for all future research
on the subject.

270 Exploring the dimension of ethnicity.
Robert F. Hill. New York: Arno Press, 1980. bibliog.
Based on sociological fieldwork amongst Polish-Americans in Pittsburgh this doctoral
dissertation at the University of Pittsburgh dealt with basic issues of identity, status,
cultural aspirations and achievements.

271 Faith and fatherland. The Polish Church in Wisconsin, 1896-1918.
Anthony J. Kuźniewski. Notre Dame: University of Notre Dame,
1980. 171p. bibliog.
Based on a doctoral dissertation this is a study of how the Polish community in
Wisconsin attempted to gain Polish-speaking bishops for its dioceses in the period
before the First World War.

272 **Polish radio broadcasting in the United States.**
Joseph Migala. New York: Columbia University Press, 1987. 309p.
(East European Monographs no. 216). bibliog.
Migala demonstrates the importance to the Polish community of possessing their own mass media especially radio, which was an important means of socio-communal integration as well as of influencing American public opinion. The book is based on the author's doctoral dissertation submitted to the department of journalism at Warsaw University.

273 **The transplanted family. A study of social adjustment of the Polish immigrant family to the United States after the Second World War.**
Danuta Mostwin. New York: Arno Press, 1980. 345p. (American Ethnic Groups Series). bibliog.
A Columbia University doctoral dissertation based on questionnaires from about 2,000 Polish post-Second World War immigrants to the USA. Mostwin investigated how they, and in particular their family groups, responded to their totally new environment.

274 **Polish folkways in America: community and family.**
Eugene E. Obidinski, Helen Stankiewicz Zand. Lanham, New York: University Press of America, 1987. 154p.
Although the strict academic value of its questionnaire base can be queried this is a highly informative study on the manner and extent of the transplantation of Polish ways of life and doing things to the USA from 1910 onwards and particularly during the interwar period. It covers a wide range of aspects such as food, family life, customs and holidays, the influence of English on the Polish language, community traditions and behaviour.

275 **Polish Detroit and the Kolasiński affair.**
Lawrence D. Orton. Detroit: Wayne State University Press, 1981. 229p.
A colourful academic study of the controversial career of Father Dominik Kolasiński set against the background of the beginnings and growth of the Polish community in Detroit in the last two decades of the nineteenth century. The regional, cultural and economic differences in original background are highlighted as well as the ecclesiastical and personal squabbles of a Polish community in the making and in the process of asserting itself. Orton also throws light on the reactions of established Americans and other ethnic groups especially the Germans. See also Edward A. Skendel, *The Kolasiński story* (Grand Rapids, Michigan: Littleshield Press, 1979. 126p).

276 **Polish Catholics in Chicago, 1850-1920.**
Joseph J. Parot. DeKalb, Illinois: Northern Illinois University Press, 1981. 298p. maps. bibliog.
A detailed study, based on original parish sources, of the Polish community in Chicago and the early development of its religious life which was marked by schisms and serious conflicts between the local community, the Chicago clergy and the Catholic hierarchy.

277   One hundred years young. A history of the Polish Falcons of America,
      1887-1987.
      Donald E. Pienkos.   New York: Columbia University Press, 1987.
      348p. (East European Monographs no. 231). bibliog.

A history to mark the centenary of the Polish Falcons of America, a fraternal
insurance organization which ranks about twentieth in size amongst such bodies and
which is also the fourth largest amongst Polish-American fraternal societies. A
significant ethnic body, it has about 30,000 members in about 150 local lodges
concentrated primarily in sixteen states. The book is amply illustrated with
photographs of its most prominent leaders and its varied group activities.

278   PNA. A centennial history of the Polish National Alliance of the United
      States of America.
      Donald E. Pienkos.   New York: Columbia University Press, 1984.
      485p. bibliog.

A detailed historical study of the growth of an important American Polonia
organization with biographies of its main leaders.

279   For God, country and Polonia. One hundred years of the Orchard Lake
      schools.
      Frank Renkiewicz.   Orchard Lake, Michigan: Center for Polish
      Studies and Culture, 1985. 177p. bibliog.

A history to mark the centenary of the Polish orientated Orchard Lake schools,
originally situated in Detroit (St. Mary's High School, St. Mary's College and the
Seminary of Saints Cyril and Methodus). The occasion was also marked by a reprint of
the original 1959 edition of Joseph Swastek, *The formative years of the Polish seminary
in the United States* (Orchard Lake: Center for Polish Studies, 1985. 127p.).
Renkiewicz also published a wider overview of the North American Polonia in *The
Polish presence in Canada and America* (Toronto: The Multicultural History Society of
Ontario, 1982. 412p.).

280   Polish-Black encounters: a history of Polish and Black relations in
      America since 1609.
      Joseph A. Wytrwal.   Detroit: Endurance Press, 1982. 538p. bibliog.

An ambitious attempt to overview the above relationship from earliest times with an
emphasis on the post-Second World War period. This is, however, a somewhat
superficial, newspaper based analysis stressing conflict rather than collaboration.

Australia

281 **Poles in Australia and Oceania, 1790-1940.**
Lech Paszkowski. Sydney: Australian National University Press,
1987. 429p. bibliog.
A much expanded and revised translation of the author's *Polaccy w Australia i Oceania, 1790-1940* published in Polish in London in 1962. The book contains a historical overview of Polish emigration to Australia up to 1940, which includes very detailed biographical material on individual Poles and associations, as well as pen-portraits of the thirty-seven Poles who made the most notable impression on Australia. The latter include not only the well-known explorer and geographer Sir Paul Edmund Strzelecki, but also a wide range of Australian Poles from the arts (the violinist, Stanisław Tarczyński) to journalists, engineers, policemen, politicians and aristocratic exiles. The anthropologist, Bronisław Malinowski is included because of his sejourn in Australasia from 1914-20 when he carried out the fieldwork for his most important works. Paszkowski's study deals with the early period of limited immigration as the number of Poles in Australia is estimated at under 8,000 in 1891 rising to 22,781 in 1947 and only then escalating to around 122,000 by 1982. See also Paszkowski's, *Social background of Sir Paul Strzelecki and Joseph Conrad* (Melbourne: Australia Felix Literary Club, 1980. 56p.).

282 **Polish people and culture in Australia.**
Edited by Roland Sussex, Jerzy Zubrzycki. Canberra: Department of
Demography, Institute of Advanced Studies, Australian National
University, 1986. 223p.
This volume is divided into seven chapters with topics ranging from the demography of Polish settlement, Polish migrants in Hobart, Tasmania, and the difficulties of their cultural survival, the problems of bilingualism and of maintaining the Polish language among children, to the achievements of the explorer Sir Paul Strzelecki. The editors assert that the dominance of the Anglo-Australian language and ethos threatened Polish identity and ethnicity in the past, causing much individual suffering, but believe that the problem has now been allayed by the growth of multi-culturalism in Australia.

Great Britain

283 **Notes from a Welsh diary.**
Josef Herman. London: Free Association Books, 1988. 50p.
Contains reproductions of fifty drawings and paintings by a Polish artist (born 1911, Warsaw) who settled in the Welsh mining village of Ystradganlais from 1944-55 setting up a flourishing studio there. Herman has had a number of retrospective exhibitions and his work is on show in a number of British art galleries. He was awarded an O.B.E. for his artistic activity in 1981.

284 **The Polish airforce in Lincolnshire.**
Michael J. Ingham. Nettleham, Lincoln: Beckside Design, 1988. 48p. bibliog.

An account of the bases, personnel, losses, memorials and insignia of the Polish aircrews and their units stationed in Lincolnshire during the Second World War. The coverage is, therefore, mainly of the 300, 301, 302, 303, 305, 306, 309, 316 and 317 squadrons with the greatest attention being given to the first two as well as to the Blyton, Hemswell, Kirton and Ingham (later Cammeringham) bases. Ingham also produced *The Airforce memorials of Lincolnshire* (Nettleham, Lincoln: Beckside Design, 1988.) which lists forty-four memorials to the various Allied units by village. The Polish memorials and Sikorski's burial-place in Newark in the adjoining county of Nottinghamshire are described on p. 43. So is the Warsaw Air Bridge Memorial to the 250 airmen of various Allied nationalities who died while attempting to fly supplies to the Warsaw Uprising of Summer 1944.

285 **Polonia Restituta.**
Kazimierz Sabbat, Mieczysław Sas-Skowroński, Krzysztof Barbarski, Edited by Peter Bander Van Duren. Gerrouds Cross, England: Van Duren, 1989. 71p.

A brochure commissioned by the 'British Friends of Free Poland' to commemorate the Golden Jubilee of the Polish University (PUNO) in 1989. The volume contains a historical overview by Kazimierz Sabbat to justify the claim that the Government-in-Exile which he headed as President until his death in July 1989 was the legitimate continuation of the sovereign government of Poland; a description of *emigré* orders and decorations by Barbarski and of PUNO's work by its Rector.

286 **The formation of the Polish community in Great Britain 1939-50.**
Keith Sword with Norman Davies, Jan Ciechanowski. London: School of Slavonic and East European Studies, University of London, 1989. 498p. bibliog.

The book is made up of three main sections. Davies covers 'The growth of the Polish community in Britain, 1939-50', Ciechanowski 'The politics of the Polish Government-in-Exile, 1939-50' and Sword 'The resettlement of Poles in Britain, 1945-50'. The work is somewhat bitty, being composed of a large number of sub-chapters, but it contains a wealth of fascinating information.

287 **Between two cultures; migrants and minorities in Britain.**
Edited by James L. Watson. Oxford: Blackwell, 1977. 338p.

The chapter entitled 'The Poles: an exile community in Britain' is by Sheila Petterson-Hórko, a social anthropologist sympathetic to Poland. She had an extensive knowledge of the Polish community in Britain, her husband being for many years the editor of *Dziennik Polski*, the Polish daily in London. She concluded that although two thirds of the Poles resident in Britain had by then become British citizens they were still at heart an *emigré* society dreaming of a return to the homeland.

New Zealand

288   History of the Polish Settlers in New Zealand, 1776-1987.
J. W. Pobóg-Jaworowski.   Warsaw: CHZ 'Ars Polonia', 1990. 228p.
The first half is a history of Polish settlement in New Zealand concentrating on family
and ecclesiastical life. The second section is an attempt to draw up as comprehensive
and exhaustive a list as possible of all Polish arrivals and departures in New Zealand
especially in the period of heightened emigration after the Second World War.

USSR

289   Policy toward the Polish minority in the Soviet Union, 1923-89.
John Lowell Armstrong.   *Polish Review*, vol. 35, no. 1 (1990), p. 51-
65.
The Polish minority in the USSR, just before its break-up, totalled about 1,151,000. A
leading expert on Soviet nationality policies overviews official policy towards the Polish
minority showing how it has veered from the extremes of cultural and administrative
autonomy to sharp repression.

290   The fate of the Poles in the USSR, 1939-89.
Tomasz Piesakowski.   London: Gryf Publications, 1990. 359p. bibliog.
A history, of a secondary nature, of Polish-Soviet relations during the Second World
War, the repatriations of Poles from the USSR during its course and the fate of Poles
in the USSR postwar up to 1989.

Language

Texts

291 **Proceedings of the Third April Conference of university teachers of English, Cracow 1984 (April 11-15): English language and literature; methods of teaching and research.** Edited by Teresa Bałuk-Ulewiczowa, Maria Korsadowicz. Kraków: Jagiellonian University, 1986. Zeszyty Naukowe Uniwersytetu Jagiellońskiego DCCXCV. 247p.

Contains a selection of the learned papers presented at the above conference which was attended by eighty participants including twenty-five from outside Poland. The volume is divided into separate sections on language and language teaching (nine contributions) and literature (eleven papers). These cover a wide and eclectic range of topics from semantics to G. K. Chesterton, Mark Twain and Iris Murdoch.

292 **Berlitz. Polish for travellers.** Lausanne: Berlitz, 1984. 192p.

A pocket-sized phrase-book containing basic phrases for a wide range of tourist needs such as shopping, sightseeing and eating out. The book is organized into topics and contains a pronunciation guide and a quick reference section for handy access to about 1,200 phrases and 2,000 useful words.

293 **Beginner's course of Polish. (Mowimy po polsku).** Wacław Biśko (et al). Warsaw: Wiedza Powszechna, 1988. 4th ed. 326p.

A beginner's course in twenty-six chapters. The book includes a Polish-English glossary, a key to exercises and table of grammar, and is accompanied by three LPs.

294 **Selected English collocations.**
Christian Douglas-Kozłowska, Halina Dzierżanowska. Warsaw: Państwowe Wydawnictwo Naukowe, 1988. 3rd rev. ed. 256p.
A primer on the word-associations of English phraseology.

295 **Colloquial Polish.**
Bolesław W. Mazur. London: Routledge & Kegan Paul, 1983. 270p.
A useful introduction for beginners in both spoken and written Polish with an accompanying cassette. See also J. Wojtowicz, L. Szkutnik, *A Polish grammar in dialogues* (744p.), a phraseological grammar with examples in Polish and in English translation.

296 **Teach yourself Polish.**
M. Corbridge-Patkaniowska. London: English Universities Press, rev. ed., 1964. 299p. (Teach Yourself Series).
A long established and widely used beginner's course in forty-one lessons with a general glossary and key to exercises. It has gone through numerous reprints.

297 **Semiotics in Poland 1894-1969.**
Edited and introduced by Jerzy Pelc. Dordrecht, Netherlands: Reidel. 1979. 504p.
An examination of aspects of the development of sign-language in Poland, which was originally published in Polish in 1971. Another highly specialist aspect is covered by Lea Sawicka, *Verb valency in contemporary Polish* (Tübingen: Narr, 1988. 98p.).

298 **An introduction to Polish.**
Gerald Stone. Oxford: Oxford University Press, 1980. 110p.
This book provides a good start for the beginner by explaining the essentials of Polish grammar without going into complex detail. A similar work is Oscar Swan's *A concise grammar of Polish* (University of America Press, 1978). Also Stanisław Westfal, *Why learn Polish? The Polish language* (London: Veritas, 1985. 136p.).

Dictionaries

299 **Słownik minimum angielsko-polski i polsko-angielski. English-Polish and Polish-English compact dictionary.**
Katarzyna Billip, Zofia Chociłowska. Warsaw: Wiedza Powszechna, 1988. 13th ed. 144p.
A small compact dictionary designed for basic needs. Contains about 10,000 entries plus a basic phonetic guide and list of abbreviations. The medium format companion contained 50,000 words and phrases: Jan Stanisławski, Katarzyna Billip, Zofia Chociłowska, *Podręczny słownik angielsko-polski. A practical English-Polish dictionary* (Warsaw: Wiedza Powszechna, 1988. 9th ed. 914p.). A similar middle-range

Language. Dictionaries

dictionary is Janina Jaslan, Jan Stanisławski, *Kieszonkowy słownik angielsko-polski, polsko-angielski. (English-Polish pocket dictionary)* (Warsaw: Wiedza Powszechna, 1988. 5th ed. 712p.), which contains appendices on abbreviations and geographical names.

300 **Polish-English and English-Polish dictionary: Słownik polsko-angielski i angielsko-polski.**
Kazimierz Bulas, Francis J. Whitefield. The Hague: Mouton, 1961. 1,037p. Reprinted, New York: Kościuszko Foundation, 1973.
Widely regarded as the main large format rival to Stanisławski's dictionary (item 304), this work has gone through numerous editions in Poland (Warsaw, PWN) and abroad, and is colloquially known as the 'Kościuszko dictionary'.

301 **Słownik prawniczy polsko-angielski. Polish-English dictionary of legal terms.**
Institute of State and Law, Polish Academy of Sciences. Wrocław: Ossolineum, 1986. 212p.
This is a standard work in this field. Other dictionaries covering the technical terminology of specialized areas are *Angielsko-polski słownik terminologii optycznej, optelekronicznej i mechaniki precyzyjnej.* vol. 1. A-M. (An English-Polish dictionary of optical and opto-electronic terminology and of precision mechanics) (Wrocław: PWr, [Wrocław Institute of Technology], 1980. 451p.); S. Czerni, M. Skrzyńska, *English-Polish dictionary of science and technology* (Warsaw: Wydawnictwo Naukowe-Techniczne, 1983. 7th edn. 909p.); *Słownik naukowo techniczny polsko-angielski* (Warsaw: WNT, 1983. 5th edn. 846p.); Ryszard Dębicki, Jan Gliński, *Słownik agrofizyczny polsko-angielski i angielsko-polski. Polish-English and English-Polish dictionary of agrophysics* (Warsaw: Państwowe Wydawnictwo Naukowe, 1986. 396p.); *English-Polish concise technical dictionary. Mały słownik techniczny polsko-angielski* (Warsaw: WNT, 1985. 4th edn. 2 vols); *Mały słownik informatyczny angielsko-polski (English-Polish dictionary of computer science)* (Warsaw: WNT, 1991. 62p.); *Słownik skrótów elektronicznych angielsko-polski (English-Polish dictionary of abbreviations used in electronics)* (Warsaw: WNT, 1988. 150p.); and Janina Jaslan, Jan Stanisławski, *Słownik turystyczny angielsko-polski, polsko-angielski. A dictionary for tourists, English-Polish, Polish-English* (Warsaw: Wiedza Powszechna, 1981. 712p.).

302 **Notes on ships, ports and cargo.**
Barbara Katarzyńska. Gdańsk, Poland: Wydawnictwo Morskie, 1988. 294p. bibliog.
A guide to the terminology used in maritime transport.

303 **Hippocrene concise dictionary. Polish-English, English-Polish dictionary with complete phonetics.**
Iwo Cyprian Pogonowski. New York: Hippocrene Books, 3rd ed., 1991. 408p.
Contains 6,500 entries in a concise, easy to use format aimed especially at students and tourists, with a glossary of menu terms and information regarding phonetics. Also available is a medium sized dictionary by Pogonowski in the same series; *Polish-*

English/English-Polish Hippocrene practical dictionary (New York: Hippocrene Books, 1991. 4th rev. edn. 389p.). There are 16,000 entries in the Polish-English section while the English-Polish part has 15,000. A phonetic guide to pronunciation in both languages is included, with a bilingual list of abbreviations and a glossary of useful terms including gastronomic ones.

304 **Great English-Polish Polish-English dictionary. Wielki slownik polsko-angielski angielsko-polski.**
Jan Stanisławski. Warsaw: Wiedza Powszechna, rev. 10th ed., 1988. 2 vols. (1,408p + 1,728p.).
A bilingual dictionary based on 19th and 20th century literary Polish. The former contains 100,000 and the latter 80,000 words and phrases. After its thorough revision in 1978 it compared favourably with competitors especially as far as the number of idioms and equivalents are concerned. Contains technological, biomedical terms as well as regional and colloquial expressions. The supplement includes new idioms, words and meanings. An index of geographical names, abbreviations and Polish acronyms and an appendix on Elements of Polish Grammar are included. The work has been long established as the outstanding large format dictionary.

Religion

Church history

305 **The Christian community of medieval Poland. Anthologies.**
Edited by Jerzy Kłoczowski, translated by Krystyna Cenkalska.
Wrocław: Ossolineum, 1981. 243p. maps. bibliog.
A volume of Polish socio-religious history largely written by specialists from the
Catholic University in Lublin (KUL). They describe the institutional, legal and
socioeconomic aspects of the Church in medieval Poland, bringing out the most
important and novel aspects of recent Polish historiography for a non-Polish
readership.

Roman Catholicism

306 **The convent at Auschwitz.**
Władysław T. Bartoszewski.　London: Bowerdean Press, 1990.
169p.
Deals with the historical background to and the development of the controversy which
took place between 1984-89 over the proposed building of a convent for Carmelite
nuns in 1986, within the boundaries of what had been the Auschwitz camp. See also
Rittner's work, *Memory offended* (q.v.).

307 **The Roman Catholic Church in 1944-89 Poland.**
Vincent C. Chrypiński. In: *Catholicism and politics in communist societies*. Edited by Pedro Ramet. Durham, North Carolina: Duke University Press, 1990. p. 117-41.

Chrypiński concludes that the Polish Church would withstand the secularization process in Poland because of historical tradition and its standing as a 'folk-church'. It was also likely to play an important role in the initial period of post-communist politics, being especially influential on such issues as divorce, abortion and the religious education of children. It was, however, unclear what its reaction would be to the play of democratic politics and any future outbursts of socio-economic protest.

308 **The Polish Catholic Church and the elections of 1989.**
Krzysztof Kosela. *Religion in Communist Lands*, vol. 18, no 2 (1990), p. 124-37.

Discusses the support given by the Roman Catholic Church, especially through its lower clergy, to Solidarity Civic Committee candidates in the election of June 1989. This led to concern on the part of the secular intelligentsia about Church involvement in politics in order to further its moral and social aims.

309 **The Polish Church under martial law.**
Jonathan Luxmore. *Religion in Communist Lands*, vol. 15, no. 2 (1987), p. 124-66.

A detailed overview of how the Roman Catholic Church reacted calmly and realistically to prevent bloodshed, while maintaining its spiritual values, to the imposition of martial law. See also as a follow-up, Irena Korba, 'Five years underground. The Opposition and the Church in Poland since martial law', *Religion in Communist Lands*, vol. 15, no. 2 (1987), p. 167-81.

310 **Polish Pope, Polish church and Polish state.**
Tomasz Mianowicz. *Survey*. vol. 30, no. 4 (June 1989), p. 131-54.

Contrary to popular belief, Vatican policy towards the communist state in Poland was not changed dramatically by the accession of Pope John Paul II. It remained based on the search for conciliation and a *modus vivendi* designed to continue the 'Polish experiment' in co-existence begun under Cardinal Wyszyński.

311 **Cardinal Wyszyński. A biography.**
Andrzej Micewski, translated by William R. Brand, Katarzyna M. Brand. New York: Harcourt, Brace, Jovanovitch, 1984. 474p.

Micewski is a well-known Polish historian and publicist associated with Mazowiecki's *Więź* and *Znak* independent Catholic tendencies, who later became one of Wałęsa's advisers. This biography was hailed as a major work when first published in Poland. Wyszyński (1901–81) was Primate of Poland from 1948 until his death. He was instrumental in preserving the Roman Catholic Church from the onslaught of Stalinism and in extending its social autonomy which allowed it to play an increasingly crucial political role. He also fashioned the co-existence between the Catholic Church and the reformist and nationalist wings of the Polish communist leadership designed to prevent the outbreak of desperate insurrections, whose crushing, as in the nineteenth century, would have reinforced the occupying power as well as causing unnecessary loss of life.

312 **Politics and religion in Eastern Europe. Catholicism in Hungary. Poland and Czechoslovakia.**
Patrick Michel, translated from the French by Alan Braley. Oxford: Polity Press, 1991. 321p. bibliog.
Examines the tension that existed between communist political power and Catholicism as an organized religion in the three countries mentioned in the title. Shows how the former failed to annihilate the latter and how this played a decisive role in enabling individuals to resist the exercise of authoritarian power.

313 **The Catholic Church in communist Poland 1945-85. Forty years of church-state relations.**
Ronald C. Monticone. New York: Columbia University Press, 1986. 227p. (East European Monographs no. 205). bibliog.
A useful and measured overview of the relationship between the Roman Catholic Church and the communist state in postwar Poland. Based originally on a doctoral dissertation the account is largely political history; but it also gives due weight to the Church's pastoral functions and to the complex web of factors which enabled it to play a mediating role after Solidarity's emergence in 1980.

314 **Resistance, persistance and change; the transformation of the Catholic Church in Poland.**
Maryjane Osa. *East European Politics and Societies*, vol. 3, no. 2 (Spring 1989), p. 268-99.
The author shows how the the Roman Catholic Church in Poland transformed itself into a decoupled two-tier organization, made up of the Episcopal leadership at the top and an activist base of lower clergy and religious laity. This adaptive response to the consolidation of communist power widened the social base of its support. It also made it more flexible and effective than the Hungarian Church in its relations with the communist system.

315 **Religious change in contemporary Poland; secularization and politics.**
Maciej Pomian-Szrednicki. London: Routledge, 1982. 227p.
An in-depth academic examination of the Polish material concerning the issue of secularization in Poland and how this affects political life.

316 **Memory offended. The Auschwitz convent controversy.**
Edited by Carol A. Rittner, John K. Roth. New York: Praeger, 1991. 280p.
Discusses the controversy aroused amongst both Jews and Christians by the establishment of a convent for Polish Carmelite nuns in 1986 within the perimeter of what had been the Auschwitz death camp. Also of interest is Bartoszewski's *The convent at Auschwitz* (q.v.).

317 **Light and life.**
Grażyna Sikorska. London: Collins, 1989. 156p.
Biography of Father Franciszek Blachnicki (1921-87) a lecturer at the Catholic
University in Lublin. A social activist who founded the 'Oasis' and anti-abortion
movements he initially fell foul of the Catholic hierarchy because of his attempts to
attract youth away from socialist organizations through scouting and similar activities
and co-operation with other religious organizations. Cf. Sikorska's 'The Light-Life
Movement in Poland', *Religion in Communist Lands*, vol. 10, no. 1 (1983), p. 49-66.

318 **The Cardinal and the commissars: views of the English Catholic primate
on the communist takeover in Poland 1944-47.**
Keith Sword. *Polish Review*. vol. 31, no. 1 (1986), p. 49-59.
Sword shows the deep interest taken by the British Catholic Primate, Cardinal Bernard
Griffin, like his predecessors Bourne and Hinsley, in supporting the Roman Catholic
Church in Poland during the Second World War and at its close. Cardinal Griffin
visited Poland in June 1947 largely on a pastoral basis but with the general aim of
raising Polish morale. Sword, however, criticizes his over-optimistic appraisal of
postwar realities including communist persecution and his encouragement of Poles to
return home to such dangerous conditions. It would seem that Griffin's primary aims
were to support the Polish cause over its new western frontier and in fitting into
postwar allied arrangements rather than on issues of civil rights.

319 **Next to God . . . Poland. Politics and religion in contemporary Poland.**
Bogdan Szajkowski. London: F. Pinter, 1983. 264p. bibliog.
Although the study concentrates on the Solidarity and martial law periods it is prefaced
by an overview of the relations between the communist state and the Roman Catholic
Church from 1944-80. Szajkowski argues that the Catholic hierarchy had to balance
between the divergent pressures of political realism and involvement; it had to
reconcile its symbiotic relationship with the Polish national community, which involved
close support for the opposition, with the need to concentrate on its primary pastoral
mission. See also his discussion of the Law of 17 May 1989 normalizing Church-State
relations by giving the Roman Catholic Church legal status for the first time since 1945,
'New Law for the Church in Poland', *Religion in Communist Lands*, vol. 17, no. 3
(Autumn 1989), p. 196-208.

320 **A freedom within. The prison notes of Stefan, Cardinal Wyszyński.**
Stefan Wyszyński, foreword by Malcolm Muggeridge, translated by
Barbara Krzywicki-Herburt, Walter J. Zięba. London: Hodder &
Stoughton, 1985; Sutton: Aid to the Church in Need, 1986. 270p.
The prison diaries and reflections of Cardinal Stefan Wyszyński (1901-81) the Primate
of Poland; Wyszyński was first imprisoned in September 1953 and later kept under
house arrest until Summer 1956.

321 **The Vatican and Poland in the age of the Partitions; diplomatic and cultural encounters at the Warsaw Nunciature.**
Larry Wolff. New York: Columbia University Press, 1988. 282p.
(East European Monographs no. 245).

This account is based on the author's Stanford University doctoral dissertation and research in the Vatican archives on the correspondence of the three Papal Nuncios in Poland between the First and Third Partitions. Wolff concludes that the Papacy was primarily concerned to protect its interests with the partitioning powers rather than those of Poland.

322 **The Catholic-Marxist ideological dialogue in Poland, 1945-80.**
Norbert A. Żmijewski. Aldershot: Dartmouth Publishing, 1991. 179p.

Catholicism and Marxism had a primarily conflictual relationship in communist Eastern Europe, but national and historical circumstances produced a form of co-existence in Poland and even a developed dialogue during the period 1956-80. Zmijewski concentrates on the intellectual interchange between the groups and currents on both sides which wanted to deepen accommodation by building on such common philosophical ground as values of national and social solidarity. He covers the philosophical debate between Marxism and Thomism, the *Znak*, *Więź* and PAX movements and the 1970s dialogue. He concludes that the onslaught of Wojtyła and Kołakowski put paid to communist attempts in the 1980s to revive a humanist and anti-Stalinist Marxism. In 'Vicissitudes of political realism in Poland: *Tygodnik Powszechny* and *Znak*', *Soviet Studies*, vol. 43, No. 1 (1991), p. 83-106, Żmijewski has examined the political ideas and strategies of the Catholic weekly close to the Hierarchy which has appeared in Kraków since 1945 and the influential movement of the 1960s and 1970s. He shows how they manoeuvred to express their viewpoints while surviving within the confines of the communist state and its censorship.

Pope John Paul II

323 **John Paul II in Poland, 2-10 June 1979.**
Dominique Le Corre, Mark Sobotka, translated by Janusz Sikorski, Grażyna Lutos. London: Veritas Foundation, 1979. 120p.

A commemorative account of John Paul's first Papal visit to his Fatherland which aroused enormous enthusiasm and which had huge political and psychological consequences.

324 **Pope John Paul II. A man from Kraków.**
George Błażyński. London: Weidenfeld & Nicholson, 1979. 176p.

A BBC journalist, the author paints an all-round picture of the Pope and his background using a wide variety of sources.

325 **The Pope from Poland.**
Muriel Bowen & *The Sunday Times* team. London: Collins, 1980. 271p.
bibliog.

An 'action study' which presents a frank and detailed evaluation of Woytyła's life and beliefs and his actions during the first two years as Pope. The British journalists consider that his traditionalism on birth control, divorce and the limits of permitted belief and doctrine can be traced back 'chiefly to his Polish background'.

326 **Holy Father, welcome to your Fatherland for the third time.**
Edited by Czesław Dąbrowski (et al). Warsaw: Interpress, 1987.

Because of the altered political situation, the Pope's third visit to Poland in 1987 was inevitably of a more pastoral and less political character than the first two in 1979 and 1983. His personal influence, however, remained unabated as shown by the photographs and the commentary in this volume.

327 **The plot to kill the Pope.**
Paul B. Henze. London: Croom Helm, 1984. 216p.

This is an account of the attempt to kill Pope John Paul II in St Peter's Square on 13 May 1981 and the evidence produced at the trial of Mehmet Ali Agca, the would-be assassin. Henze indicates the certainty of Bulgarian complicity and the probability that the Kremlin and the KGB were the architects of the plot.

328 **Pope John Paul II. His travels and mission.**
Norman St-John Stevas. London: Faber & Faber, 1982. 160p.

A prominent British Catholic, historian and Conservative ex-Cabinet Minister, assesses the Pope's first ten foreign trips including one to Poland in 1979, as well as his overall character and mission.

329 **God's politician. John Paul at the Vatican.**
David Willey. London: Faber & Faber, 1992. 258p.

A perceptive and well-informed political history of John Paul's pontificate by a BBC journalist who accompanied him on many of his travels.

330 **The mind of John Paul II.**
George H. Williams. New York: Seabury Press, 1981. 415p. maps.

A study of the Polish influences during his life and career which formed the Pope's moral and intellectual character.

Maximilian (Rajmund) Kolbe

331 **Saint of Auschwitz: the story of Maximilian Kolbe.**
Diana Dewar. London: Darton, Longman & Todd, San Francisco: Harper & Row: 1982. 146p. bibliog.

An English journalist's popular account of Kolbe's life (1894-1941) and significance. Kolbe was canonized as a saint in 1982 for sacrificing his life in place of another victim due for extermination at Auschwitz.

332 **Maximilian Kolbe.**
Boniface Hanley. Notre Dame, Indiana: Ave Maria, 1982. 80p.

An American Franciscan scholar interprets the religious significance of the life of Saint Maximilian Kolbe. This is an accessible and very personal account.

333 **A man for others: Maximilian Kolbe, Saint of Auschwitz in the words of those who knew him.**
Patricia Treece. San Francisco: Harper & Row, 1982. bibliog.

An account based very heavily on the reminiscences of family, friends and Second World War survivors who knew him. The study is designed to bring out in intimate detail his personality and character.

Jerzy Popiełuszko

334 **The priest who had to die. The tragedy of Father Jerzy Popiełuszko.**
Roger Boyes, John Moody. London: Victor Gollancz, 1986. 204p.

A journalistic account of the circumstances of Father Popiełuszko's murder by four secret policemen in October 1984 and of the immediate repercussions of the affair.

335 **Turbulent priest. The political implications of the Popiełuszko affair.**
Paul Lewis. *Politics*, vol. 5, no. 2 (1985), p. 33-9.

Examines the political background to Popiełuszko's murder and the course of the Toruń trial of late December 1984 to February 1985 of the four secret policemen convicted of his murder. Lewis concludes that the wider political implications of the affair, and even the general responsibility, were contained very successfully by the Jaruzelski regime.

336 **A martyr for the truth: Jerzy Popiełuszko.**
Grażyna Sikorska. London: Fount, 1985. 134p. (Keston Books no 24).

A popular account of the life and work of Jerzy Popiełuszko and of the circumstances of his murder in 1984. Written by a Pole now settled in England.

National Catholic Church

337 **The Polish National Catholic Church in the United States of America**
from 1897 to 1980; its social conditioning and social functions.
Hieronim Kubiak. Kraków-Warsaw: Nakładem Uniwersytetu
Jagiellońskiego – Państwowe Wydawnictwo Naukowe, 1982. 214p.
(Scientific Bulletins of the Jagiellonian University no. 654).
A translation of a work first published in Poland in 1970 by a major Kraków University
sociologist who achieved much prominence in the early 1980s as a reform-minded
member of the PZPR Politburo. The study examines the reasons for the establishment
of the Polish National Catholic Church (PNCC) in the USA at the end of the
nineteenth century, its conflicts with the Roman Catholic Church, its sociological
development during the twentieth century and how this reflected the social adaptation
of Polish immigrants to changing American conditions. The PNCC still had about
28,000 members, 151 priests and 162 churches in the early 1960s mostly located in
traditional regions of Polish settlement in the north-east of the USA. But with social
advancement it was beginning to spread to more prosperous, notably 'sun-belt', states;
Kubiak concluded that it had established itself as a permanent force despite facing new
dilemmas stemming from the confrontation between its American reality and Polish
tradition.

Protestant churches

338 **Baptists in Poland; past and present.**
R. E. Davies. *Religion in Communist Lands*, vol. 18, no. 1 (1990),
p. 52-63.
Discusses the small Polish Baptist Union, with its membership of a few thousand, its
historical development, links with other denominations and foreign Baptist churches as
well as its prospects. The author considers the movement to be 'pietistic' and wholly
inwardly motivated in character, without much possibility of expansion.

339 **Polish Protestants; ecumenism in a dual diaspora.**
Paul Keim. *Religion in Communist Lands*, vol. 10, no. 3 (1983),
p. 295-309.
Examines the five protestant churches affiliated to the Polish Ecumenical Council and
their memberships; the (Lutheran) Evangelical-Augsburg (70,000), the Evangelical
Reform Church (4,500), the Polish Baptists (6,000), Methodists (4,500) and the
United Evangelical Church (15,000). Polish protestants had a dual character as they
lived in an overwhelmingly Catholic nation but were paradoxically assisted by the
existence of the socialist state. On later developments and their concern at growing
Roman Catholic influence see Bogdan Tranda, 'The situation of Protestants in today's
Poland', *Religion in Communist Lands*, vol. 19, nos 1-2 (Summer 1991), p. 37-44.

Orthodox and Greek Catholic churches

340 **Ukrainian Catholics and Orthodox in Poland.**
Andrew Sorokowski. *Religion in Communist Lands*, vol.14, no. 3
(1986), p. 244-61.
Estimates that there are about 350-400 thousand Ukrainian Greek Catholics and 150-200 thousand members of the Polish Autocephalous Orthodox Church in Poland. This article examines the postwar historical and organizational development of the two churches and the influence of the Solidarity period upon them.

Society

Social groups and conditions

341 **Poland's journalists: professionalism and politics.**
Jane Leftwich Curry. Cambridge, England: Cambridge University
Press, 1990. 302p. (Soviet and East European Studies series no. 66).
bibliog.
An academic study of journalists and their professional associations in the late
communist period in Poland. Curry demonstrates conclusively how their professional
interests and behaviour transformed them into an effective pressure group within the
system especially in reform-periods such as 1980-81.

342 **Towards Poland 2000: problems of social development.**
Edited by Jan Danecki, Jerzy Krycki. Wrocław, Poland:
Ossolineum, 1980. 281p.
A variety of specialists predict different aspects of Poland's social development up to
the year 2000. The contributions are grouped under four headings; social forecasting,
the socio-cultural framework, spatial studies and selected aspects.

343 **A village without Solidarity. Polish peasants in years of crisis.**
C. M. Hann. New Haven, Connecticut: Yale University Press, 1985.
208p. bibliog.
A clear and attractively presented piece of rural sociology based on exemplary
fieldwork during 1979-81 in the village of Wisłok in the Lower Beskid region of south-
eastern Poland. Hann elucidates the barriers to political participation, economic
development and toleration produced by Gierek's bureaucratic running of the largely
privately peasant-owned countryside. But Wisłok, with its substantial ethnic and
religious minorities (Ruthenian Orthodox), is probably too untypical to carry wider
generalizations about the Solidarity experience of 1980-81 in the countryside. It

remained largely passive and poorly integrated while the rest of the region became a hotbed of social contestation and the driving force behind Rural Solidarity.

344 **Social structure and self-direction. A comparative analysis of the United States and Poland.**
Melvin L. Kohn, Kazimierz M. Słomczyński. Oxford: Basil Blackwell, 1990. 256p. bibliog.
A comparative study of the effects of the social structure upon the individual personality in Poland and the USA.

345 **Equality and inequality under socialism: Poland and Hungary compared.**
Edited by Tamas Kolosi, Edmund Wnuk-Lipiński. London: Sage, 1983. 201p.
This comparative study, based on fieldwork in the late 1970s carried out by Polish and Hungarian sociologists, concluded that there were more similarities than differences in the internal stratification patterns of industrial workers in the two countries. Professional, administrative and clerical workers made up a fairly homogeneous group in Poland but their differences with the workers were primarily cultural rather than economic.

346 **Crisis and transition. Polish society in the 1980s.**
Edited by Jadwiga Koralewicz, Ireneusz Białecki, Margaret Watson.
Oxford: Berg, 1987. 184p. bibliog.
A volume of eight translated papers by pro-Solidarity Polish sociologists critical of the communist regime of the time who popularize their favoured concepts for an English readership. Koralewicz and Wnuk-Lipiński examine the problems of cognitive dissonance or social dimorphism while Marody presents survey findings on society's low level of acceptance of communist values. The volume's central pieces are Jadwiga Staniszkis' dissection of the dilemmas which produced the Polish stalemate of the mid-1980s and Andrzej Rychard's theoretical framework for the communist system's legitimation crisis.

347 **Society and deviance in communist Poland: attitudes towards social control.**
Jerzy Kwaśniewski, translated by Margaret Watson. Leamington Spa, England: Berg, 1984. 210p. bibliog.
A Polish sociological examination of how the concept of deviance was defined and applied in communist Poland. Kwaśniewski concluded that Polish society had developed a high tolerance of what would normally be regarded as social pathologies such as alcoholism, bribery and prostitution.

348 **Social groups in Polish society.**
Edited by David Lane, George Kolankiewicz. New York: Columbia
University Press, 1973. 380p.
This made a strong impact on publication because it examined the dynamics and
problems of the country as a projection of its social structure rather than its mode of
government. The book covers a wide range of Polish social groups: private sector
farmers, industrial workers, the cultural and technical intelligentsia, managers and the
political elite.

349 **People's Poland. Patterns of social inequality and conflict.**
Władysław Majkowski. Westport, Connecticut: Greenwood Press,
1985. 234p. bibliog.
A detailed examination of the light thrown on the problems of class and inequality by
the four workers' revolts in communist Poland (Poznań 1956, Baltic seacoast 1970,
Radom/Ursus 1970 and August 1980 nationwide).

350 **Social change and stratification in Eastern Europe; interpretative
analysis of Poland and her neighbours.**
Aleksander Matejko. New York: Praeger, 1974. 272p. bibliog.
A comprehensive and extremely detailed academic study of the rapidity and depth of
social transformation in postwar Poland up to the early Gierek period. Poland's
experience is contrasted with that of the rest of Eastern Europe.

351 **Women in contemporary Poland. A sketch to a portrait.**
Krystyna Niedzielska. Warsaw: Wydawnictwo Spółdzielcze, 1985.
50p.
An essay for a popular readership illustrating the many-faceted roles of women in
modern Poland.

352 **Ways of life in Finland and Poland. Comparative studies on urban
populations.**
Edited by J. P. Roos, Andrzej Siciński. Aldershot, England: Gower
Press, 1987. 203p.. bibliog.
This joint Polish-Finnish sociological investigation carried out during the 1980s is a
successor to E. Allardt and Włodzimierz Wesołowski, *Social structure and change.
Finland and Poland. Comparative perspective* (Warsaw: PWN, 1978. 392p). The study
concluded that in Finland the social situation was conducive to a settled and private
way of life whereas Polish conditions produced a continuous struggle and conflict in all
social activities from shopping to fixing even the simplest matter.

353 **Women and social movements in Poland.**
Renata Siemieńska. *Women and Politics*, vol. 6, no. 4 (1986), p. 5-35.
Siemieńska argues that the political activity of Polish women was largely conditioned
by the country's highly specific history and the hierarchy of values in Polish society.
The processes of feminine mobilization and participation were, therefore, very
irregular and far from being part of a linear development.

354 **Social stratification in Poland. Eight empirical studies.**
Edited by Kazimierz M. Słomczyński, Tadeusz K. Krauze. Armonk,
New York: M. E. Sharpe, 1986. 189p. bibliog.

The editors, assisted by other Polish sociologists, present theoretical discussions and
empirical findings on such issues as social equality and mobility, perceptions of the
social structure, social and occupational status, values and class images, and worker
radicalism. This is a sequel to Słomczyński & Krauze, *Class structure and social
mobility in Poland* (New York: M. E. Sharpe, 1978).

355 **Social structure and mobility; Poland, Japan and the United States.
Methodological studies.**
Kazimierz M. Słomczyński. Warsaw: IFIS – PAN, 1989. 182p.
bibliog.

A highly theoretical and comparative discussion of social stratification in the three
countries mentioned in the title.

356 **Polish society.**
Jan Szczepański. New York: Random House, 1970. 214p.

This celebrated essay by an influential Polish academic and political adviser still
provides a succinct and readable account of the dynamics and aspirations of the
pluralist-nationalist middle stage of communist Poland's life.

357 **Private Poland. An anthropologist looks at everyday life in Poland.**
Janine Wedel. New York: Facts on File, 1986. 256p. bibliog.

A knowledgeable presentation, based on genuine experience, of the realities of Polish
life, particularly the various fixing activities which were necessary to get even the most
simple things done in the post-1976 period.

358 **The unplanned society. Poland during and after communism.**
Edited, annotated and introduced by Janine Wedel. New York:
Columbia University Press, 1992. 271p.

Contains seventeen chapters by Polish writers, mainly sociologists, on the role of social
groups, notably the protective social circle (środowisko) in the transition from
communism to a fully plural society.

Social and ethical issues

359   **Aids and human rights: an international perspective: by independent
scholars from 14 different countries including the Soviet Union, USA,
Poland, East Germany, Sweden, Greece, Finland and Great Britain.**
Edited by Martin Breum, Aart Hendricks.   Copenhagen: Akademisk
Forlag, 1988. 174p. (Publications of the Danish Centre for Human
Rights no. 6).

An international symposium on the legal and moral issues raised by the treatment of
HIV and Aids sufferers in fourteen countries. The Polish chapter (p. 115-21) is by
Zofia Kuratowska, who became a well-known Democratic Union Senator after 1989,
and Marek Nowakowski of Warsaw University. They confirm that Aids, with sixty-four
cases of HIV infection and three deaths by March 1988, had not, by then, spread
widely in Poland. But the Polish state, regarding it as a very serious potential problem,
had already legislated a number of prophylactic and medical measures. The issue was
to arouse much fear and intolerance in Poland in the early 1990s and direct opposition
to the siting of hostels for Aids victims, even for children, in various locales.

360   **A question of life: its beginning and transmission: a moral perspective of
the new genetics in the West, the USSR, Poland and East Germany.**
Patrick O'Mahony.   London: Sheed & Ward, 1990. 253p. (Christian
Classics). bibliog.

A discussion by a Catholic priest of the ethical implications of new reproductive
techniques such as *in vitro* fertilization, embryo-freezing, surrogacy, and cloning as
well as abortion in the light of the 1984 recommendations of the Warnock Committee
in the UK. The author compares the Secularist and Utilitarian views of the West with
the Marxist approaches of East Germany and the USSR. The chapter on Poland is
short (p. 196-211) and confirms that the use of such techniques had not advanced very
far there. The main controversial isssue consequently was the high abortion rate;
Poland's Catholic character turned it into an ethical as well as a practical question
unlike the situation in the USSR and Protestant East Germany.

Social Services, Health and Welfare

361 **Social policy in the new Eastern Europe. What future for socialist welfare?**
Edited by Bob Deacon, Julia Szalai. Aldershot, England: Avebury, 1990.

The Polish contributors are Mirosław Księżopolski, Lena Kolarska-Bobińska, Magdalena Sokołowska and Andrzej Rychard. Part B compares the possibilities for independent social policy in Poland and Hungary. See also the chapter on 'Social Policy in Poland' by Frances Millard (p. 118-43) in Bob Deacon's, *The New Eastern Europe. Social policy, past, present and future* (London: Sage, 1992. 198p.). This volume covers social policy in Eastern Europe in general and in Poland, Bulgaria, Czechoslovakia, Hungary and the former USSR in particular.

362 **Health for all by the year 2000. Polish strategy and tactics.**
Government Commission's Report on Health for All. Warsaw: Polish Medical Publishers, 1991. 55p. bibliog.

This report was part of a much wider-reaching United Nations programme. It now reads as a very optimistic document given the economic constraints of the 1990s.

363 **Assist and befriend or direct and control; a report on probation services in Poland and England.**
Edited by John Harper, John Simmonds, Thelma Wilson, Maria Ziemska. London: North East London Polytechnic, 1982. 211p. (Sponsored by North East London Polytechnic, Warsaw University, the Polish Ministry of Justice and the South Eastern Regional Staff Development Unit, UK).

A report made up of nineteen short chapters on various aspects of the probation services and their legal-penal frameworks in the two countries. Written by a group of Polish and English academics and probation officers who exchanged visits and collaborated together on this project, the information was collected during the year 1979-80. The description of their mutual contacts is of peripheral interest but there is a useful central core of information and discussion about the main subject.

364 **Social welfare in Britain and Poland.**
Edited by Julian Le Grand, Włodzimierz Okrasa. London School of Economics, Suntory-Toyota International Centre for Economics and Related Disciplines (STICERD), 1988. (Occasional Paper no 12).

One of a series of papers relating to Poland published by the Centre. Other papers of interest include: Frances Millard, *Social welfare and the market* 1989 (Occasional Paper no. 15); and Włodzimierz Okrasa, *Social justice and the redistributive effect of social expenditure in Poland*, 1987 (Welfare State Discussion Paper no. 18). STICERD also published the proceedings of the British-Polish conference on social welfare in Eastern and Western Europe, *Social welfare in Britain and Poland* (1987. 266p. bibliog.).

365 **Poland.**
Ewa Les. In: *Social welfare in socialist countries*. Edited by John Dixon, David Macarov. London: Routledge, 1992. p. 156-83.

An essay which presents the historical origins of welfare in Poland; the welfare state; political and social environments; finance; care of the elderly, personal social services, the disabled and handicapped, sick and injured, children and youth. The information deals only with the communist period up till the end of 1988, and concludes that, although the scope of Polish welfare benefits were considerable, their real value was kept low by inflation and poor productivity.

366 **Panel services for offenders. Comparative studies of England and Poland, 1984-85.**
Edited by Thelma Wilson. Aldershot, England: Avebury, 1987. 103p. bibliog.

Six English (London Polytechnic) specialists, who visited Poland in 1979-84 during the course of this joint-project compare the English and Polish probation services and their different aims, political and legal-administrative frameworks. A companion study to Harper (item no. 363).

Politics

367 **Poland. The role of the press in political change.**
Madeline K. Albright. New York: Praeger, 1983. 147p. (Washington Papers no. 102). bibliog.
A high-powered analysis of the dynamic relationship between communication and power during the Solidarity period when the communist control of the mass media was seriously undermined.

368 **Political legitimacy and crisis in Poland.**
William P. Avery. *Political Science Quarterly*, vol. 103, no. 1 (Spring 1988), p. 111-30.
Argues that the legitimacy crisis of Poland's political system could only be resolved by bringing its political institutions and procedures into closer conformity with its mainstream national values and traditions. Political instability in Poland and her neighbours is likely due to the absence of political confidence and legitimacy which lowers public tolerance on specific issues.

369 **The strikes of June 1976 in Poland.**
Michael Bernhard. *East European Politics and Societies*, vol. 1, no. 3 (1987), p. 363-92.
An in-depth examination of the wave of at least 1,430 strikes in June 1976 which forced the Government to rescind its proposed price increases. A good analysis is included of the events in Radom, Płock, and the Ursus tractor plant outside Warsaw which concludes that the strike-wave was more national in character, although not as intense, as in 1970-71.

370 Poland's politics: idealism versus realism.
Adam Bromke. Cambridge, Massachusetts: Harvard University
Press, 1967. 316p. bibliog.

This proved to be one of the most influential discussions of the dynamics of Polish history for almost two decades after its publication. Bromke argues that Polish political thought and practice since the Partitions has been dominated by the clash between romantic nationalism and positivist realism. The response to Poland's international position, and the issue of how either to gain or protect her independence, produced cyclical swings; periods of excessive emphasis on full independence, even great Power aspirations, as in Piłsudski's era were followed by periods of accommodation to external realities as in the postwar communist period up to Gierek. The examination of political currents in the first half of the life of communist Poland is still invaluable.

371 Poland. The protracted crisis.
Adam Bromke. Oakville, Ontario: Mosaic Press, 1983. 260p.
(Extended edition of *Poland: the last decade*, 1981. 189p.).

A collection which brings together, very usefully, the academic articles published at various times between 1971 and 1982 by a leading expert on Polish politics. Some of the articles on the Gierek period (especially chapters 3, 4, 5 and 7) are regarded as authoritative by specialists in the field.

372 The grand failure. The birth and death of communism in the twentieth
century.
Zbigniew Brzezinski. London: Macdonald, 1990. 278p.

In this seminal work Brzezinski sets out, in broad terms, the ten dynamics of disunion which led to the collapse of communism, the breakup of the USSR and its 'Organic Rejection' in Eastern Europe. Chapters nine and ten concentrate on Polish society's self-emancipation from Soviet rule and the development of pluralism during the 1980s.

373 Devant la Guerre. Les Réalités. (Before the war. The true situation.)
Cornelius Castoriadis. Paris: Fayard, 1981. 2nd ed. 285p.

An influential French social analysis of the growing weight of the military within the Soviet stratocracy, and of how this pushed the Kremlin towards external aggression and domestic repression in its *bloc*, notably Poland in the early 1980s.

374 Local officials of the Polish United Workers Party, 1956-75.
Jane Cave. *Soviet Studies*, vol. 33, no. 1 (1981), p. 125-41.

A detailed sociological examination of the composition of the local officials of the Polish communist party over a twenty year period. It aims to elucidate the extent to which their educational qualifications and expertise had improved. The level of the former was certainly raised and this led to conflicts between younger and older generations of officials especially in the late 1960s.

Politics

375 **Poland. Communism. Nationalism, Anti-Semitism.**
Michael Chęciński, translated in part by Tadeusz Szafar. New York: Karz-Cohl, 1982. 289p.

A defecting Polish officer's analysis of the sinister role of the security police in postwar Poland and its complex relationship with the nationalist and authoritarian currents within the communist party. Chęciński concentrates on the way Moczar's Partisan faction used the Jewish issue in 1967-68 to challenge Gomułka and to carry out a purge of both Jews and liberal communists.

376 **Poland's military burden.**
Michael Chęciński. *Problems of Communism*, vol. 32, no. 3 (May-June 1983), p. 31-44.

Chęcinski demonstrates how the Soviet imposed military-industrial build-up from 1949 onwards slowed down Poland's economic and consumption growth and impeded economic reform. These factors contributed substantially to Poland's continuing political unrest.

377 **Poland since 1956; readings and essays on Polish government and politics.**
Edited by Tadeusz N. Cieplak. New York: Twayne, 1972. 482p.

An old and venerable volume which remains one of the most useful collections of documents and analyses on the Gomułka period, 1956-70.

378 **The black book of Polish censorship.**
Edited and translated by Jane Leftwich Curry. New York: Random House, 1984. 451p.

An important collection of the Censorship Bureau's directives, bans and appraisals during the 1974-77 period taken abroad by a defecting censor from the Kraków office.

379 **The psychological barriers to reform in Poland.**
Jane L. Curry. *East European Politics and Societies*, vol. 2, no. 3 (Fall 1988), p. 484-509.

The basic thesis is that economic reform in Poland in the late 1980s was rendered impossible by the very conditions which made it neccesary. While the international bloc and domestic situations now favoured communist reform leaderships, the balance of internal Polish social forces and the economic balance mitigated against its possible success.

380 **Conscientious objection and the Freedom and Peace Movement in Poland.**
Gareth Davies. *Religion in Communist Lands*, vol. 16, no. 1 (1988), p. 4-20.

An examination of the Freedom and Peace (WiP) movement's struggle during the 1980's to gain the legal right of conscientious objection in Poland.

381 **Eastern Europe, Gorbachev and reform. The great challenge.**
Karen Dawisha. Cambridge, England: Cambridge University Press,
1990. 2nd ed. 319p.

The much revised and expanded second edition supplies the answer to the question
posed in the 1988 edition; would Gorbachev's reforms ensure communism's survival in
Eastern Europe? Dawisha examines the reasons for systemic collapse and Soviet
withdrawal in 1989 trenchantly and comprehensively, and situates Polish developments
in the context of Eastern Europe as a whole. She also covers the major issues
concerning the region's domestic and international evolution before the collapse of
Soviet communism and the break-up of the USSR in 1991 rendered another edition
necessary.

382 **No-choice elections.**
Jerzy Drygalski, Jacek Kwaśniewski. *Soviet Studies*, vol. 42, no. 2
(1990), p. 295-315.

An examination of local elections and elections within the Polish communist party
during the 1950-79 period. It shows how the party controlled such elections in order to
block the free articulation of interests and currents and to put on a show of
participation designed to build up its legitimacy.

383 **The Communist Party of Poland: an outline of history.**
Marian Kamil Dziewanowski. New York: Columbia University Press,
1977. 2nd ed. 419p. (Russian Research Centre Studies no. 32). bibliog.

A pioneering, but now badly dated, history of the revolutionary socialist movement in
Poland. The pre-1948 material is still quite useful but the main section on the Polish
United Workers' Party was not updated sufficiently in the second edition.

384 **Crisis and political ritual in postwar Poland.**
Andrzej Flis. *Problems of Commmunism*, vol. 37, no. 3-4 (May-August
1988), p. 43-54.

Flis argues that since communist ideology regarded the socialist system as perfect any
attack on it was considered to be profane by the communist authorities. There was
therefore a gnostic discontinuity of the sacred versus the profane, in the communists'
view of reality which explained the banning of political opposition and their deep
attachment to political ritual.

385 **Roman Dmowski; party, tactics, ideology, 1895-1907.**
Alvin Marcus Fountain. Boulder, Colorado: Columbia University
Press, 1980. 240p.

An important study of the early ideas and policies of Roman Dmowski during the key
1895-1907 formative period when the National Democratic Party (*Endecja*) was
established. Dmowski was the father-figure of modern Polish integral nationalism. His
movement was a major force in the interwar period and remains highly influential in
post-communist Poland.

386 **Civil Society in Poland and Hungary.**
    Janina Frentzel-Zagórska. *Soviet Studies*, vol. 42, no. 4 (1990), p. 759-77.

The article contrasts the different development of Civil Soviety in Poland since the emergence of Solidarity and its increased momentum in Hungary in the 1980s. It concludes that the post-communist free societies in both countries will continue to develop as a result of their highly specific domestic evolutions and circumstances. See also the author's 'The dominant political culture in Poland', *Politics*, vol. 20, no. 1 (1985), p. 82-98.

387 **The political systems of the socialist states. An introduction to Marxist-Leninist regimes.**
    Robert K. Furtak. Brighton, England: Harvester Press, 1986. 308p.

A serious legal-institutional textbook introduction to the comparative state framework of communism, examining all communist systems across the board. The author is a distinguished German scholar.

388 **The failure of authoritarian change: reform, opposition and geo-politics in Poland in the 1980s.**
    Andre W. M. Gerrits. Aldershot, England: Dartmouth, 1990. 260p.

Examines the interplay between the Kremlin, the domestic Polish communist leadership and Polish society and opposition groups during the 1980s. Basing his account on a thorough examination of the best sources Gerrits produces a challenging interpretation of the relationship between Jaruzelski's *regime* and the doctrine of alleged Polish limited sovereignty. He explains the steps which led from martial law to the Round Table very convincingly.

389 **In defence of my country.**
    Jędrzej Giertych. London: Veritas Foundation Press, 1981. 732p.
    (Publications of the Roman Dmowski Society no. 19). maps.

Giertych, Dmowski's disciple and the main postwar emigré Polish National Democrat leader, sets out his credo and principles for a Polish nationalist state with ethnically based frontiers. His case is supported by a range of Polish, Russian and German documents.

390 **Is Hungary the future of Poland?**
    Zvi Gitelman. *East European Politics and Societies*, vol. 1, no. 1 (Winter 1987), p. 135-59.

This seminal article discussed why the Mexican model of One-Party pluralism had turned out to be not relevant to the Polish case. Gitelman concentrated on the extent to which Kadar's Hungarian long-term reform strategy had been debated in Poland and outlined the differences and the obstacles which stood in the way of Poland successfully adopting such a strategy.

391　On cultural freedom. An exploration of public life in Poland and America.
Jeffrey C. Goldfarb.　Chicago: Chicago University Press, 1982. 173p.

A highly original comparison of the very different threats to cultural freedom in 1970s Poland and the USA (political censorship versus commercial constraints and marginalization). Goldfarb shows how the Polish film and theatre, in particular, managed to remain lively and creative, and even to some extent autonomous. Communist attempts to exert political control through a wide variety of supports and constraints resulted in a more dynamic and balanced relationship with cultural creators than in other communist countries because of the Polish party's loss of legitimacy and self-confidence. See also his *The persistence of freedom; the sociological implications of Polish student theatre* (Boulder, Colorado: Westview Press, 1980. 159p.).

392　Polish paradoxes.
Edited by Stanisław Gomułka, Anthony Polonsky.　London: Routledge, 1990. 274p.

An outstanding collection of essays by an impressive set of contemporary Polish writers (Walicki, Jedlicki, Król, Holzer, Jerschina, Staniszkis, et al). It constitutes both an intellectually high-powered analysis and a valuable source of information on communism's death-throes in the 1980s. The editors argue that 'paradox' is a key feature of Polish politics. Apparent opposites have been blended together by a long-drawn out struggle for national independence and democracy which has created a highly original and resilient political culture. This has survived numerous political forms in the past and will also mould the post-communist system.

393　Perestroika. New thinking for our country and our world.
Mikhail Gorbachev.　London: Fontana-Collins, 1989. rev. ed. 354p.

The authoritative expression of the changes in the international environment and in Eastern Europe which Gorbachev aimed to bring about through his communist reformism and international security and disarmament negotiations. Gorbachev's account makes interesting reading in the light of what actually happened. The book was also published in Polish as *Przebudowa i nowe myślenie dla naszego kraju i dla całego świata.* (Warsaw: Państwowy Instytut Wydawniczy, 1988).

394　Central and Eastern Europe. The opening curtain?
Edited by William E. Griffith.　Boulder, Colorado: Westview Press, 1989. 458p.

The eighteen chapters by high-flying specialists make this one of the most comprehensive and relevant symposia on the varied presssures, domestic and external, facing the communist system in Eastern Europe in the last phase of its existence.

395　Democracy in a Communist party. The Polish experience since 1980.
Werner G. Hahn.　New York: Columbia University Press, 1987. 367p. bibliog.

The question of whether internal party democracy was possible and whether the democratic element could be rebalanced against the normally dominant Leninist centralist pole was a major theoretical political science issue during the 1980s. Hahn's detailed examination is the major case-study of such an attempt outside Yugoslavia and before Gorbachev became more radical. The Polish United Workers' Party responded to the 1980-81 crisis by attempting to mobilize its mass membership (3 million at the outset) through competitive elections for party committees and for the delegates to its Extraordinary Ninth Congress in July 1981. Its statute and programme, embodying the aim of internal party democracy, were overwhelmed by political polarization and economic collapse and the imposition of martial law in December 1981. But the strategy produced some revival of political caucuses which, backed by the military, underpinned the Jaruzelski *regime* in the early 1980s.

396 **Return to Poland.**
Denis Hills. London: Bodley Head, 1988. 278p.

The author spent the period from 1935 to the outbreak of war in September 1939 in Poland, before escaping through Romania. This book is an account of his impressions during his second return visit in 1985, which ended in his expulsion by Christmas. An obstreperous journalist, and alleged British Intelligence Officer, Hills had previously achieved world-wide notoriety by being sentenced to death by Idi Amin in Uganda.

397 **Coercion and control in communist society; the visible hand in a command economy.**
Maria Hirszowicz. Brighton, England: Harvester Press, 1985. 226p. bibliog.

A wide-ranging development of the ideas first set out in *The bureaucratic Leviathan*, this is basically a sociological essay on the various social, economic and bureaucratic contradictions bedevilling the communist system in the last phase of its life in Poland and Eastern Europe.

398 **The bureaucratic Leviathan; a study in the sociology of communism.**
Maria Hirszowicz. Oxford: Martin Robertson, 1980. 208p.

A penetrating sociological examination, based largely on Poland, of the institutional dynamics of communism as a system of power. The author is a distinguished Polish scholar who has taught at a British university since leaving Poland after the events of 1968.

399 **Politics in the communist world.**
Leslie Holmes. Oxford: Clarendon Press, 1986. 457p. bibliog.

Holmes' account had deservedly established itself as the best single-authored textbook on comparative communism by the time the system collapsed in Eastern Europe. It situates the development of Polish politics and government within the context of the wider communist experience admirably.

400 **Isaac Deutscher. The man and his work.**
Edited by David Horowicz. London: Macdonald, 1971. 254p. bibliog.

A collective work on Deutscher's revolutionary marxist, but non-Stalinist, career and writings. The most specifically Polish section is by Daniel Singer which covers his life up till his final departure from Poland in April 1939.

401 **Changing values and political dissatisfaction in Poland and the West.**
Ronald Inglehart, Renata Siemieńska. *Government and Opposition*,
vol. 23, no. 4 (Autumn 1988), p. 440-57.
A survey carried out in Poland five months before Solidarity's re-legalization shows a
surprising similarity in the intergenerational shift from materialist to post-modernist
attitudes when compared with data collected in eight western countries in the mid-
1970s. Polish post-materialists were however more dissatisfied and were more likely to
take part in protest activities. It is argued that underlying cultural change must be
considered along with the deteriorating economy as giving rise to crisis.

402 **Exiled Governments; Spanish and Polish. An essay in political sociology.**
Alicja Iwańska. Cambridge, Massachusetts: Schenkman, 1981. 130p.
bibliog.
An instructive sociological comparison between the governments-in-exile opposed to
Franco's Spain and to communist Poland.

403 **Polish broadcasting studies in search of a raison d'être.**
Karol Jakubowicz. *European Journal of Communications*, vol. 4, no. 3
(September 1989), p. 267-85.
Demonstrates how at the time of writing Polish broadcasting was 'languishing in limbo'
and how it still had to come to terms with the democratization required to break the
communist monopoly and organization of the mass media. *Glasnost* was still
proceeding far too slowly and the Polish audience was still living in a state of stress and
anomie which produced 'protective-escapist' reactions.

404 **Poland and the politics of permissable pluralism.**
George Kolankiewicz. *East European Politics and Societies*, vol. 2,
no. 1 (Winter 1988), p. 152-83.
Solidarity created the values, identity and terms on which social incorporation into the
communist system can take place. In the past selective inclusion or co-option has
proved a viable policy for the regime.

405 **Poland. Politics, economics and society.**
George Kolankiewicz, Paul Lewis. London: F. Pinter, 1988. 210p.
bibliog.
Two well-established and knowledgeable British academics produced what is now
widely regarded as the most authoritative student textbook on communist Poland just
as the system was about to undergo fundamental transformation in 1989. The authors
argue that Poland's complex historical and socio-cultural diversity produced a wide
variety of structural forms of communist rule. They examine these under the self-
explanatory headings of history and traditions, social structure and welfare, structures
of political rule, international politics and a concluding examination of the challenges
to communist power. Poland's crisis-ridden postwar development is attributed to lack
of support for the Soviet model which produced unstable and unorthodox balances
between the communist state and a recalcitrant society.

Politics

406 **Evolution after revolution; the Polish press in transition.**
Tadeusz Kowalski. *Media, Culture and Society*, vol. 10, no. 2 (April 1988), p. 183-96.
A growing divergence between the aims and expectations of people active in political and cultural life and the legal-organizational framework of the mass media developed in Poland during 1980-81. Kowalski explains how martial law was unsuccessful in repressing such aspirations for reform in the mass media which forced the authorities to move towards accommodation.

407 **Andrzej Krauze's Poland.**
Andrzej Krauze, preface by George Mikes. London: Nina Karsov, 1981. 95p.
Andrzej Krauze, one of Poland's most famous political cartoonists, achieved prominence with his drawings for the Warsaw weekly *Kultura* during the 1970s. This anthology of eighty-three of his political cartoons, only fifteen of which were published in the Polish press, has English and Russian translations of his Polish captions. They deal largely with the 1980-81 crisis period and include the famous drawings of the communist wolf blaming the sheep for not co-existing with him. See also *A year of martial law. Cartoons by Andrzej Krauze* (Paris: Kontakt, 1982. 47p.). Mikes places Krauze in the same class as the British cartoonists Vicky and Low. A later example of his work is *Culture shock*, edited by Michael Rosen and illustrated by Andrzej Krauze (London: Viking, 1990. 117p.).

408 **An open letter to the Party.**
Jacek Kuroń, Karol Modzelewski. London: International Socialism, [n. d.]. 74p.
Written in 1965, this is historically one of the most important critiques of state-socialism and the power and privilege of the communist elite. Its authors, who were imprisoned for writing it, subsequently became major opposition and Solidarity leaders. Also published as *Solidarność: the missing link* (London: Bookmarks, 1982).

409 **Eastern Europe. Political crisis and legitimation.**
Edited by Paul G. Lewis. London: Croom Helm, 1984. 202p.
In this work academic specialists discuss the application of the concept of legitimacy to the politics of Hungary, Czechoslovakia, Poland and the GDR in the early 1980s. The editor argues, tautologically, that the delegitimization of communist regimes was 'the major cause of system disintegration and political crisis in Eastern Europe'.

410 **Obstacles to the establishment of political legitimacy in Poland.**
Paul Lewis. *British Journal of Political Science*, vol. 12, no. 2 (April 1982), p. 125-47.
Argues that the Gierek regime collapsed because the institutional conditions of the communist state led to the failure of its strategy of attempting to gain legitimacy through rapid economic growth and consumer satisfaction. Despite the Extraordinary Congress of July 1981 the communist system's prospects for achieving political legitimacy are weak.

411 **Political authority and Party Secretaries in Poland 1975-86.**
Paul G. Lewis. Cambridge, England: Cambridge University Press, 1989. 344p.

Lewis argues, in this heavily documented monograph, that the Polish communist leadership's failure to gain political legitimacy and to carry through reforms was caused by the highly specific shortcomings of its provincial party committees. The contradictory political and socio-economic dynamics and organizational party confusion caused by Gierek's early 1970s local government reforms made it impossible to carry out essential economic adjustments in the late 1970s. Institutional blockages within the communist party led to its partial replacement by the military during martial law and was a crucial factor in its eventual abdication from power in 1989.

412 **The Polish Party apparatus: changes in provincial First Secretaries 1975-84.**
Paul Lewis. *Soviet Studies*, vol. 38, no. 3 (1986), p. 369-86.

A summary presentation of the argument in the author's *Political authority and Party Secretaries in Poland 1975-86* (q.v.) which discusses the failure of the communist leadership to carry out necessary reforms.

413 **KOR. A history of the Workers' Defense Committee in Poland.**
Jan Józef Lipski, translated by Olga Amsterdamska, Gene A. Moore. Berkeley, California: University of California Press, 1985. 561p.

An authoritative descriptive political history of the Workers' Defense Committee from its establishment after the Radom and other repressions of 1976 to its dissolution at the Solidarity Congress in Autumn 1981, written by a prominent academic dissident and socialist (PPS) leader. For the development of the intellectual-opposition current after KOR's self-dissolution at the Solidarity Congress in September 1981, see Robert Żuzowski's 'KOR after KOR, the intelligentsia and dissent in Poland, 1981-87', *Polish Review*, vol. 33, no. 2 (1988), p. 167-89.

414 **Politics and society in Eastern Europe.**
Joni Lovenduski, Jean Woodall. London: Macmillan, 1987. 474p. maps. bibliog.

This work had just established itself as the best student textbook on the subject when communism collapsed. The authors introduce a wide range of concepts, discussing how these apply to Eastern Europe and referring the readers to the relevant literature which sums up the state of knowledge on each aspect. Poland's postwar development is assessed quite economically within its comparative regional and communist context.

415 **The crises of communism; its meaning, origins and phases.**
Rett R. Ludwikowski. Washington, DC: Pergamon-Brasseys, 1986. 84p.

A short but detailed analysis which identifies the features of Polish developments during 1980-81 which constitute aspects of the general crisis of communism. A foreign policy report written for the Institute of Foreign Policy Analysis in Cambridge, Massachusetts, by a Professor of Law at the Catholic University of America.

Politics

416 **Poland's politicised army. Communists in uniform.**
George Malcher. New York: Praeger, 1984. 287p.
An excellent analysis of how the 'political military' emerged in Poland and how it was used by Jaruzelski to suppress Solidarity during martial law.

417 **Public opinion and political change in Poland 1980-82.**
David S. Mason. Cambridge, England: Cambridge University Press, 1985. 275p. (Soviet and East European Studies series). bibliog.
A major academic study of the development of public opinion polling in Poland and the light thrown on popular attitudes and the basic political issues and events by the surveys carried out during the 1980-81 crisis and the first year of martial law. It provides reliable and indispensable source-material as well as high quality analysis. See also Mason's 'Solidarity, the Regime and the public', *Soviet Studies*, vol. 35, no. 4 (1983), p. 533-45.

418 **Un autre visage de l'Europe.** (Another face of Europe.)
Tadeusz Mazowiecki, translated by E. Morin-Aguilar, preface by Jean-Marie Domenach. Montricher, Switzerland: Les Editions Noir sur Blanc, 1989. 214p.
A French-language translation of fifteen of Mazowiecki's articles published during 1971-87 when he was editor of the Catholic monthly *Więź*. They provide a heavy and difficult insight into his underlying Personalist views of the Mounier type and into his general approach to such large issues as the reform of the Roman Catholic Church, the concept of a broad Europe and its relationship to human rights in Eastern Europe, and the 1979 papal visit to Poland. But they gave few pointers to his specific policy preferences and to explaining his performance as Prime Minister from August 1989 to December 1990.

419 **Leadership and succession in the Soviet Union, Eastern Europe and China.**
Edited by Martin McCauley, Stephen Carter. Basingstoke, England: Macmillan, 1986. 256p. bibliog.
Academic specialists assessed the top party and state leaderships and the succession processes in all eight communist East European states, China and the USSR. The Polish chapter by Sanford (p. 40-63) examines the six (pre-1986) successions to the post of First Secretary of the Polish United Workers' Party (PZPR) as well as the patterns of office-holding in the offices of the Chairmen of the Council of Ministers and the Council of State. The argument is that the Polish case was highly original because of the continuing interplay between normal types of 'closed' internal mechanisms and the more 'open' social pressures external to it.

420 **The captive mind.**
Czesław Miłosz, translated by Jane Zielonko. New York: Knopf, 1953. Reprinted, New York: Octogon, 1981. 251p.
A political treatise in literary form which purports to show the psychological reactions of Polish intellectuals to the Stalinist cultural policies which attempted to limit their expression. Miłosz's work is praised and extensively read and quoted on the impact of dialectical materialism upon intellectual life in the 1947-52 period.

421 **Black book of Polish censorship.**
Aleksander Niczów. South Bend, Indiana: AND Books, 1982. 169p.
The volume's main value lies in the English language translation of the Main
Censorship Board's instructions (p. 85-169) earlier published in Polish as *Czarna
Księga Cenzury PRL* (London: Aneks, 1977). This work formed the basis for Curry's
The black book of Polish censorship. (q.v.) in a greatly expanded and edited form.

422 **Towards a corporatist solution in Eastern Europe: the case of Poland.**
David Ost. *East European Politics and Societies*, vol. 3, no. 1 (1989),
p. 152-74.
Ost argued against the totalitarian interpretations of post-1956 Polish politics and
society. He believed that Jaruzelski was attempting to manage the state-society conflict
of the late 1980s through neo-corporatist means. The aim was to allow civil society the
independence which it demanded, and which the economy required, while allowing the
communist party to dominate the formal-institutional political processes.

423 **Modernization and political tension management; a socialist society in
perspective; case-study of Poland.**
Dennis Clark Pirages. New York: Praeger, 1972. 260p. bibliog.
A pioneering work in its time based on original research at Warsaw University. It
identified the political techniques resorted to by communist regimes in late 1960s and
early 1970s Poland to manage the social strains of rapid industrialization.

424 **Political opposition in Poland, 1954-77.**
Peter Raina. London: Poets and Painters Press, 1978. 584p. bibliog.
A chronicle and a description of opposition movements in Poland from 1954-77. Raina
depicts a dissident movement with varied and contradictory components. This was not
only tolerated by the ruling communist party but sometimes actually influenced the
course of events and occasionally even obtained concessions and compromises.

425 **Worker power and party politics in Poland: political mobilization of the
Polish working class.**
Robin Alison Remington. *Punjab Journal of Political Science*, vol. 4,
no. 2 (July-December 1980), p. 167-83.
An analysis of the impact of the rise of an independent trade union movement on the
Polish communist party and the character of working class mobilization in Poland since
1956. Argues against the inevitablity of these events either ending in the collapse of
Polish communism or a Soviet invasion; Solidarity's rapid growth has, however,
produced a revolutionary constituency which raises problems for moderate leadership.

426 **The Party Statutes of the Communist world.**
Edited by William B. Simons, Stephen White. The Hague: Martinus
Nijhoff, 1984. 543p.
Contains translations of the statutes of what were then the sixteen ruling communist
parties. Dietrich Loeber and Stephen White argue the case for the increasing
institutional significance of such rules in their important introductory essays. Each
statute is prefaced by a short overview of its historical development and a select

Politics

bibliography. The democratizing Polish United Workers' Party statute passed by its Extraordinary Ninth Congress in July 1981 (p. 325-61) is described by Sanford in his introduction as one of 'the most reformist in its implications of any that have been adopted by ruling parties in communist political systems'.

427 **The governments of Communist Eastern Europe.**
Harold Gordon Skilling. New York: Crowell, 1966. 256p. maps.
bibliog.

Skilling's broad account was the standard textbook on Eastern European politics for two decades until it was superceded by Lovenduski & Woodall (item no. 414).

428 **The liberation of one.**
Romuald Spasowski. New York: Harcourt, Brace, Jovanovitch, 1986. 687p.

Spasowski, was the Polish ambassador to Washington and a former Deputy-Foreign Minister, who defected on the declaration of martial law in December 1981. This represents his *apologia pro vita sua* as well as his analysis of the development and crises of communism in postwar Poland.

429 **Communist regimes in Eastern Europe.**
Richard Felix Staar. Stanford, California: Hoover Institution Press, 1989. 5th rev. ed. 369p.

This student textbook went through successive revised editions. It adopted a chapter per country approach; the section on communist Poland covers major aspects of constitutional, party-state, institutional and socio-economic life as well as external relations with both the capitalist world and other East European states.

430 **Mechanisms of repression in Poland during martial law.**
Andrzej Świdlicki. *Polish Review*, vol. 29, no. 1-2 (1984), p. 97-126.

This article is effectively a summary of the argument and material in Świdlicki's book, *Political trials in Poland 1981-86* (q.v.).

431 **Political trials in Poland 1981-86.**
Andrzej Świdlicki. London: Croom Helm, 1988. 426p.

Useful as a comprehensive compendium and reference work on the institutions, agents, legal procedures and general mechanisms used by the Jaruzelski regime to repress opposition during the State of War (martial law) of December 1981-83.

432 **The shattered dream.**
Alexander Szurek, translated by Jacques & Hilda Grunblat. New York: Columbia University Press, 1989. 382p. (East European Monographs no. 213).

The memoirs of a Polish Jewish communist (died 1978) who was General Świerczewski's ('Comrade Walter') adjutant during 1936-38 in the International Brigade fighting on the Government side in the Spanish Civil War. It also provides interesting material on the experience of such Spanish Civil War veterans and dedicated communist activists in postwar Poland up till his forced emigration in 1969.

433 **Ideology in a socialist state. Poland 1956-83.**
Ray Taras. Cambridge, England: Cambridge University Press, 1984.
299p. (Soviet and East European Studies series). bibliog.
Taras defines the role of ideology in a socialist state and examines how it functioned in selected issue-areas in Poland between 1956-82. He concludes that although Marxism-Leninism was revised substantially in Poland, particularly on the 'operative' level, this was insufficient to prevent a long drawn-out ideological crisis which contributed to the cyclical recurrence of political and social conflicts.

434 **Leadership change in communist states.**
Edited by Ray Taras. London: Unwin Hyman, 1989. 210p. bibliog.
A somewhat uneven symposium whose chapters on China, Vietnam and Cuba remain the most relevant. Taras attempts to broach crucial, though somewhat neglected, factional and clientelist approaches borrowed from comparative political studies of traditional authoritarian systems.

435 **Official etiologies of Polish crises: changing historiographies and factional struggles.**
Ray Taras. *Soviet Studies*, vol. 38, no. 1 (1986), p. 53-68.
Contrary to the prevalent Western approaches of the time Taras presented the explanations for crises in communist systems advanced by the East European leaders themselves. He concentrates, in particular, on the 1983 Kubiak Report and follows it in arguing that more profound socio-economic factors, not the mistakes of individual leaders, had produced the crises in Poland.

436 **The Polish crisis and Myrdal's model of circular causation.**
Jacek Tarkowski. *Political Studies*, vol. 36, no. 3 (September 1988), p. 463-74.
Myrdal's model of economic underdevelopment as a self-reinforcing rather than a self-correcting process is highly applicable to Poland whose backwardness affects every walk of life; it is a permanent rather than a transient feature. The predicament of how to break the vicious circle of self-perpetuating backwardness poses intractable problems for reformers.

437 **The new regime: the structure of power in Eastern Europe.**
Marek Tarniewski. London: Alison & Busby; New York: Schocken, 1981. 224p.
The author, a critical oppositionist to the communist regime, understandably concentrates on the relationship between upheavals and the power-structure in post-1956 Poland.

438 **Combat motivation of the Polish armed forces.**
Edmund Walendowski. Basingstoke, England: Macmillan, 1988. 154p. bibliog.
A US Intelligence Analyst writes up his doctoral dissertation as a study of the reliability of the Polish armed forces in the event of a NATO-Warsaw Pact conflict in the last years of communism.

Politics

439 **The patterns of bureaucratic elite recruitment in Poland in the 1970s and 1980s.**
Jacek Wasilewski. *Soviet Studies*, vol. 42, no. 4 (1990), p. 743-58.
Argues, on the basis of a detailed examination of the data on the composition of the bureaucratic elite, that the criteria and methods of its recruitment remained unchanged in the 1970s compared with the 1980s and that *nomenklatura* considerations still predominated. The model of the loyal expert therefore did not replace that of the party-specialist which continued to prevail; an astounding degree of stability was thus maintained in the functionary class.

440 **The evolution of communism.**
Adam Westoby. Cambridge, England: Polity Press, 1989. 333p. bibliog.
One of the clearest and most controlled historical overviews and syntheses of the communist experience in power from its establishment until just prior to its collapse. Part four on the problems and crises of communist states and societies in their last phase in Eastern Europe and the USSR is a remarkably balanced and prescient *envoi*.

441 **The Communists of Poland: an historical outline.**
Jan B. de Weydenthal. Stanford, California: Hoover Institution Press, 1978. 2nd ed. 217p. bibliog.
This volume examines the history of the communist movement in Poland from its foundation in 1893 more analytically than Dziewanowski's study (item no. 383) which it largely supersedes. This is a well-documented account which presents a reasonably objective evaluation of the Polish United Workers' Party postwar development. It is particularly useful on the problems, aspirations, errors and contradictions of the Gierek period.

442 **The soldier and the nation. The role of the military in Polish politics, 1918-85.**
Jerzy J. Wiatr. Boulder, Colorado: Westview Press, 1988. 204p. bibliog.
Part One deals with the political role of the military during the inter-war period and throughout the Second World War. Part Two discusses the relationship between the military and the ruling communist party in fairly basic terms; there are the beginnings of an interesting comparison between the two cases of military intervention in 1926 and 1981 at the end.

443 **Political ideas in contemporary Poland.**
Jan Zielonka. Avebury, England: Gower, 1989. 210p. bibliog.
A collection of essays presented as an interpretative study of the varied political ideas, values and programmes which collided during the last decade of communist rule in Poland. The overviews of the contribution of Catholic and Workers' Defense Committee ideas to the concept of Civil Society repeat well-travelled ground but the short discourses on Solidarity's values and strategies and Jaruzelski's corporatist attempts to produce communist-led reform provide more Polish material and better insights.

Law, Institutions and Administration

444 **The Polish Parliament at the summit of its development.**
Edited by Władysław Czapliński, translated by Janina Dorosz.
Wrocław, Poland: Ossolineum – PAN, Committee for Historical
Sciences, 1985. 214p. (Polish Historical Library no. 6).
Contains ten chapters by noted Polish constitutional historians such as Władysław
Konopczyński, Konstanty Grzybowski, Juliusz Bardach and Stanisław Kutrzeba on
aspects of the mature Gentry-Parliament (Sejm) of the sixteenth to seventeenth
centuries. Topics include the Sejm's election, composition and procedure, the
development of the unanimity principle, the legislative process, reform proposals and a
comparison of the functioning of the English and Polish parliaments at this time.

445 **Constitutions, elections and legislatures of Poland 1493-1977. A guide to
their history.**
Jacek Jędruch.   Washington, DC: University Press of America, 1982.
589p. bibliog.
A comprehensive, if somewhat basic, source-book on Polish parliamentarianism and its
development between 1493-1977. Includes about 100 biographies of the major
legislators in each period, photographs, lists of presiding officers, parliamentary
compositions and chronologies of constitutional highlights.

446 **General principles of law of the Polish People's Republic.**
Edited by Leon Kurowski. Warsaw: Państwowe Wydawnictwo
Naukowe, 1984. 404p.

A specialist work which contains detailed chapter discussions by a number of experts
on fifteen sectors of Polish Law ranging from Constitutional, Administrative, Financial
and Civil to Agricultural, Insurance, Transportation and Penal Law.

447 **Civil code of the Polish People's Republic.**
Introduced by Ewa Łętowska, Józef S. Piątkowski, translated by
Aleksander Makowski. Warsaw: Wydawnictwo Prawnicze, 1981.
284p.

A full translation of the 1964 Civil Code, as amended in 1971, which was only partially
replaced after the fall of communism. The introductory commentary is very detailed
(p. 5-101) and one of its state-lawyer authors (Łętowska) went on to achieve a great
reputation as Poland's Ombudsman (Spokesman for Civil Rights, 1987-92).

448 **Administration in People's Poland.**
Edited by Janusz Łętowski, translated by Stanisław Tarnowski.
Wrocław: PAN Institute of State and Law, Ossolineum, 1980. 276p.

Contains chapters by seven Polish specialists on the organization and procedures of the
state administration in communist Poland as well as on the role of civil servants.

449 **Communist ideology, law and crime. A comparative overview of the
USSR and Poland.**
Maria W. Los. Basingstoke, England: Macmillan, 1988. 353p. bibliog.

A Canadian academic examines the connection between the ideology, state and
economic organization of communist Poland and the forms of crime and its control
compared with the same problem in the USSR. She concentrates on demonstrating
similarities and the extent of the influence of the Soviet experience upon Poland.

450 **The institutional development of a minimal parliament: the case of the
Polish Sejm.**
David M. Olson, Maurice Simon. In *Communist Legislatures in
Comparative Perspective* edited by Daniel Nelson, Stephen White.
London: Macmillan, 1982. p. 47-84.

Confirms in detail that the activities of the Sejm (parliament) had expanded
considerably since 1956 even though its full democratic potential was limited by the
communist framework.

451 **Communist local government; a study of Poland.**
Jarosław A. Piekalkiewicz. Athens, Ohio: Ohio University Press,
1975. 282p. bibliog.

This was the authoritative study of how the communist model of local government had
been adapted over the postwar period to Polish conditions. Still useful in these
historical terms and for its discussion of Gierek's local government reform, the

Law, Institutions and Administration

problems of participation and the size and organization of socio-economic micro-regions.

452 **Decentralization and local government. Danish-Polish comparative study.**
Edited by Jerzy Regulski (et al). New Brunswick, New Jersey; Oxford: Transaction Books, 1988. 271p. bibliog.

Academic papers contributing towards a comparative study of local government in Poland and Denmark edited by a scholar who became the Minister for Local Government in the Mazowiecki Government.

453 **Sejm elections in communist Poland: an overview and a reappraisal.**
George Sakwa, Martin Crouch. *British Journal of Political Science*, vol. 8, no. 4 (October 1978), p. 403-24.

A detailed discussion of the processes of communist party control of candidate-selection and of parliamentary (Sejm) elections in Poland from 1952 to 1972. An authoritative examination of the mechanisms and significance of 'crossing-off', made possible by having up to half more candidates on the voting-list sponsored by the Front of National Unity than the seats available. The article explains why this phenomenon, which was highly significant in the crisis election of January 1957 declined thereafter; it situates the process within the context of the communist party's relations with Polish society in both 'settled' and 'unsettled' periods.

454 **The constitutions of the communist world.**
Edited by William B. Simons. Leiden, Netherlands: Sijthoff & Noordhoff, 1980. 644p.

Translations of the mature communist constitutions of Poland (1952) and fourteen other communist states. The volume includes background historical information covering the evolution of the fundamental laws of each country. For the constitutions at an earlier period see: *Constitutions of the communist party states*, edited by Jan F. Triska. (Stanford, California: Hoover Institution Press, 1968. 541p.). Writing the post-communist constitution proved an exceptionally difficult and long drawn-out problem in Poland. For the course of the controversy see Wojciech Sokolewicz, 'The Polish Constitution in a time of change', *International Journal of the Sociology of Law*, vol. 20 (1992), p. 29-42.

455 **The Supreme Court of the Polish People's Republic.**
Włodzimierz Skrzypiński, translated by Michał Jankowski. Warsaw: IWZZ, 1988. 24p.

Originally published as a manual for internal use, this pamphlet provides a guide to the functioning and internal organization of the Supreme Court.

456 **Rule by the people. A study of local councils.**
Maria Vischer. Berne: Peter Lang, 1989. 222p. (European University Studies, Series XXII Sociology). bibliog.

An academic dissertation on the theory and practice of government by the local councils in Poland based mainly on the period between the 1958 and 1975 reforms.

457 **Code of Criminal Procedure of the Polish People's Republic.**
Edited by S. Waltos.   Warsaw: Polish Academy of Sciences, Institute
of State and Law – Wydawnictwo Prawnicze, 1979. 262p.

For a translation of the Criminal Code, also of April 1969, see *The Penal Code of the Polish People's Republic* (London: Sweet & Maxwell, 1973. 139p. [The American series of foreign penal codes no. 19]).

458 **Local politics in Poland. 20 years of research.**
Edited by Jerzy Józef Wiatr.   Warsaw: UN Institute of Sociology,
1986. 267p.

A number of academic papers which attempt to go a little beyond the normal type of legal-description which long predominated in this field, and to show the dynamics of Polish local politics. Edited by a well-known political sociologist who kept within, but always at the outer party boundaries, of communist reform ideas for over three decades.

Solidarity and Poland
in the 1980s

459 **Poland 1980-81. Solidarity versus the Party.**
Nicholas G. Andrews. Washington, DC: National Defense University
Press, 1985. 351p. maps.
A competent and straightforward political history concentrating on the domestic
aspects of the 1980-81 crisis. Purports to take the conflict between Solidarity and the
Polish Communist Party as its central theme. This book has little original to offer
despite the author's direct experience resulting from his diplomatic posting to Warsaw
at that time.

460 **Civil society against the State.**
Andrew Arato. *Telos*, no. 47 (Spring 1981), p. 23-47.
An influential demonstration of the role of Civil Society in challenging the communist
system in Poland and how this affected the possibility of political and economic reform.
For a further development of his theme which also discusses the consequences of
martial law see, 'Empire vs Civil Society: Poland, 1980-81', *Telos*, no. 50 (Winter 1981-
82), p. 19-48.

461 **The Polish August. What has happened in Poland.**
Neal Ascherson. Harmondsworth, England: Penguin Books, 1981.
316p. bibliog.
One of the earliest and most widely read accounts by a British journalist. About half
the book is basic interpretative historical background while the course of the crisis is
only covered up to the end of 1980. Contains translations of the Szczecin and Gdańsk
Agreements.

462 **The Polish Revolution. Solidarity 1980-82.**
Timothy Garton Ash.   London: Jonathan Cape, 1983. 398p. bibliog.
London: Granta – Penguin, 1991. 422p.

The author's personal capacity to marry his academic background with a colourful literary style and very competent political journalism combine to make this the most widely read account of the Polish events of 1980-81. For a withering critique of its academic plausibility see Richard Spielman's article, 'The Eighteenth Brumaire of General Wojciech Jaruzelski', *World Politics*, vol. 37, no. 4 (1985), p. 561-85.

463 **The uses of adversity. Essays on the fate of East-Central Europe.**
Timothy Garton Ash.   London: Granta Books in association with Penguin Books, 1991. 304p.

A major work of intellectual history on the decomposition of communist power in Eastern Europe in the mid to late 1980s. The essays most directly concerned with Poland are on the Pope's 1983 visit, the Polish intelligentsia, a superb comparison of Claude Lanzmann's *Shoah* with Edgar Reitz's, *Heimat*, Poland's place in East-Central Europe and the prospects for reform or revolution.

464 **Festival of the oppressed. Solidarity, reform and revolution in Poland 1980-81.**
Colin Barker.   London: Bookmarks, 1986. 192p.

Although written from a committed extreme left (British Socialist Workers) point of view this is an excellent account of Solidarity's development against the background of the 1980-82 crisis in Poland. Barker sympathises with the Fundamentalist revolutionary minority rather than with Wałesa's Pragmatic majority. The latter attempted to incorporate the movement in the Polish system, through reformist self-limitation.

465 **Solidarność. From Gdańsk to military repression.**
Colin Barker, Kara Weber.   London: International Socialism no. 15, 1982.

A lively account of the political history of the sixteen months of Solidarity's existence, written from a British Far Left standpoint. Section two contains the International Socialist analysis of Polish state capitalism in crisis.

466 **Polish politics. Edge of the abyss.**
Edited by Jack Bielasiak, Maurice D. Simon.   New York: Praeger, 1984. 366p.

One of the most comprehensive and influential symposia on the Polish crisis of 1980-81. The fifteen chapters by specialists cover a wide range of political, social, economic, military, cultural and external aspects.

467 Solidarity's self-organization: the crisis of rationality and legitimacy in
Poland 1980-81.
Jack Bielasiak, Barbara Hicks. *East European Politics and Societies*,
vol. 4, no. 3 (1990), p. 489-512.

Solidarity's principles of self-organization and pluralism challenged communist party
rule in 1980-81. This explains why the movement could not be incorporated
successfully into the latter's structures of rule and why it eventually undermined
Jaruzelski's legitimating strategies by 1988. See also Grzegorz Bakuniak, Krzysztof
Nowak, 'The creation of a collective identity in a social movement. The case of
Solidarność', *Theory and Society*, vol. 16, no. 3 (1987), p. 401-29.

468 Poland's Solidarity movement.
Edited by Lawrence Biondi, Frank Mocha. Chicago: Loyola
University of Chicago, 1984. 236p.

A symposium of papers presented at a conference on Solidarity held in the Loyola
University in April 1982. Contributors include Leszek Kołakowski, George Lerski
and Jerzy Milewski.

469 Sisyphus and martial law. Reflections on martial law.
Edited by J. L. Black, John W. Strong. Winnipeg, Manitoba: Ronald
P. Frye, 1986. 191p. (Carleton series in Soviet and East European
Studies no. 9). bibliog.

Contains eleven important academic papers on the Polish crisis and the repercussions
of the imposition of martial law from December 1981 to Summer 1983.

470 My brother Lech Wałęsa.
Walter Brolewicz, introduced by Lech Wałęsa. London: Robson
Books, 1983. 120p.

Confusingly for non-Poles this is written not by his brother, but by his cousin, an
engineer from the branch of the family resident in the USA. Brolewicz got to know
Wałęsa directly in 1982-83 and paints a very basic and simple picture of the man and
his family circumstances with almost no political content.

471 Eastern Europe in the aftermath of Solidarity.
Adam Bromke. New York: Columbia University Press, 1985. 206p.
(East European Monographs no. 183).

A reconsideration of Eastern Europe, concentrating on Poland's place in the East-
West conflict, after the Polish upheaval of 1980-81. The appendices include a
translation of the historical section on postwar communist crises contained in the 1983
'Kubiak Report' and Aleksander Hall's 'New Realist' evaluation of Poland's prospects,
a viewpoint echoed by Bromke.

472 **Poland's upheaval: an interim report.**
Adam Bromke. *The World Today*, vol. 37, no. 6 (June 1981),
p. 211-18.

The popular movement for change in Poland in 1980-81 presented the most massive working class challenge ever to the communist state. Although it produced wide ranging communist concessions the emergence of free trade unions undermined the communist party's legitimacy by refuting its claim to be the authentic spokesman for the working class.

473 **Poland. Genesis of a revolution.**
Edited by Abraham Brumberg. New York: Vintage Books, 1983.
322p.

A widely read symposium by a number of well known writers which originally appeared in *Survey*. It was highly influential in creating Western values regarding the Polish Crisis.

474 **On trial in Gdańsk. A transcript of the proceedings against Adam
Michnik, Bogdan Lis, Władysław Frasyniuk, May-June 1985.**
Edited and introduced by Jane Cave, translated by Jane Cave, Roman
Dumas. Washington, DC: Poland Watch Centre, 1986. 190p.

Contains the transcript of the trial of three major Solidarity activists in 1986 for having engaged in illegal activities. Although they were sentenced to between three and a half and two and a half years imprisonment they were amnestied soon afterwards. The volume also contains short biographical notes and commentaries by Lis and Michnik.

475 **The crystal spirit. Lech Wałęsa and his Poland.**
Mary Craig. London: Hodder & Stoughton, 1986. 320p. maps.

A popular presentation of Poland's historical experience during the last century. It attempts to place Solidarity and Wałęsa in that context. Among other biographies of Wałęsa of a similar ephemeral publicist character, is: Mary Craig's, *Lech Wałęsa: the leader of Solidarity and campaigner for freedom and human rights in Poland.* (Dublin: Wolfhound, 1989. 64p.).

476 **Poland: Solidarity: Wałęsa.**
Michael Dobbs, K. S. Karol, Dessa Trevisan. Oxford: Pergamon
Press, 1981. 128p.

A glossily produced and amply illustrated celebration of the Solidarity experience by three well known journalists. Trevisan introduces the historical background, Karol sets out the basic political history before Spring 1981 while Dobbs attempts an early assessment of Wałęsa's career as 'the symbol of the Polish August'.

477   The Polish dilemma. Views from within.
Edited by Lawrence S. Graham, Maria K. Ciechocińska.   Boulder,
Colorado: Westview Press, 1987. 258p.

This collection of translated chapters by major Polish social scientists (Pajestka,
Markiewicz, Wiatr, Sokolewicz and Reykowski) is still valuable as a source of detailed
information. It also conveys the mid-1980s viewpoint of sections of the critical
intellectual establishment on the nature of the crisis facing their country.

478   Jaruzelski. Prime Minister of Poland. Selected speeches: interview with
Robert Maxwell and a biographical sketch.
Wojciech Jaruzelski.   London: Pergamon, 1985. 136p. (Leaders of the
Modern World Series).

A glossy and attractively produced volume which seeks to popularize Jaruzelski's
views, character and career to an English language readership. Unfortunately the
result is mainly a testament to Maxwell's megalomaniac desire to ingratiate himself
with world leaders and to play a role on the world stage. It is, however, better than the
volumes on Ceausescu, Honecker and Husak in the same series.

479   Mad dreams, saving graces. Poland: a nation in conspiracy.
Michael T. Kaufman.   New York: Random House, 1989. 207p.

An American journalist, who first arrived in in Poland in 1984, gives a lively account of
the events which he lived through during the last years of communism in Poland.

480   The birth of Solidarity. The Gdańsk negotiations 1980.
Edited and translated by Antony Kemp-Welch.   Basingstoke,
England: Macmillan, 1983. 213p. 2nd rev. ed, 1991. 261p.

Contains the full text of the negotiations between the Polish Government Commission
and the Inter-factory Strike Committee at the Gdańsk shipyard in late August 1980 as
well as the final agreement. It also has a section by Tadeusz Kowalik on the role of the
Working Group of Experts and short profiles of the main participants. The second
edition is mainly expanded by a new chapter on Solidarity's history prior to its
assumption of power in 1989 (p. 200-24).

481   Professionals, power and Solidarity in Poland. A critical sociology of
Soviet-type society.
Michael D. Kennedy.   Cambridge, England: Cambridge University
Press, 1991. 421p. bibliog.

Kennedy presents a theory of Soviet-type societies based on an analysis of the threat to
Polish communist power and its capacity to transform itself raised by the emergence of
Solidarity. He also produces a major examination of Solidarity's internal composition
and conflicting strategies.

482   The roots of Solidarity. A political sociology of Poland's working class
       democratization.
       Roman Laba.   Princeton, New Jersey: Princeton University Press,
       1991. 247p. bibliog.
Describes the emergence of Solidarity in 1980, arguing that it generated a new form of
workers' democracy in opposition to Leninist bureaucratic elitism. More controversially it claims that Solidarity developed an 'endogeneous working-class generated
character' through industrial struggle during the 1970s.

483   **Worker roots of Solidarity.**
       Roman Laba. *Problems of Communism*, vol. 35, no. 4 (July-Aug.
       1986), p. 47-67.
Laba attacks the argument that intellectuals provided the main impetus in the
formation of Solidarity. His thesis is that the workers' demands of 1970-71 all reflected
the demands of politically conscious coastal workers for free trade unions well before
the Workers' Defense Committee and the Roman Catholic Church became politically
active. Even more controversially he claims that such demands involved an early
systemic critique of the Leninist state's power and privileges going well beyond the
alleged workers' socialist reformism of 1980.

484   **Poland under Jaruzelski.**
       Edited by Leopold Labedz.   New York: Charles Scribner, 1984. 432p.
A collection of articles on Solidarity and martial law which were first published in two
special issues of *Survey* (London).

485   **Konspira. The Solidarity underground.**
       Maciej Łopiński, Marcin Moskit, Mariusz Wilk, translated by Jane
       Cave, afterword by Lawrence Weschler.   Los Angeles: University of
       California Press, 1990. 261p.
An English translation of the 1984 Polish emigré edition. This volume, a collection of
tape-recorded interviews with key Solidarity activists like Bujak, Frasyniuk, Lis and
Hall is a major primary source for Solidarity's internal debates over strategy and tactics
during the martial law period of December 1981-83. It also contains useful judgements
on the Solidarity experience of 1980-81 especially on its actions during the run-up to
martial law.

486   The Polish August. Documents from the beginnings of the Polish
       workers' rebellion. Gdańsk – August 1980.
       Edited by Oliver Macdonald.   Seattle, Washington: Left Bank Books,
       1981. 177p.
The editor of *Labour Focus on Eastern Europe* brings together in one volume
translations of documents on the outbreak of the Polish crisis, mainly from Gdańsk to
the Registration Dispute, first published in his journal (vol. 4, nos. 1-3).

487 Solidarity as a new social movement.

David S. Mason. *Political Science Quarterly*, vol. 104, no. 1 (Spring 1989), p. 41-58.

Although the 1980-81 Solidarity was a novelty in communist Poland it resembled social movements elsewhere especially 'new social movements' in the West. Such features as post-materialism, popular alienation with large centralized bureaucracies, pressures for grassroots participation and non-violent methods are susceptible to comparative study. For a contrasting view on Solidarity's Christian ethos, and on the religious basis of its definition of human dignity by a well-known Polish sociologist, see Ireneusz Krzemiński (translated by Irena Korba). 'Solidarity – the meaning of the experience', *Religion in Communist Lands*, vol. 14, no. 1 (Spring 1986), p. 4-16.

488 Solidarity. Poland's independent trade union.

Denis McShane. Nottingham, England: Spokesman, 1981. 172p.

A very basic account of Solidarity's organization and functioning, primarily as a trade union, during the first year of its life.

489 Letters from prison and other essays.

Adam Michnik, translated by Maya Latyńska, foreword by Czesław Miłosz. Berkeley, California: University of California Press, 1985. 354p.

Contains translations of twenty essays written by Adam Michnik. The writings are grouped under three sub-periods of his career as one of the founders of the Workers Defense Committee (1976-80), a major Solidarity adviser (1980-81) and the period of his internment or imprisonment for much of 1982-85. They include major documents such as 'The Polish War', 'On Resistance', 'The New Evolutionism' and 'Maggots and Angels'.

490 Poland after Solidarity. Social movements versus the state.

Edited by Bronisław Misztal. New Brunswick, New Jersey: Transaction Books, 1985. 167p. bibliog.

A collection of chapters on the conflicts between social movements and the Polish state in the early 1980s, notably by Jack Bielasiak on Solidarity's strategy, Paul Lewis on party-state institutionalization and Bogdan Szajkowski on the Roman Catholic Church. The second section concentrates on wider comparative and theoretical issues. A similar academic symposium is Robert F. Miller's *Poland in the 1980s. Social Revolution against Real Socialism* (Canberra: Politics Department, Australian National University, Occasional Paper no. 18, 1984. 180p.).

491 A prisoner of martial law. Poland, 1981-1982.

Jan Mur (pseud.), translated by Lillian Vallee. New York: Harcourt, Brace, Jovanovitch, 1984. 311p. maps.

The journal of a Solidarity activist interned under martial law in the Strzebielinek camp in Gdańsk province from December 1981 to August 1982. Political and philosophical reflections rather than prison-literature.

492 **Poland. A crisis for socialism.**
Martin Myant. London: Lawrence & Wishart, 1982. 254p.
A sharp and perceptive analysis of the 1980-81 crisis in Poland, placing it in a wider historical perspective, which is written from a British leftwing viewpoint. Myant has a critical, although fair, attitude towards both communist and Solidarity failures. His prediction that East Europe's future lay not 'in the restoration of capitalism but in a democratization of the existing socialist countries' sounds quaint today places him in excellent company.

493 **Poland. Economic collapse and socialist renewal.**
Domenico Mario Nuti. *New Left Review*, vol. 130 (Nov.-Dec. 1981), p. 23-36.
Nuti argues that martial law was neither a revolution nor a counter-revolution and that it served Soviet interests better than direct military occupation. Austerity and inflation, it is suggested, are the preconditions for Polish economic recovery alongside economic reform and workers' self-management.

494 **The Polish Crisis: economic factors and constraints.**
Domenico Mario Nuti. In: *The Socialist Register 1981*, edited by Ralph Miliband, John Savile. London: Merlin Press, 1981, p. 104-41.
This article reviews in detail the basic aspects of the Polish economic crisis in the 1970s and how it triggered off the 1980 outburst. The author considers how the economic constraints conditioned the possibility of recovery and reform by influencing developments within both Solidarity and the communist party. Nuti concludes that while systemic weakness similar to the Polish were potentially dangerous to other communist systems, none of them faced anything like the intensity of the exogenous factors which combined to create the explosive situation in Poland.

495 **Solidarity and the politics of anti-politics. Opposition and reform in Poland since 1968.**
David Ost. Philadelphia, Pennsylvania: Temple University Press, 1990. 279p. bibliog.
Ost locates Solidarity within the context of the 'New Left' movement since 1968 and interprets its comparative significance with verve and literary style. He demonstrates how the movement maintained its unity during the 1980s by side-stepping divisive political choices in favour of a moral-systemic rejection of communism until the communist elite abdicated power in 1989. Depth of analysis is, however, sacrificed to clarity of argument in Ost's examination of the various deals of a largely corporatist nature, encouraged by the Roman Catholic hierarchy, which were in practice attempted with the communist authorities during 1980s. Also of interest is his 'Indispensable ambiguity: Solidarity's internal structure', *Studies in Comparative Communism*, vol. 21, no. 2 (Summer 1988), p. 192-201.

496   **The Solidarity source book.**
Edited by Stan Persky, Henry Flam.   Vancouver: New Star Books,
1982. 262p. bibliog.

Contains a representative sample, presented in largely chronological order, of
translations of Polish documents and writings concerning Solidarity's origins and its
development up till the Bydgoszcz crisis of March 1981. The material on the Solidarity
Congress and the period preceding martial law is very slight.

497   **The Summer before the frost. Solidarity in Poland.**
Jean Yves Potel, translated from the French by Phil Markham.
London: Pluto Press, 1982. 226p.

A lively and popular journalistic account of the first phase of the 1980 Polish crisis,
which is most valuable as a description of the Baltic seacoast strikes and negotiations.
The author includes a translation of the Twenty One Demands (p. 219-20), short
biographical notes on the main participants and a basic chronology of events. This
book was first published in French as *Scènes de gréves en Pologne* (Paris: Stock, 1981),
and also as *The Promise of Solidarity. Inside the Polish workers' struggle*, 1980-82 (New
York: Praeger, 1982).

498   **Poland 1980: from 'premature consumerism' to labour solidarity.**
Alex Pravda. *Soviet Studies*, vol. 34, no. 2 (1982), p. 167-99.

A detailed examination of the very wide range of factors which led to the explosion of
blue collar workers' protest in Summer 1980 in Poland. It also analyses the reasons
why labour was likely to become a major factor of change in mature communist
systems.

499   **Independent social movements in Poland.**
Peter Raina.   London: London School of Economics – Orbis Books,
1981. 632p. bibliog.

An extremely useful collection of translations of key documents on urban and rural
social movements in Poland before August 1980 and on the early period of Solidarity's
life. The documents include key Workers' Defense Committee (KOR), Confederation
for an Independent Poland (KPN) and Solidarity documents as well as the texts of the
Gdańsk and Szczecin agreements and the Solidarity statute. They are linked together
by explanatory analysis by a major Polish specialist with a proven track record in
presenting such documentation.

500   **Poland 1981. Towards socialist renewal.**
Peter Raina.   London: George Allen & Unwin, 1985. 472p. bibliog.

The usual Raina mixture of linked commentary, analysis and translation of key
documents. This is the most comprehensive documentary collection on the Polish crisis
of 1980-81. The material is presented both chronologically to cover the political history
and thematically in order to highlight the main issues and trends.

501 **Solidarity and Poland. Impacts East and West.**
Edited by Steve W. Reiquam.   Washington, DC: Wilson Center Press,
1987. 60p.

Publishes summary-reports of the papers presented at a conference on 'The legacy of
Solidarity' held at the Woodrow Wilson International Centre in February 1987.
Contributors include Kolankiewicz, Najder, Bialer and Brzezinski.

502 **August 1980. The strikes in Poland.**
Edited by William F. Robinson.   Munich: Radio Free Europe
Research; October 1980. 447p.

The first section contains Radio Free Europe analyses and reports on the political,
social and economic situation in Poland in Summer-Autumn 1980. The second section
presents translations of original Polish documents including strike information bulletins
and the texts of the Szczecin and Gdańsk agreements.

503 **The Polish challenge.**
Kevin Ruane.   London: BBC Publications, 1982. 328p.

A popular and sensibly written account of the Solidarity period of 1980-81 by a well-
known British television journalist. The translated text of the Gdańsk Agreement is
included along with Jaruzelski's broadcast of 13 December 1981 announcing martial
law as well as the Military Council of National Salvation's (WRON) proclamation of
the same date.

504 **The other Europe.**
Jacques Rupnik.   London: Weidenfeld & Nicholson – Channel Four
Books, rev. ed. 1989. 291p. bibliog.

Hailed as a masterpiece this book is authoritative as well as very readable, examining
the national and 'European' factors which resisted, modified and eventually overthrew
Soviet communism in Eastern Europe in 1989. Rupnik's examination of the 'organic
rejection' process is marked by lucidity, comprehensive sweep and intimate knowledge
of the East European detail, especially cultural and intellectual trends.

505 **Resource-mobilization in a Marxist-Leninist society; the case of Poland's
Solidarity movement.**
Christine Sadowski. *Journal of Communist Studies*, vol. 4, no. 2 (1988),
p. 181-202.

The application of resource-mobilization theory to Solidarity demonstrates the linkage
of groups and organizations which became genuine political actors within it. Social
networks emerged to circumvent the bureaucratic authoritarian structures of the
communist state. The Polish Leninist system proved vulnerable to the development of
movements from below as it was weakened by economic crisis and cleavages within its
ranks.

506 **Military Rule in Poland. The rebuilding of communist power 1981-83.**
George Sanford. London; Croom Helm, 1986. 288p. bibliog.
The first part of the book examines the development of the Political Military in Poland
and its role during the 1980-81 crisis against the backdrop of the theoretical issue of the
role of military apparats in communist systems. The second section deals in detail with
why martial law was imposed, the mechanisms of its application and lifting and its
effect upon the communist party, the Roman Catholic Church and the Solidarity
underground. The rebuilding of communist power described in this study did not save
communism in Poland but it allowed the Jaruzelski regime to survive until 1989.

507 **Polish communism in crisis.**
George Sanford. London: Croom Helm, 1983. 249p. bibliog.
A detailed academic study of the politics of the communist elite during the 1980-81
crisis. The main argument is that the Kania centrists played for time very successfully.
By postponing the Extraordinary Ninth Congress until Summer 1981 they managed to
control the party-reforms promised there and to retain control of the levers of power in
a way that mollified the Kremlin, and perhaps prevented a Soviet invasion. The cost
was the lack of social credibility and ground-roots party membership mobilization as
well as the absence of common ground with Solidarity which led to martial law at the
end of 1981.

508 **The Polish communist leadership and the onset of the State of War.**
George Sanford. *Soviet Studies*, vol. 36, no. 4 (Oct. 1984), p. 494-512.
The Polish United Workers' Party (PZPR) top leadership divided into about eight
main currents in its response to Solidarity's challenge in 1980-81. The dominant group,
however, led by First Secretary Stanisław Kania, renewed and rallied the pro-Soviet
apparats and caucuses through a controlled process of Leninist democratization
culminating in the July 1981 Ninth Congress. Martial Law was imposed because a
radicalized Solidarity and an economically desperate society refused to support PZPR-
led reform and this, therefore, led to temporary military dominance. For the
controversy over the Jaruzelski regime's prospects see Paul Lewis, 'The PZPR
leadership and political developments', *Soviet Studies*, vol. 37, no. 3 (1985) p. 437-9
and Sanford's rejoinder 'Interpreting the Polish Crisis', *Soviet Studies*, vol. 37, no. 4
(Oct. 1985), p. 541-3.

509 **The Solidarity Congress 1981. The Great Debate.**
Edited and translated by George Sanford. Basingstoke, England:
Macmillan, 1990. 270p. bibliog.
The eighteen day long Solidarity Congress of September-October 1981 stands as the
best record of the movement's extremely varied intellectual and political composition.
This edition is made up of a mixture of verbatim translations of all the main speeches
plus summaries of subsidiary ones and of the entire course of the congress proceedings.
The appendices include lists of speeches by foreign and other invited non-delegates,
sermons by clerics, messages received and sent by the congress, its resolutions and
declarations as well as data on the election and composition of the committees which it
mandated. The index contains a list of all the delegates' names and their contribution
to the congress.

510 **Polish paradox. Communism and self-renewal.**
William E. Schaufele. New York: Foreign Policy Association, 1981.
74p. maps. bibliog.
Schaufele, the American ambassador to Poland from 1977 to 1984, reviews the Solidarity period in the light of his personal and professional experience.

511 **Nice promises. Tim Sebastian in Poland.**
Tim Sebastian. London: Chatto & Windus, 1985. 225p.
A light and entertaining account of his experiences in Poland during the martial law period written by a well-known British television journalist. The title is a short translation of a well-known Polish folk-saying.

512 **Death of the dark hero. Eastern Europe, 1987-90.**
David Selbourne. London: Jonathan Cape, 1990. 274p.
A disillusioned British socialist (an ex-Ruskin College, Oxford, workers' education tutor) recounts his florid impressions of Eastern Europe just before the collapse of communism. The chapter on Poland (p. 178-209) covers his travels and meetings in the country between the Round Table and the June 1989 elections.

513 **The road to Gdańsk. Poland and the USSR.**
Daniel Singer. New York: Monthly Review, 1981. 256p.
A committed socialist and veteran journalist situates the 1980 Polish Crisis within the historical framework of workers' and intellectual opposition in the Soviet *bloc*.

514 **Poland's self-limiting revolution.**
Jadwiga Staniszkis, edited by Jan Gross. Princeton, New Jersey:
Princeton University Press, 1984. 352p.
These difficult papers, written as the Polish crisis of 1980-81 unfolded, by the *enfant terrible* of Polish sociology are undoubtedly full of deep and piercing insights. The work is most notable for developing the concept of Solidarity's 'self-limitation' as a technique of survival within the Soviet backed Polish communist system in order to allow free trade unions and social pluralism to survive. Staniszkis also published the following much discussed, and influential, articles: 'The evolution of class protest in Poland; sociological reflections on the Gdańsk-Szczecin case', *Soviet Studies*, vol. 33, no. 2 (1981), p. 204-31, a seminal demonstration of how the forms of working class protest had evolved from populist protest, to corporatist representation on to a rapidly changing type of autonomous class-based representation in the explosion of Summer 1980; 'On remodelling the Polish economic system', *Soviet Studies*, vol. 30, no. 4 (October 1978), p. 547-52; 'Martial law in Poland', *Telos*, vol. 54 (1982-3), p. 87-100; 'The obsolescence of Solidarity', *Telos*, no. 80 (Summer 1989), p. 37-50.

515 **Class struggles in classless Poland.**
Stanisław Starski. Boston: South End Press, 1982. 253p.
Starski is the pseudonym of a Polish sociologist whose critical analysis of social discontent and class struggle in the Polish crisis of 1980-81 was published by an American Far Left press during martial law. It contains an academic critique of state-socialism rooted in the realities of Polish working class movements and demands. This work provides much useful detailed information as well as theoretical analysis.

516 **Brinkmanship in Poland.**
Tadeusz Szafar. *Problems of Communism*, vol. 30, no. 3 (May-June 1981), p. 75-81.
The spontaneous protest against price increases in Summer 1980 turned into a significant political transformation which permitted political pluralism. The problem was whether free trade unions would be able to co-exist with the Polish communist party's monopoly in the remaining spheres.

517 **The Polish ordeal. The view from within.**
Andrzej Szczypiorski, translated by Celina Wieniewska. London: Croom Helm, 1982. 154p.
An autobiographical-historical analysis of the long-term background to the 1980 crisis, together with some slight coverage of the Solidarity period itself (p. 111-40). The author was a noted opposition journalist who became one of Solidarity's leading intellectual lights and one of its Senators in 1989.

518 **Poland's path.**
Tad Szulc. *Foreign Policy*, vol. 72 (Fall 1988), p. 210-29.
Examines Poland's peaceful evolution from a totalitarian communist regime towards political pluralism, a decentralized economy and respect for human rights. The sequence of events since the emergence and suppression of Solidarity in the early 1980s and the developing dialogue between the government and the opposition suggests that the Poles are constructing 'a Polish way away from socialism'.

519 **Candle for Poland. 469 days of Solidarity.**
Leszek Szymanski. San Barnardino, California: Borgo Press, 1982. 128p. bibliog.
A popularly written, committed presentation of the Polish Crisis up till the imposition of martial law. Contains some documents and biographies of key figures.

520 **Five months within Solidarity: a first hand report from inside Hotel Morski.**
John Taylor. London: Wildwood House, 1981. 123p.
A mundane account, by an unemployed British trade unionist, of the five months which he spent from September 1980 to February 1981 in Solidarity's headquarters in Gdańsk.

521 **The spirit of Solidarity.**
Józef Tischner, translated by Marek B. Zaleski, Bejamin Fiore, introduction by Zbigniew Brzezinski. New York: Harper & Row, 1984. 126p.
A series of short homilies and philosophical essays by a cleric who became a major influence on the Solidarity movement. This volume was much praised as expressing Solidarity's ethical and social justice aspirations.

522 **Solidarity. The analysis of a social movement. Poland 1980-81.**
Alain Touraine, François Dubet, Michel Wieviorka, Jan Strzelecki.
translated from the French by David Denby. Cambridge, England:
Cambridge University Press: Paris: Éditions de la Maison des Sciences
de l'Homme; 1983. 203p. bibliog.

The most influential early sociological analysis of Solidarity based on interviews with
union militants at the factory level carried out by a distinguished Franco-Polish team.
Argues that Solidarity went through periods dominated successively by economic,
social and political demands which reflected its complex character as a trade union, a
social movement and a political force.

523 **Poland. The state of the nation. Reports by the Experience and Future
discussion group (DiP) Warsaw.**
Edited by Michael Vale. London: Pluto Press, 1981. 231p.

The two reports on the state of Poland in the late 1970s were based on questionnaires
circulated among the population and interpreted by a critical-reformist intelligentsia
team originally sponsored by the Gierek regime. Their highly influential findings and
conclusions were widely regarded as identifying the pressures, discontents and regime
mistakes which caused the 1980 explosion. See also *Poland Today. The State of the
Republic*, introduced by Jack Bielasiak in *International Journal of Politics* (Summer-
Fall 1981) (New York: M. E. Sharpe. 231p.).

524 **A way of hope.**
Lech Wałęsa. New York: Henry Holt, 1987.

Wałęsa's reminiscences of his life and career in opposition give an important
psychological insight, but are only a very basic and unreliable guide to his political
activities. This work, by various unattributed hands, is successful neither as an
autobiography nor a pen-portrait. Also published as *A Path of Hope* (London: Collins
Harvill, 1987. 325p.), and in French, *Un chemin d'éspoir* (Paris: Fayard, 1987. 606p.).

525 **The paradoxes of Jaruzelski's Poland.**
Andrzej Walicki. *Archives Européens de Sociologie*, vol. 26, no. 1
(1985), p. 167-92.

A major discussion which aroused much controversy because of its political realist
analysis of the Jaruzelski regime as a relatively restrained, and certainly not
totalitarian, 'lesser evil'. It was immeasurably superior to its predecessors and held the
possibility of domestic evolution in a reform-pluralist direction notably in the economic
sphere.

526 **Solidarity. Poland in the season of its passion.**
Lawrence Weschler. New York: Simon & Schuster, 1982. 221p.
(Reprinted as *Poland. From Solidarity through the State of War*.
Detroit: Pantheon, 1984. 263p. maps).

An American journalist writes up his purple prose from the *New Yorker* in the form of
a book on the Polish situation between May and December 1981. Includes a
background chronology and documents such as the 21 Gdańsk Demands of August
1980. A slighter work by a British journalist is Tim Sharman, *The rise of Solidarity*
(Hove, England: Wayland Publishers, 1986).

527 **The Polish drama 1980-82.**
Jan B. de Weydenthal, Bruce D. Porter, Kevin Devlin. Lexington, Kentucky: Lexington Books, 1983. 351p.

This extremely sound analysis is divided into three sections each covering the 1980-81 period: Weydenthal examines Polish internal developments, Porter covers Soviet policies towards Poland and East European responses while Devlin discusses Eurocommunist reactions.

528 **The book of Lech Wałęsa.**
Translated by Celina Wieniewska, Jacek Laskowski, Bolesław Taborski. Harmondsworth, England: Penguin, 1982. 203p.

A collection of impressions, reminiscences and assessments of Wałęsa together with an interview with him. Although some big names like Andrzej Wajda, the film director, Jerzy Kołodziejski, the Gdańsk province governor who collaborated with him in 1980-81 and Andrzej Drzycimski, his future presidential press-spokesman, contributed the volume is little more than a series of outline sketches and preliminary biographical material.

529 **Policy and politics in contemporary Poland: reform, failure and crisis.**
Edited by Jean Woodall. London: F. Pinter, 1982. 200p.

The editor introduces eight chapters by specialists with a discussion of the theoretical relationship between 'Developed Socialism' and 'Socialist Renewal'. The politics section, dealing largely with the 1980 crisis has contributions by Schopflin, Sanford, Kolankiewicz and Lewis while the policy aspects are covered by Blazyca, Kolankiewicz, Tomiak and Russell-Hodgson.

Post-Communist Poland (1989-)

530 **We the people. The revolutions of 89.**
Timothy Garton Ash. Cambridge, England: Granta Books, in
association with Penguin, 1990. 156p.

This is the usual Ash mixture of vivid journalistic reporting and direct experience of
political history, intended for the general reader. The account of events and
personalities Ash experienced in Warsaw, Budapest, Berlin and Prague during the
collapse of communism constitutes a colourful historical record.

531 **Surge to freedom. The end of communist rule in Eastern Europe.**
James F. Brown. London: Adamantine Press, 1991. 330p.

An ex-Radio Free Europe director chronicles the momentous events of 1989 in
separate chapters on all the Eastern European countries. The chapter on Poland
(p. 71-98) contains a great deal of historical background but little discussion of the
Round Table and the installation of the Mazowiecki Government. A very adequate
student textbook which provides historical background and political analysis of the
reasons for communism's collapse in Eastern Europe. Also of interest is Mark
Frankland's *The Patriots' Revolution. How East Europe won its freedom* (London:
Sinclair-Stevenson, 1990. 352p.). This is a more popular political analysis of the
reasons for the collapse of communism in Eastern Europe. Frankland argues that the
structural constraints and the cultural inheritance of the past are of primary importance
in shaping the new character of the nations of Eastern Europe. This is most strongly
visible in Poland's case (p. 160-88).

532   Escape from socialism. The Polish route.
      Edited by Walter D. Connor, Piotr Płoszajski.   Warsaw: IFIS
      Publishers, 1992. 312p.

A very high-powered symposium by some of the most noted Polish and American
academic specialists on the specific and practical political and social problems facing
Poland in its exit from socialism. The previous black-and-white interpretations of the
anti-communist struggle are now being replaced by the complex and messy interplay of
normal democratic and market politics mediated by the conflicts between parties and
interest groups and the clashes between competing political ideals.

533   The Polish political scene (1989).
      Andrzej Friszke. *East European Politics and Societies*, vol. 4, no. 2
      (Spring 1990), p. 305-41.

Gives a good picture of the currents within Solidarity and the other political forces
which were emerging in the first phase of the making of the post-communist political
party-system in Poland.

534   The rebirth of history. Eastern Europe in the age of democracy.
      Misha Glenny.   London: Penguin, 1990. 244p. map.

This book was one of the earliest and most widely read accounts of the course of the
1989 revolutions and their likely consequences. The work is organized into chapters on
each individual country. Glenny emphasizes the rebirth of historical factors; he
concentrates very presciently on the re-emergence of traditional nationalism and
national minority conflicts in the region which had to some extent been kept down by
communist rule. He has correspondingly less to say on the problems of democratization and marketization. The chapter on Poland (p. 50-71) is competent but Glenny's
real expertise is demonstrated in his coverage of the Balkan countries.

535   The Revolution of 1989: the unbearable burden of history.
      Jerzy Jedlicki. *Problems of Communism*, vol. 39, no. 4 (July-
      Aug. 1990), p. 39-45.

The author, a distinguished Warsaw University historian, while welcoming the rebirth
of national historical consciousness caused by the collapse of communism warns that
the effort needed to rectify the region's backwardness compared to Western Europe
might set up up strains which would endanger democratization. The too rapid and
intensive imposition of capitalist solutions, in particular, might hinder rather than help
the 'return to Europe'.

536   The collapse of State Socialism. The case of Poland.
      Bartolomiej Kamiński.   Princeton, New Jersey: Princeton University
      Press, 1991. 264p. bibliog.

A well-written and documented account of the political and socio-economic processes
which led to the ending of communist rule in Poland in 1989. Kamiński presents the
thesis of systemic failure but argues that Polish communist crisis management was
more effective than is often assumed. Post-communist development would also be
dominated by Poland's local circumstances and very specific inheritance within the
general parameters of democratization and marketization. See also his 'The dying

command economy. Solidarity and the Polish crisis', *Journal of Contemporary Studies*, vol. 8, no. 1 (1985), p. 5-35.

537 Non-competitive elections and regime-change. Poland 1989.
Paul Lewis. *Parliamentary Affairs*, vol. 43, no. 1 (January 1990), p. 90-107.

Sets out the background to the contractual election of June 1989 and its consequences in the form of Jaruzelski's election as President and the formation of a Solidarity-led Government by Tadeusz Mazowiecki. Contains a detailed examination of the election results.

538 Apathy and the birth of democracy.
David S. Mason, Daniel N. Nelson, Bohdan M. Szlarski. *East European Politics and Societies*, vol. 5, no. 2 (Spring 1991), p. 205-33.

Deals with the extent, reasons for and consequences of growing political apathy and demobilization in post-communist Poland and the threat which this poses to successful democratization and economic development.

539 The legacy of real socialism and Western democracy.
Edmund Mokrzycki. *Studies in Comparative Communism*, vol. 24, no. 2 (June 1991), p. 211-16.

Examines the difficulties facing Poland in her attempt to adopt a parliamentary democracy and a market economy. Shows how the socialist social structure impeded this process by producing real interests opposed to liberal reforms and ideas.

540 Poland
Martin Myant, George Sanford. In: *Handbook of Reconstruction in Eastern Europe and the Soviet Union*. Edited by Stephen White. London: Longman, 1991. p. 147-82.

Part of a reference guide which provides detailed information and analysis on East European developments in the first 18 months or so following the collapse of communism in Eastern Europe. Academic specialists cover each of the seven East European countries plus Germany, the USSR, Comecon and the Warsaw Pact in separate chapters. The country chapters include coverage under the following standard headings: post-communist government lists, a chronology of events, short biographies of principal personalities, political overview, the media and foreign relations (Sanford); economic overview, key economic sectors and foreign economic relations (Myant).

541 Poland
Zbigniew Pełczyński, Sergiusz Kowalski. *Electoral Studies*, vol. 9, no. 4 (1990), p. 346-54.

An analysis of the Sejm and Senate elections of June 1989 which concentrates on the details of the electoral system and the results in terms of voting behaviour. The discussion of the political background goes up to the May 1990 local elections and the split within Solidarity's Civic Committees caused by the 'War at the Top' between Wałęsa and Mazowiecki.

542   **The New Eastern Europe. Western responses.**
      J. M. C. Rollo with Judy Batt, Brigitte Granville, Neil Malcolm.
      London: Royal Institute of International Affairs – F. Pinter, 1990.
      137p. (Chatham House Papers).
An early, but highly influential, study by a team of specialists based at the British
Royal Institute of International Affairs. They examine the political, economic, and
international problems facing post-communist Eastern Europe and the most
appropriate Western responses. The main sections specifically on Poland are by Judy
Batt (p. 12-19) and Rollo/Granville (p. 47-9).

543   **Democratization in Poland 1988-90. Polish voices.**
      Edited and translated by George Sanford.   Basingstoke, England:
      Macmillan, 1992. 203p.
The editor defines the 1989 events in Poland as a 'Negotiated Revolution' in his
introductory overview. A representative spread of Polish academics, both Solidarity
sympathizers and reform-socialists, then discuss various aspects of the 1988-90 period
in terms of the mechanisms of the communist abdication of power and the initial
dynamics of democratic transition.

544   **Poland.**
      George Sanford. In: *New Political Parties of Eastern Europe and the
      Soviet Union*. Edited by Bogdan Szajkowski.   London: Longman,
      1991. p. 175-217.
Contains a historical introduction to the making of the new party system which began
to emerge with democratization after 1989. The bulk of the chapter is a directory guide
to sixty-nine political party organizations giving, where appropriate, information and
analysis concerning location, membership, leadership, programme, historical development and current situation. The volume covers all the East European and Baltic states
as well as the USSR in the same format.

545   **'Political Capitalism' in Poland.**
      Jadwiga Staniszkis. *East European Politics and Societies*, vol. 5, no. 1
      (Winter 1991), p. 127-41.
Discusses the four steps of privatization, de-monopolization, creation of sound money
and of inter-sectional links in the economy necessary to introduce what the author
defines as 'political capitalism' into Poland; she analyses the problems rendering this
endeavour problematical and examines the wider patterns of change taking place
within post-communist elites and societies in 'Patterns for change in Eastern Europe',
East European Politics and Societies, vol. 4, no. 1 (Winter 1990), p. 77-97.

546 **The dynamics of the breakthrough in Eastern Europe. The Polish experience.**
Jadwiga Staniszkis, translated by Chester A. Kisiel, foreword by Ivan Szelenyi. Berkeley, California: University of California Press, 1991. 303p.

One of Poland's foremost sociologists argues that communism's collapse in Eastern Europe and what she terms the 'Ontological opening' towards democratic capitalism was caused by the interplay between systemic failure and the Gorbachev 'Globalist' faction's mistakes. Her strongly Polish-based analysis and material provides essential insights for understanding the formidable barriers to the full development of democracy and a market economy. It also contains important material on the development of forms of property ownership in Poland during the late 1980s. Staniszkis examines the development of so-called 'nomenklatura capitalism', the process by which some communist politicians and managers used their control of state economic assets to transform themselves into independent entrepreneurs.

547 **The Times guide to Eastern Europe. Inside the other Europe.**
Keith Sword. London: Times Books, 1991. rev. 2nd ed. 298p. appendices.

A overview guide to the detail of post-communist developments in the erstwhile Soviet *bloc*. Poland is covered throughout and in p. 117-32.

Foreign Relations

General

548 **Final Report: diplomatic memoirs.**
Józef Beck. New York: Robert Speller. 1957. 278p.
Beck, Poland's Foreign Minister from 1932-39, was largely responsible for the conduct of her foreign affairs after Piłsudski's death in 1935. These papers, written during his exile in Romania after 1939, are an unpolished, but truthful exposition of the theory and practice of Piłsudski's foreign policy. Beck had been one of his closest confidants and agents but his reputation was blackened unjustly by his political adversaries after the September 1939 defeat. His reliance on bilateral agreements can be criticized but these memoirs deserve to be considered on their merits in presenting the theory of the two equal German and Soviet enemies of interwar Poland.

549 **Poland and the coming of the Second World War. The diplomatic papers of A. J. Drexel Biddle Jr, United States ambassador to Poland 1937-39.**
Edited by Philip Cannistraro, Edward D. Wynot, Theodore P. Kovaloff. Columbus, Ohio: Ohio State University Press, 1976. 358p.
Biddle's career and period as US ambassador to Poland in the crucial two years before the outbreak of the Second World War is introduced by the editors. The documents reproduced are from Biddle's final report and a selection of his diplomatic papers.

550 **The eagle and the small birds; crisis in the Soviet Empire from Yalta to Solidarity.**
Michael Charlton. London: BBC Publications, 1984. 192p.
A well-known BBC journalist produces a vivid history based on interviews, overviewing the whole of the postwar relationship between the USSR and the Eastern European countries within its *bloc*. The main Polish interviewees are the Katyń survivor, Stanisław Świaniewicz, the courier from Warsaw, Jan Nowak and ambassador Edward Raczyński. Together with academics such as Brzezinski, Bialer,

125

Kolakowski and Davies, and Western officials they throw a revealing light on key episodes like Katyń, the Warsaw Uprising, Yalta and the 1956 Polish 'October'.

551 **Soviet and United States signalling in the Polish crisis.**
Thomas M. Cynkin. Basingstoke, England: Macmillan, 1988. 263p.

A major academic study of how the American and Soviet superpowers signalled their intentions in order to manage the international repercussions of the 1980-81 Polish crisis.

552 **Foreign policy of Poland, 1919-39.**
Roman Dębicki, foreword by by Oskar Halecki. London: Pall Mall Press: New York: Ungar, 1962. 192p. bibliog.

A brief, but well-organized and clear survey of Poland's interwar diplomatic history. The author, a high ranking interwar diplomat and Foreign Ministry official, bases his account of the European diplomatic scene as seen from Warsaw on both official and private sources as well as on personal experience. He does justice to Poland's quest for security and national independence in the pre-1926 democratic period as well as during the periods when Auguste Zaleski (1926-32) and the controversial Józef Beck (1932-39) were Foreign Ministers.

553 **Limits of influence. The Kremlin and the Polish crisis 1980-81.**
Andre Gerrits. *Bulletin of Peace Proposals*, vol. 19, no. 2 (June 1988), p. 231-39.

Gerrits argues that Soviet influence on the actual strategy of the Polish Communist Party in its handling of the 1980-81 crisis was slight, although it caused tension in their relations and continuing speculation. The Polish authorities were relatively independent of the Kremlin in conducting their internal affairs while the latter by 1981 was incapable of controlling crises in Eastern Europe.

554 **Eroding empire. Western relations with Eastern Europe.**
Edited by Lincoln Gordon. Washington, DC: Brookings Institution, 1987. 359p.

J. F. Brown sets out the East European scene and assesses the region's connection with Western Europe. Other specialists examine the view from Washington, Bonn, Paris, London, Vienna and Rome giving ample attention to Polish aspects. Gordon argues that the Soviet Empire in Eastern Europe was disintegrating at a significant pace and that Western policy should be directed towards aiding and accelerating the process.

555 **Soviet-East European relations. Consolidation and conflict, 1968-80.**
Robert L. Hutchings. Madison, Wisconsin: University of Wisconsin Press, 1987. 2nd ed. 314p. bibliog.

A detailed and comprehensive study of the relations between the USSR and its East European allies in the period between the invasion of Czechoslovakia and the rise of Solidarity. Hutchings examines the restructuring of the Warsaw Pact and the main dimensions of Soviet-East European relations at both the inter-party and the inter-state levels; political and military relations within the Warsaw Pact; and economic, ideological and cultural relations. He correctly forecast a decade of instability despite Brezhnev's efforts to consolidate the Soviet position in Eastern Europe.

556   **The Great Powers and Poland 1919-45. From Versailles to Yalta.**
      Jan Karski.   Washington, DC: University Press of America, 1985.
      695p. bibliog.
A thoroughly documented study of the crucial period in Poland's history when her fate
was heavily dependent upon the changing interplay in the relationships between the
Great Powers.

557   **Eastern Europe in transition: a chance or a threat to peace.**
      Edited by Wojciech Kostecki.   Warsaw: Polish Institute of
      International Affairs, 1991. (IPRA [International Peace Research
      Association] team on changes in Eastern Europe). 146p.
Publishes the proceedings of an IPRA symposium held in Warsaw in October 1991.
The theme addressed by the Polish specialists was whether the changes in Eastern
Europe would strengthen peace and security on the continent, or whether they would
be the source of tensions and conflicts which would endanger the Pan-European
process of collaboration.

558   **Poland in the perspective of global change.**
      Edited by Antoni Kukliński.   Warsaw: Polish Institute of International
      Affairs, 1991. (Polish Association for the Club of Rome; Globality
      versus Locality series no. 1). 231p.
The main contributors are Zdzisław Sadowski on 'the Great Transition' and Jan
Szczepański on post-communist political and social change in Poland. The editor
makes much play of Michael Porter's idea of successful firms as national 'diamonds' set
out in his *The competitive advantage of nations* (Macmillan, 1990).

559   **Rapacki plan. The 1957 proposal to denuclearize Central Europe and its
      rejection.**
      James R. Ozinga.   Jefferson, North Carolina; London: Macfarland,
      1989. 193p. bibliog.
A thorough study making out the case for the missed benefits of the plan proposed at
the UN by Polish Foreign Minister, Adam Rapacki, in October 1957, for a
denuclearized zone in West and East Germany, Poland and Czechoslovakia. The plan,
envisaged as leading on to disengagement and disarmament in conventional weapons,
was rejected, in too cavalier a fashion, by the Western Powers as 'a naive and empty
gesture' favouring Soviet military and political interests.

560   **International relations studies in Poland.**
      Longin Pastusiak.   Warsaw: Polish Institute of International Affairs,
      1989. 81p.
An overview of Polish approaches to the study of international relations and the main
scholars working in the field, written by a noted specialist (particularly on the USA and
Polish-Western relations) and Social Democratic (SdRP) Sejm Deputy.

561 **The Great Powers and the Polish question, 1941-45: a documentary study of Cold War origins.**
Edited by Antony Polonsky. London: London School of Economics and Political Science, 1976. 282p. maps.

An analysis of the complex tangle of inter-allied relations over the Polish Question during the Second World War. It is largely made up of a collection of documents from various US, British, Polish and Russian sources, many of them published for the first time. It can be read together with the older study of the Polish Question and its effect upon inter-allied relations by Edward J. Rozek, *Allied wartime diplomacy: a pattern in Poland* (New York: Wiley, 1958. 481p. bibliog.).

562 **In search of Poland. The superpowers' response to Solidarity 1980-89.**
Arthur R. Rachwald. Stanford, California: Hoover Institution Press, 1990. 149p. bibliog.

A perceptive analysis of the key actors (communist institutions, Roman Catholic Church and the opposition) in the Polish Question towards independence and domestic political transformation during the 1980s.

563 **Poland between the superpowers. Security versus economic recovery.**
Arthur R. Rachwald. Boulder, Colorado: Westview Press, 1983. 154p. bibliog.

A brisk overview of the postwar period which examines the linkage between Poland's international environment and her domestic policies. Rachwald argues that the main goals were to achieve security through alliance with the USSR, full recognition of the Oder-Neisse frontier and domestic political and economic development. He concludes that the communist elites sacrificed the latter by adopting the unacceptable Soviet model which caused recurrent crises in order to achieve the first two aspirations.

564 **Poland challenges a divided world.**
John C. Rensenbrink. Baton Rouge, Louisiana: Louisiana State University Press, 1988. 246p. bibliog.

A very prescient analysis of the challenge to Soviet hegemony in Eastern Europe posed by Solidarity and of the possibility of internal transformation in Poland itself.

565 **From confidence to disarmament.**
Edited by Adam Rotfeld, introduced by Philip Noël-Baker. Warsaw: Państwowe Wydawnictwo Naukowe, 1986. 298p.

A consideration by a team of Polish specialists of the Polish view of the problems of arms limitation and disarmament and the prospects for international confidence-building at a crucial stage of the CSCE (Conference on Security and Confidence-building in Europe) process in the mid-1980s. The appendices contain a list of the most important arms-limitation and disarmament agreements and a critical appraisal of the East-West balance of military forces.

566 **Poland's place in Europe. General Sikorski and the origin of the Oder-Neisse Line, 1939-43.**
Sarah Meiklejohn Terry. Princeton, New Jersey: Princeton University Press, 1983. 394p. bibliog.

A careful and detailed study of the dilemmas facing General Władysław Sikorski, as Prime Minister of the Polish Government-in-Exile in London. He attempted to achieve a rapprochment with the USSR on terms that would satisfy both his supporters and the Western Allies. Terry argues that his failure to safeguard Poland's independence and the eventual emergence of Poland's revised western frontier on the Oder-Neisse line under Soviet auspices was probably inevitable given Stalin's policy and the lack of resolute Western opposition to it.

567 **Polish diplomacy 1914-45. Aims and achievements, together with a bibliographical essay on works dealing with recent diplomatic history.**
Piotr Stefan Wandycz. London: School of Slavonic Studies – Orbis Books, 1988. 139p. (Third M. B. Grabowski Memorial Lecture).

An overview of the problems facing Polish foreign policy in the interwar and Second World War periods. Wandycz explains the aim and achievement somewhat tritely in terms of spiritual and national survival. See also his 'Poland's place in Europe in the concepts of Piłsudski and Dmowski', *East European Politics and Societies*, vol. 4, no. 3 (1990), p. 451-68.

568 **On the border of war and peace: Polish intelligence and diplomacy in 1937-39 and the origins of the Ultra secret.**
Richard Andrew Woytak. New York: Columbia University Press, 1980. 168p

Tells the story of how a group of brilliant young Polish mathematicians succeeded in breaking the German 'Enigma' code thus making a great contribution to Allied intelligence and the war-effort.

Polish-British

569 **England's Baltic trade in the early seventeenth century. A study in Anglo-Polish diplomacy.**
Jacek K. Fedorowicz. Cambridge, England: Cambridge University Press, 1980. 334p. maps. bibliog.

A detailed study, based on a revised Cambridge University doctoral dissertation, of economic relations between England and the Polish Commonwealth with an explanation of the reasons for its decline. See also Artur Attman, *The Struggle for Baltic Markets, 1558-1618* (Göteborg, Sweden: Kungl, 1979. 231p. bibliog.).

570 **Poland in the British Parliament, 1939-45.**
Edited by Wacław Jędrzejewicz, Pauline C. Ramsey. New York:
Józef Piłsudski Institute, 3 vols. 1946-63. bibliog.
Provides the stenographic record (Hansard) of British parliamentary debates and attitudes to the Polish Question during the Second World War. This still remains an authoritative primary source of documentation.

571 **March 1939: the British guarantee to Poland: a study in the continuity of British foreign policy.**
Simon K. Newman. London: Oxford University Press, 1976. 253p.
bibliog.
Explains why Britain chose to oppose Germany at that particular time on the issue of Poland. Newman argues that the British Government was simply following traditional policy on the continental balance of power in switching from appeasement to the commitment to Poland.

572 **Britain, Poland and the Eastern Front 1939.**
Anita Prazmowska. Cambridge, England: Cambridge University
Press, 1987. 231p. (East European Studies series). bibliog.
A thoroughly documented study, based on both British and Polish primary sources, of the diplomatic relations between Britain and Poland from March to September 1939. Prazmowska demonstrates the hand to mouth nature of the British response to mounting German aggression in her guarantee to Poland and in her inability to build an Eastern Front around this. But Prazmowska merely demolishes a straw-man by refuting charges that British support led to a Polish hard-line in rejecting German demands over Danzig which provoked the final aggression and war.

573 **A fateful meeting at Elsinore.**
Paweł Skwarczyński, edited by Wacław W. Soroka. Stevens Point,
Wisconsin: University of Wisconsin-Stevens Point, Office of Academic
Support Programs, 1982.
Skwarczyński, a distinguished Polish historian, spent much of the postwar period as an academic at the School of Slavonic Studies, London University. One of his last works before his death, this book was published by a colleague. The study concerns the persecution of a Jesuit priest, Father James Bosgrove, in Elizabethan England and the Polish representations made in order to effect his release.

574 **British reactions to the Soviet occupation of Eastern Poland in September 1939.**
Keith Sword. *Slavonic and East European Review*, vol. 69, no. 1
(1991), p. 81-101.
A detailed examination of the British Foreign Office's reaction to the Soviet occupation of Poland from 17 September 1939 onwards. British policy was to keep an open mind on Poland's erstwhile eastern frontier while maintaining Anglo-Soviet links. Sword argues that the latter, after July 1941, made it possible for Britain to influence Stalin on on such issues as the release and repatriation of substantial numbers of Poles out of the USSR.

575 **British policy in relation to Poland in the Second World War.**
Starusław Zochowski. New York: Vantage Press, 1988. 207p.
A retired Second World War Polish army officer, now living in Australia, argues that
the Western Powers betrayed their Polish ally during the Second World War and
handed the country over to Soviet servitude.

Polish-Czechoslovak

576 **Poland and Czechoslovakia; can they find that they need each other.**
Stephen E. Medvec. *Polish Review*, vol. 36, no. 4 (1991), p. 451-69.
The article overviews Polish-Czech relations in the twentieth century but concentrates
on the late 1980s to illustrate the issues which either bind or divide the two nations. It
concludes that there is a good basis for collaboration over political, regional security,
economic and environmental issues especially as they have no really serious territorial
or national minority disputes. Loose talk over the Cieszyn issue only reflects traditional
psychological-historical animosities which have little basis in specific disputes.

577 **Czechoslovak-Polish Confederation and the Great Powers, 1940-43.**
Piotr Stefan Wandycz. Bloomington, Indiana: Indiana University
Press, 1956. 152p. (Slavic and East European series no. 3). bibliog.
This study, which gained renewed topicality after the collapse of communism,
examines the attempt at the end of the Second World War to reorganize East-Central
Europe on a federal basis. It elucidates the varied reasons for Polish-Czechoslovak
conflicts and misunderstandings despite a fairly close common ancestry. These
torpedoed efforts to achieve closer unity just as much as Soviet opposition.

Polish-French

578 **Diplomat in Paris, 1936-39: papers and memoirs of Juliusz
Łukasiewicz, ambassador of Poland.**
Edited by Wacław Jędrzejewicz. New York: Columbia University
Press, 1970. 408p. maps. bibliog.
The Polish ambassador to France in the late 1930s, Łukasiewicz, was one of Foreign
Minister Józef Beck's closest confidants. His papers are therefore a very valuable
source on Beck's policy of 'balance' designed to avoid military conflict by keeping
Germany and the USSR apart and on the weakening of the Franco-Polish alliance
which was the responsibility of both partners in this period. Cf. George Sakwa, 'The
"Renewal" of the Franco-Polish Alliance in 1936 and the Rambouillet Agreement',
Polish Review, vol. xvi, no. 2 (Spring 1971), p. 45-66.

579 **France and her Eastern allies, 1919-25.** French-Czechoslovak-Polish
relations from the Paris Peace Conference to Locarno.
Piotr Stefan Wandycz.   Minneapolis, Minnesota: University of
Minnesota Press, 1962. 454p.

A massively detailed diplomatic study of France's establishment of an alliance system
with Poland and Czechoslovakia after the First World War designed to keep Germany
and the USSR apart. Within a few years though France, under British pressure, began
to lose interest in Eastern Europe in favour of a policy of reconciliation with Germany
that eventuated at Locarno. Wandycz argues that although this was justified during the
Weimar period it laid the seeds for appeasement in the 1930s. The follow-up study by
Wandycz, a similarly massive examination of the complex tangle of French-Polish-
Czechoslovak relations from Locarno up till the Remilitarization of the Rhineland, is
The Twilight of the French Eastern Alliances, 1926-36 (Princeton, New Jersey:
Princeton University Press, 1988. 537p.).

Polish-German

580 **The evolution of blitzkrieg tactics. Germany defends itself against
Poland, 1918-39.**
Robert M. Citino.   Westport, Massachusetts: Greenwood Press, 1987.
224p. (Contributions in Military Studies no. 61). bibliog.

Citino argues that the Versailles limitations on the strength of the German Army
during the Weimar period forced its military leadership to develop new mobile
strategies and tactics in planning for a defensive war against Poland. This was the
basis for Hitler's later *Blitzkrieg* which crushed brave but poorly led, equipped and
deployed Polish forces in the September 1939 campaign. Consequent German
contempt for Slav military capabilities led the Nazis to underestimate the magnitude of
the task of attempting to defeat the USSR in 1941.

581 **Diplomat in Berlin, 1933-39. Papers and memoirs of Józef Lipski,
ambassador of Poland.**
Edited by Wacław Jędrzejewicz.   New York: Columbia University
Press, 1968. 679p. bibliog.

The papers of the Polish ambassador to Berlin from 1933-39 have been arranged
chronologically by a former Polish cabinet minister who became a university professor
in the USA. Lipski, one of the main architects of the Polish-German non-aggression
pact of 26 September 1934, implemented Beck's policy of bilateral negotiation with
Germany in order to undercut Western attempts both to appease Germany and to gain
the USSR as their main ally in Eastern Europe to Poland's detriment.

582   **Germany and Poland: from war to peaceful relations.**
Władysław Wszebor Kulski.   New York: Syracuse University Press,
1976. 336p. bibliog.
An overview of a thousand years of mutual hostility between Germany and Poland.
Beginning with prehistoric settlement the study concludes with Ostpolitik as applied to
Poland and the impact of German-Polish relations on European security after the
signing of the treaties confirming the Second World War frontiers in the early 1970s.

Polish-Haitian

583   **Poland's Caribbean tragedy. A study of Polish legions in the Haitian war
of independence 1802-1803.**
Jan Pachoński, Reuel K. Wilson.   New York: Columbia University
Press, 1986. 378p. (East European Monographs no. 199). bibliog.
Napoleon cynically sent the Polish Legion which had fought for him in the Rhineland
to Santo Domingo in 1801 to put down the uprising of black slaves led by Toussaint
l'Ouverture against French colonial rule. Most of the Poles perished there through
cholera and in the fighting on the island. The episode, however, failed to shake the
Poles' belief that the Emperor would help them regain their independence. This study
brings together a Canadian and a Polish scholar in an interesting collaboration.

Polish-Indian

584   **Poland-India. Political, economic and cultural problems.**
Władysław Góralski, translated by Lech Petrowicz.   Warsaw:
Interpress, 1987. 70p.
A publicist, but fairly informative overview, not just on their bilateral economic and
cultural links but especially on their mutual efforts to establish non-aligned links
outside the East-West conflict.

Polish-Lithuanian

585 **Polish-Lithuanian relations: past, present and future.**
Stephen R. Burant. *Problems of Communism*, vol. 40, no. 3 (May-June 1991), p. 67-84.

Polish-Lithuanian relations, which had lain dormant during fifty years of Soviet domination, were re-activated by the Lithuanian declaration of independence of March 1990. Although they had historically been part of the same state for four centuries they had been divided by territorial and national minority disputes in the interwar period. Burant hopes that shared democratic values will now assuage Lithuanian fears of their larger neighbour; he argues that this should aid the amicable resolution of current disputes, notably the treatment of the Polish minority in Lithuania, as well as in the establishment of regional collaboration.

586 **The Polish ultimatum to Lithuania in March 1938.**
George Sakwa. *Slavonic and East European Review*, vol. 55, no. 2 (April 1977), p. 204-26.

A detailed examination based on Polish Foreign Ministry as well as other diplomatic documents. It shows how Foreign Minister Józef Beck took advantage of a frontier incident and the *Anschluss* of Austria in March 1938 to force Lithuania to re-establish the diplomatic relations which had been broken off for most of the interwar period. The satisfaction of this limited and justified demand and the opening of their frontier yielded Poland few tangible methods but Beck's forceful methods were much criticized in the West. The episode demonstrates his determination to defend Poland's regional interests independently and bilaterally according to the principles bequeathed to him by Piłsudski; but it remains debatable whether by doing so he also jeopardized the real, and not just declaratory, Western support which was essential to assuring his country's long-term security.

587 **The great powers, Lithuania and the Vilna question.**
Alfred Erich Senn. Leiden, Netherlands: Brill, 1966. 239p.

A well-researched and impartial assessment, by a Lithuanian-American scholar, of Polish-Lithuanian relations in the period after the Polish-Soviet War. The question of Vilna (Wilno, Vilnius) was one of the most inflammable and intractable in inter-war Eastern Europe. Vilna, the capital city of the former Grand Duchy of Lithuania was then predominantly Polish with a strong Jewish minority, but it was surrounded by a mixed Lithuanian-Belorussian-Polish population. Its seizure by General Lucjan Zeligowski on Piłsudski's orders (it was his birthplace) in October 1920 and its formal annexation poisoned subsequent Polish-Lithuanian relations which remained frozen until the events of early 1938 discussed in the previous item.

Polish-Pakistani

588 **Polish-Pakistan relations 1947-87.**
Moonis Ahmar. *Journal of European Studies*, vol. 4, no. 1 (January 1988), p. 41-62.
Ahmar overviews Poland's relations with Pakistan since 1947 and demonstrates that bilateral relations have improved over the years, especially in shipping and trade. Poland was one of the few communist countries to establish good relations with Islamic Pakistan and this provides an excellent platform for further improvement.

Polish-Russian and Soviet

589 **Polish-Soviet relations, 1932-39**
Bohdan Budurowycz. New York: Columbia University Press, 1963. 229p. bibliog.
An objective account of Poland's efforts to maintain a balanced relationship and bilateral collaboration with her eastern neighbour during the 1930s despite the legacy of ideological and national distrust and territorial conflict engendered by the Polish-Soviet War of 1920.

590 **Continuity and change in Soviet East-European relations. Implications for the West.**
Edited by Marco Carnovale, William Potter. Boulder, Colorado: Westview Press, 1989. 238p.
An important symposium which assesses the early impact of Gorbachev's accession to power on Soviet-East European relations. Symptomatic of the extent and rapidity with which the 1989-91 changes caught the western academic community by surprise was Andrzej Korboński's prediction that he did 'not expect radical changes in Soviet relations with Eastern Europe, at least in the foreseeable future'.

591 **Russia's retreat from Poland 1920. From permanent revolution to peaceful co-existence.**
Thomas C. Fiddick. London: Macmillan, 1990. 348p. bibliog.
A detailed, but not particularly perceptive, academic study of the political and diplomatic course and consequences of the Soviet-Polish War of 1920 considered largely from the viewpoint of the development of Soviet policy. See also James M. McCann, 'Beyond the Bug; historiography of the Soviet-Polish War of 1920', *Soviet Studies*, vol. 36, no. 4 (1984), p. 475-93.

592 Documents on Polish-Soviet relations, 1939-45.
General Sikorski Historical Institute, preface by Edward Raczyński.
London: Heinemann, 2 vols, 1961-67.

Volume I (1939-April 1943) covers diplomatic negotiations, agreements and correspondence between the Polish Government-in-Exile and the USSR. Volume II (May 1943-August 1945) deals with these contacts against the backgound of US-British-Soviet relations. In addition the Polish embassy in Washington published in 1944 a collection of official documents entitled *Polish-Soviet relations, 1918-39* (251p.) which covered the Soviet-Polish War of 1920, the 1921 Riga peace treaty, the Sikorski-Maisky agreement of 1941 and the Katyń massacre.

593 Conversations with the Kremlin and dispatches from Russia.
Stanisław Kot, translated by Harry C. Stevens. London: Oxford University Press, 1963. 285p.

Professor Kot, a distinguished cultural historian, became Sikorski's ambassador in the USSR after the re-establishment of diplomatic relations between Poland and the USSR in 1941. His papers remain an important historical record of the failed attempt to preserve the *emigré* government's interests against overwhelming Soviet and Allied pressures to the contrary.

594 Moscow and the Polish crisis. An interpretation of Soviet politics and intentions.
Sidney I. Ploss. Boulder, Colorado: Westview Press, 1986. 200p.

A somewhat superficial and old-fashioned Kremlinological type of examination of Soviet policies and reactions to the Polish Crisis of 1980-81; it does not go much beyond the basic political history and press coverage and is rather sparse in its interpretation of the Polish side of the crisis.

595 Polish-Soviet relations.
George Sanford. In: *The end of the Outer Empire. Soviet-East relations under Gorbachev, 1985-90.* Edited by Alex Pravda. London: Sage – RIIA, 1992, p. 94-119.

Argues that the Polish and Soviet communist elites made a last-ditch attempt to move away from neo-Stalinism and to put their relationship on the sounder footing of arguments of equality and mutual advantage. The drive to eliminate psychological blockages through the 'blank-spots' campaign, however, proved inadequate even though it boosted Gorbachev's popularity in Poland.

596 Addressing 'blank spots' in Polish-Soviet relations.
Thomas S. Szajna. *Problems of Communism*, vol. 37, no. 6 (Nov.-Dec. 1988), p. 37-61.

Examines the work of the Joint Polish-Soviet Historical Commission in clarifying the 'blank spots' in their past relations. Slow progress, lagging behind events, fuelled the suspicion that the communist-dominated body was designed to control and limit the processs of re-evaluation, especially over the most sensitive issue of all, the Soviet massacre of Polish reserve officers in Katyń in 1940. See also Elizabeth Kridl Valkenier, 'Glasnost and filling in the "blank spots" in the history of Polish-Soviet relations, 1987-90', *Polish Review*, vol. 36, no. 3 (1991), p. 247-68.

597 **Perestroika; the Polish influence.**
Elizabeth Teague. *Survey*, vol. 30, no. 3 (October 1988), p. 39-58.
Workers' unrest and the rise of Solidarity in Poland in 1980-81 stimulated the debate over political and economic reform in the USSR. It influenced the Soviet elites towards Perestroika by acting as a warning of the consequences of ignoring popular discontent.

598 **Solidarity and the Soviet worker. The impact of the Polish events of 1980 on Soviet internal politics.**
Elizabeth Teague. London: Croom Helm, 1988. 378p. bibliog.
Teague demonstrates that Solidarity's rise in Poland alarmed the Soviet leadership and led to various standard of living concessions to Soviet workers. The bulk of the Soviet population remained quiescent although Teague argues that this only masked a deep malaise. The Polish events, however, sparked off much unrest in the USSR's western borderlands where Ukrainians, Belorussians and Balts expressed deep anti-Russian feelings.

599 **Soviet policy in Eastern Europe.**
Edited by Sarah Meiklejohn Terry. New Haven, Connecticut: Yale University Press, 1984. 375p.
This symposium by eleven American academic high-fliers was regarded as the most authoritative discussion of Soviet-East European relations in the early 1980s. The much recycled, largely historical chapter on Polish-Soviet relations by Andrzej Korboński contains only slight coverage of the Solidarity and martial law periods. It illustrates the Kremlin's unpleasant choices of the time between repression or compromise, and between ideological principles or political and military stability.

600 **Soviet decisionmaking and the Polish crisis.**
Richard Weitz. *East European Quarterly*, vol. 22, no. 2 (June 1988), p. 191-212.
Confused Soviet behaviour during the 1980-81 crisis resulted from divisions within different sectors of the Soviet elite. Secretary-General Brezhnev played a key role in the formation of Soviet foreign policy. Weitz demonstrates that he, along with other East European communist allies, was more involved in the imposition of martial law in Poland than is commonly believed.

601 **From crisis to crisis. Soviet-Polish relations in the 1970s.**
Vladimir Wozniuk. Ames, Iowa: Iowa State University Press, 1987. 176p. bibliog.
Wozniuk's study of the post-1956 Polish-Soviet relationship examines the multi-layered complexity of the Gierek era in order to produce a more flexible interpretative framework for the concept of Soviet oversight. The 1956 and 1980-81 crises in Poland produced major disagreements between the Polish and Soviet elites over the extent to which the former should make concessions to Polish society.

Polish-Swedish

602 **Relations between Poland and Sweden over the centuries. A collection of studies.**
Edited by Zenon Cieselski. Wrocław, Poland: Ossolineum, 1990. 160p. bibliog.
A varied and wide-ranging collection of studies on Polish-Swedish relations. The volume covers an eclectic number of historical episodes and individuals but also includes some interesting material.

603 **Polish-Swedish literary contacts.**
Edited by Maria Janion, Nils Ake Nilsonn. Stockholm: Almquist & Wiksell, 1988. 127p.
Papers presented by a number of Polish and Swedish scholars and writers at a symposium held in Warsaw in September 1986 showing the varied literary and intellectual links between the two countries.

604 **Swedish contribution to the Polish Resistance Movement during World War Two, (1939-42).**
Józef Lewandowski. Uppsala, Sweden: Almquist & Wiksell, 1979. 114p. (Acta Universitatis Upsaliensis. Studia Slavica Upsaliensis no. 20).
The author introduces his historical examination with a bibliographic overview of the writing on the subject. He concentrates on German pressure to prevent the activity of Polish Intelligence in neutral Sweden and of individual Swedes from collaborating with the Resistance in Poland. Some of the latter were sentenced to death in 1943, and although the sentences were not carried out, the Germans used them as a form of blackmail on the Swedish Government. Relevant German and Polish documents are included in the appendix.

Polish-Ukrainian

605 **Poland and the Ukraine: past and present.**
Edited by Peter J. Potichnyj. Edmonton, Alberta: Canadian Institute of Ukrainian Studies, 1980. 364p.
These seventeen contributions to a McMaster University conference represent the Ukrainian view of the historical relationship between the two quite closely related Slav peoples. Because of its geopolitical position the Ukraine had to balance her relations with Muscovy and Poland, but religious and social differences made her prefer the former during the seventeenth century. This led to the eventual incorporation of the Ukraine into the Russian and Soviet empires. Some Ukrainian leaders, like Semeon Petlura later sought to establish a federation with Poland but majority feeling usually favoured traditional alliances with Germany, Turkey or Sweden as the means by which to achieve full national self-determination. Although this was delayed until 1991 the

study suggests that the new Ukrainian national consciousness is friendlier towards Poland than in the past.

Polish-United States

606 **From Potsdam to Poland. American policy towards Eastern Europe.**
Stephen A. Garrett. New York: Praeger, 1986. 237p.
bibliog.

Argues that the East European communities in the USA had relatively little influence over American foreign policy towards the region because of their diversity and disunity. They contributed just as much towards the normalization of relations as to any attempts to liberate communist Eastern Europe. Garrett's examination of the role of the Polish-American lobby, of such bodies as the Polish-American Congress and of the issue of sanctions against Poland following the imposition of martial law in December 1981 illustrates the above thesis. He marshals the evidence judiciously in favour of his preferred policy goal of 'Finlandization' for the region.

607 **Bitter legacy. Polish-American relations in the wake of World War II.**
Richard C. Lukas. Lexington, Kentucky: University of Kentucky
Press, 1982. 191p. maps. bibliog.

Discusses the various levels of the Polish-American relationship during the Second World War, concentrating on the postwar issues of the Yalta and Potsdam agreements as they affected Poland and specific issues of repatriation, settlement and relief.

608 **The strange allies. The United States and Poland, 1941-45.**
Richard C. Lukas. Knoxville, Tennessee: University of Tennessee
Press. 1978. 230p. bibliog.

A clear, well-documented and objective presentation of the American attitude towards Poland in the Second World War. It describes the gradual erosion of Poland's special moral and political position following the German invasion of the USSR and the conflict between the Polish and Soviet governments over Katyń. Roosevelt appeared to support Poland, for electoral reasons, but he did not hesitate to sacrifice her interests; he gave priority to the Soviet war-effort, and then to achieving a general postwar settlement between the Great Powers. Efforts by Polish Americans to secure the territorial integrity based on interwar frontiers and the real independence of their 'old country' therefore proved fruitless.

609 **Poland, the United States and the stabilization of Europe 1919-33.**
Neal Pease. New York: Oxford University Press, 1986. 238p. bibliog.

This academic study demonstrates the difficulties encountered by the newly independent Polish state, in the period between Versailles and Hitler's takeover of power, to gain United States support for a policy of stabilization in Europe which would protect Poland's basic interests.

610 **The United States and Poland.**
Piotr Stefan Wandycz. Cambridge, Massachusetts: Harvard
University Press, 1980. 465p. bibliog.
A history of Polish-American relations designed to increase mutual comprehension
between the two nations by explaining past misunderstandings and disappointments.
Wandycz situates his theme against the broader background of Polish history but
emphasizes developments since Poland regained her independence.

Economy and Economic History

611 Economic reforms in the Soviet Union and Eastern Europe since the 1960s.

Jan Adam. Basingstoke, England: Macmillan, 1989. 264p. bibliog.

A high-powered academic overview of the problems of the introduction of economic reforms in the East European economies since the full establishment of the Stalinist model. Adam, a professor at Calgary University, concentrates on changes in the management structures in the state industrial sector. Chapter 6 examines the Polish economic reform of 1973 and chapter 9 that of 1982 in detail.

612 Private enterprise in Eastern Europe. The non-agricultural private sector in Poland and the GDR, 1945-83.

Anders Aslund. New York: St Martin's Press; London: Macmillan, 1985. 294p.

An extremely detailed and comprehensive study of how private enterprise survived and functioned in the non-agricultural sector of the economy in communist Poland compared with the same experience in the German Democratic Republic. Aslund concluded, too pessimistically, that the Polish private sector faced greater objective economic difficulties as well as a stronger possibility of repression for ideological reasons. See also his 'The functioning of private enterprise in Poland', *Soviet Studies*, vol. 36, no. 3 (1984), p. 427-44.

613 Poland. Into the 1990s. Economy and society in transition.

Edited by George Blazyca, Ryszard Rapacki. London: Pinter, 1991. 148p.

A team of Polish specialists, mainly economists from the former Main School of Economics and Statistics in Warsaw, produce eleven crisp reports on the first phase of Poland's transition to a market economy. These cover a wide range of sectors from

141

energy, agriculture, housing, the environment, prices and incomes, capital investment and banking to foreign trade and external debts. This is a valuable guide to the post-communist economic transformation implemented by Finance Minister Leszek Balcerowicz, his IMF influenced 'shock-therapy' policies and to the prospects of maintaining the financial stability achieved in early 1990.

614 Poland to the 1990s. Retreat or reform?
George Blazyca. London: Economist Intelligence Unit, 1986. 136p.

A comprehensive examination of the state of the Polish economy in the mid-1980s. Concludes that while it might 'muddle on' this would cause sharp social instability. In *Poland's next five years; the dash for capitalism* (London: Economist Intelligence Unit, 1991. 67p. Economist Special Report no. 2110) Blazyca sets out the political and economic background to the great economic changes. He concentrates on the key transformation issues of privatization, joint ventures, debt management, foreign trade restructuring and Poland and the EEC. Blazyca's scenarios for the future are realistically pessimistic about the short-term prospects of avoiding political and social fragmentation but generally optimistic about longer-term developments.

615 The Polish road to capitalism.
Edited by George Blazyca, Ryszard Rapacki. London: Pinter, 1991. 192p.

Examines the strategy of Finance Minister Leszek Balcerowicz and Poland's first postwar non-communist Government, implemented during 1990 with the active involvement of Western Governments and the IMF, for a rapid 'big-bang' move towards capitalism and financial stabilization.

616 Global challenges and East European responses.
Edited by Paweł Bożyk. Warsaw: The United Nations University – Polish Scientific Publishers, 1988. 367p.

Contains seventeen papers by East European and some Swedish scholars summarizing the first stage of a United Nations University research project. Its main themes were the identity problems of Real Socialism, faced by such challenges as the shift from autarchy to a more open and competitive market economy and the global pressures for modernization.

617 Cracow's early development.
Frank W. Carter. *Slavonic and East European Review*, vol. 61, no. 2 (1983), p. 197-225.

An authoritative illustrated examination of the establishment and early growth of the town of Kraków from its earliest basic settlement in the sixth century AD to its major development from the ninth to the thirteenth centuries. With the building of the Wawel castle and cathedral in the eleventh century it became the seat of the Polish monarchy and a flourishing commercial and cultural centre blessed by its favourable natural position in Southern Poland.

618 Cracow's wine trade (fourteenth to eighteenth centuries).
Frank W. Carter. *Slavonic and East European Review*, vol. 65, no. 4 (1987), p. 537-78.

Traces out the development of Kraków's wine trade over the centuries. These patterns were altered by changing political alliances but Turkish occupation of Balkan territory did not affect it as much as is often supposed.

619 The Polish transformation; programme and progress.
Centre for Research into Communist Economies. London: CRCE, 1990. 83p.

In the first two parts Polish economists (J. Beksiak, T. Gruszewski, A. Jędraszczyk and J. Winiecki) discuss the 1989 Beksiak Report, commissioned by the Sejm on the initial economic programme of the Mazowiecki Government. O. Blanchard and R. Layard then discuss the Polish anti-crisis and systemic transformation measures comparing them with Western experience, such as post Second World War reconstruction programmmes, in such fields as privatization, taxation and anti-inflation policy.

620 Plans and disequilibria in centrally planned economies. Empirical investigation in Poland.
Wojciech Charemza, Mirosław Gronicki. Warsaw: Państwowe Wydawnicto Naukowe; Amsterdam: North Holland: 1988. 187p. bibliog.

A highly specialist econometric analysis of the disequilibria problems faced by the Polish command economy.

621 Poland. The economy in the 1980s.
Edited by Roger Clarke. Harlow, England: Longman, 1989. 149p. (Perspectives on Eastern Europe).

A review of the attempts since 1981 to reform the Polish economy and to pull the country out of the crisis which had engulfed it. A joint collaboration between Glasgow and Warsaw Universities; the contributors are Martin Myant, Andrew Duncan and William Wallace for the former and Jerzy Eysmontt, Lena Kolarska-Bobińska, Mieczysław Socha (among others) for the latter.

622 Crisis in the East European economy. The spread of the Polish disease.
Edited by Jan Drewnowski. London: Croom Helm, 1982. 192p.

Domenico Mario Nuti, in an exhaustive analysis of the various factors causing the Polish economic crisis of the early 1980s, concludes that it had a systemic character (p. 18-64). Stanisław Gomułka (p. 65-71) agrees but argues that the crisis was only more open and intense in Poland than elsewhere in Eastern Europe.

623 East-West technology transfer: study of Poland 1971-80.
Zbigniew Marian Fallenbuchl. Paris: OECD, 1983. 199p.

This well-known specialist on the Polish economy, with numerous publications to his credit on the subject, discussed the problems of economic transformation in Poland just before communism collapsed in *The Polish economy in the year 2000; need and outlook for systemic reforms*, (commentary by Paul Marer. Pittsburg: University of

Economy and Economic History

Pittsburg Center for Russian & East European Studies, 1988. 49p. [Carl Beck Papers no. 607]). The legal and financial-institutional framework at that moment of time can be guaged from Natalia Gajl, *Reforms of legal and financial system of public enterprises in Poland and other socialist countries* (Wrocław: Ossolineum, 1988. 286p. Łódź Academic Society [Papers of the Department of Historical and Social Sciences no. 93]). On managerial aspects see Perry T. Puzyrewski, *Polmart 1989. A management blueprint for Poland's reform* (Macroman, 1989. 252p.).

624 **The Polish economy under martial law.**
Zbigniew Marian Fallenbuchl. *Soviet Studies*. vol. 36, no. 4 (1984), p. 513-27.

The reply challenging Fallenbuchl's argument was George Blazyca who set out the contrary case that the martial law measures did lead to a significant degree of adjustment and stabilization, 'The Polish economy under martial law. A dissenting view', *Soviet Studies*, vol. 37, no. 3 (1985), p. 428-36.

625 **Growth, innovation and reform in Eastern Europe.**
Stanisław Gomułka. Madison, Wisconsin: University of Wisconsin Press, 1986. 288p.

A heavily Polish-based and very extensive examination of the economic aspects mentioned in the title. This major study includes additional material by Włodzimierz Brus and Jacek Rostowski.

626 **The management perspective on Poland's economic crisis and recent attempts at reform.**
Richard Hunter. *Polish Review*, vol. 31, no. 4 (1986), p. 299-313.

Examines the background and the course of the introduction of economic reform from above in Poland from February 1982 onwards, and the attempt to combine some aspects of a market system with managerial-dominated state enterprises. See also Stanisław Gomułka, Jacek Rostowski, 'The reformed Polish economic system, 1982-83', *Soviet Studies*, vol. 36, no. 3 (1984), p. 386-405.

627 **The economic history of Eastern Europe, 1919-75.**
Edited by Michael Kaser, E. A. Radice. Oxford: Oxford University Press, 3 vols, 1985-86.

The three volumes are entitled 1. *Economic structure and performance between the two wars*. 1985; 2. *Interwar policy, the war and reconstruction*. 1986; 3. *Institutional change within a planned economy* (Edited by Kaser alone). 1986. Top specialists like Włodzimierz Brus, Jaroslaw Krejci, Gyorgi Ranki and others contribute to what has been praised as the most comprehensive and intensive academic examination of the subject which gives full coverage to Poland.

628 **The politics of economic reforms in Eastern Europe.**
Andrzej Korboński. *Soviet Studies*, vol. 41, no. 1 (January 1989), p. 1-19.

Examines the way in which communist elites in Poland, Hungary and Czechoslovakia attempted to resolve their developmental crisis through economic reform. Such attempts to come to terms with problems of distribution, participation and penetration by western states, however, generated severe new problems. The gravity of the crisis, resulting from the failure to achieve a new balance, was particularly deep in Poland which stagnated for fifteen years.

629 **Regional studies in Poland. Experiences and prospects.**
Edited by Antoni Kukliński for the PAN Committee for Spatial Economy and Regional Planning. Warsaw: Państwowe Wydawnictwo Naukowe, 1986. 380p. bibliog.
This is a specialist examination of regional economic planning structures, mechanisms and problems.

630 **An economic theory of the feudal system. Towards a model of the Polish economy 1500-1800.**
Witold Kula. London: Verso; Atlantic Highlands, New Jersey: Humanities Press, 1976. 192p. maps.
An explanation of the feudal roots in the making of the early modern Polish economy with an emphasis on developing new methodology.

631 **The Polish economy in the twentieth century.**
Zbigniew Landau, Jerzy Tomaszewski, translated by Wojciech Roszkowski. London: Croom Helm, 1985. 346p. (Contemporary Economic History of Europe series). bibliog.
A readable and knowledgeable overview, concentrating on the post-Second World War communist war.

632 **Creating a market economy: the case of Poland.**
David Lipton, Jeffrey Sachs. Brookings Papers on Economic Activity no. 1 (1990), p. 75-147.
The authors argue that post-communist politicians in Poland, along with those in Hungary and Czechoslovakia, have abandoned any idea of a Third Way in the form of Market Socialism. They are working, with amazing rapidity to create a fully fledged market economy based on private property. The bulk of their study is an in-depth analysis of Finance Minister Leszek Balcerowicz' policies in early 1990 which controlled inflation and stabilized the domestic level of the złoty, the Polish currency. They also present their prescriptions for further rapid marketization.

633 **The relationship between changes in consumption and politics in Poland.**
Bogdan Mieczkowski. *Soviet Studies*, vol. 30, no. 2 (1978), p. 262-9.
A short essay, which made a great impact by arguing that there was an inverse relationship between the power of the communist party and levels of consumption in the postwar Polish experience. The more self-confident the party felt the more it would direct investment towards its own industrial-military priorities; the less sure and the more challenged it felt, the more it would assign to social consumption.

634   **Central planning in Poland.**
John Michael Montias.   New Haven, Connecticut: Yale University
Press, 1962. 410p. Reprinted, Westview: Greenwood Press, 1974.
tables. bibliog.

A classic study of the establishment of the Soviet Stalinist command economy in
Poland and of the Polish attempts to reform and modify the economic planning, pricing
and investment mechanisms in a new economic model after 1956.

635   **The decay of socialism and the growth of private enterprise in Poland.**
Jacek Rostowksi. *Soviet Studies*, vol 41, no. 2 (1989), p. 194-214.

Argues that, contrary to Aslund's predictions, private economic activity was likely to
continue to expand in Poland because of the collapse of the socialist alternatives. He
forecast a move towards a 'mixed economic kleptocracy' as in Mexico rather than
towards the classical Western mixed economy.

636   **Poland. Stagnation, collapse or growth. A report by an independent
group of economists in Poland.**
Commentary by Jacek Rostowski. Preface by Andrzej Brzeski.
London: Centre for Research into Communist Economies, 1988. 100p.
(The State of Communist Economies no. 3).

A group of anonymous Warsaw economists examine the state of the Polish economy in
1985 and, again, in 1986 from the point of view of the prospects of economic reform.
They conclude that the economic recovery of 1982-84 had run out of steam: unless the
'Second Stage' of the economic reform, announced in October 1987, became more
radical Poland would be condemned to political crisis and socio-economic stagnation.

637   **Debt and development.**
Jeffrey Sachs.   Warsaw: Foreign Trade Research Institute, 1990. 28p.
(FTRI paper no. 6).

Sachs was a Harvard economics professor who was highly influential in encouraging
Minister of Finance, Leszek Balcerowicz, to go for a 'big-bang' policy of financial
rigour and austerity and a rapid move towards capitalism in 1989-90. Here he sets out
his views on how Poland could break out of its constraints of external debt and other
barriers to economic development.

638   **The planned economies of Eastern Europe.**
Alan H. Smith.   London: Croom Helm, 1983. 249p. bibliog.

A historical overview and an assessment by a well-established specialist at the School
of Slavonic Studies, London University. The main sections are: the origins and
operation of central planning; wages, retail trade and consumer equilibrium; and
international economic relations.

639   **The year 1990 – between inflation and recession and the perspectives of
the Polish economy in 1991 and after.**
Władysław Welfe.   Łódź, Poland: Wydawnictwo UZ, 1991. 26p.

A collection of papers presented at the Project LINK meeting in Manila, Philippines,
in November 1990.

640   The distorted world of Soviet-type economies.
       Jan Winiecki.   London: Routledge, 1988. 230p. bibliog.

A highly influential analysis of the system-specific economic distortions characteristic of Soviet-type economies and their effect upon economic performance. Winiecki draws widely on Polish sources and information.

Finance, Banking and Statistics

641 **Biographies of Polish statisticians.**
Jan Berger (et al), for the Polish Statistical Association, translated by
Leszek Podbielski. Warsaw: Central Statistical Office, 1989. 107p.

Contains the biographies of forty-two major individuals who contributed to the
development of Polish statistics during the last five centuries. The collection starts with
Jan Długosz (1415-1480) and concludes with Zbigniew Pawłowski (1930-81).

642 **Country reports. Central and Eastern Europe, 1991.**
European Communities – Commission. Luxemburg: Office for
Official Publications of the European Communities, 1991. 184p.
(Statistiches Bundesamt, Wiesbaden).

Includes official statistics on Poland, along with the other East European countries,
covering the main economic and social sectors from population to the national
accounts.

643 **Concise statistical yearbook of the Polish People's Republic.**
Warsaw: Główny Urząd Statystyczny, 1947- . maps.

This statistical yearbook, published throughout the history of Communist Poland
provided statistical data across the whole range of political, demographic, social,
economic and cultural sectors. Although the data were challenged as unreliable at
times, there was a marked improvement in accuracy after 1970, and again after 1980.
The 1970s also saw the inclusion of an increasing amount of comparative data designed
to show how Poland measured up to other countries. The *Rocznik Statystyczny*
(Annual Yearbook) was not published in English but included the full range of
statistical material; the 51st edition for 1991, for example, was 596p. in length.

644 **Facts about Poland.**
Warsaw: Interpress, 1980- . 206p.
An irregular series revised at various times during the 1980s. It provides concise general information and statistical data about all aspects of Polish economic, social, political and cultural life.

645 **Foreign exchange law of February 15, 1989.**
Warsaw: Interpress, 1989. 10p.
This pamphlet contains the English-language text of the above law which was the first major step towards official domestic currency convertibility.

646 **Stabilization policy in Poland. Challenges and constraints.**
Grzegorz W. Kołodko. Warsaw: Instytut Finansowy, 1989. 33p.
(Institute of Finance Working Paper no. 3). bibliog.
A study of the measures taken to grapple with the problem of mounting hyper-inflation in Poland in 1989. Paper no. 2 in the same series was written by an economist who was briefly to become Minister of Finance in early 1992; Karol Lutkowski, *Some crucial aspects of the IMF adjustment programs. Their relevance to Poland's economic problems*, 1989. 17p. Also Mikołaj Breitkop, *Foreign direct investment in Poland.* (Warsaw: Instytut Finansowy, 1990. 25p. [IF Working Papers no. 13]).

647 **National income and outlay in Czechoslovakia, Poland and Yugoslavia.**
Jaroslaw Krejci. London: Macmillan, 1982. 122p. bibliog.
An extremely detailed statistical comparison, written by a major academic, which is invaluable as a source of the most reliable information available on the subject.

648 **Poland 1990. Statistical data.**
Warsaw: Główny Urząd Statystyczny, 1991. 100p.
An irregular, but useful, GUS series, containing material on all aspects of Polish life. See also *Poland 1987. Statistical data* (Warsaw: GUS, 1987. 102p.).

649 **Socialist banking and monetary control: the experience of Poland.**
Tadeusz M. Podolski. Cambridge, England: Cambridge University Press, 1972. 392p. bibliog. (Soviet and East European Studies Series).
An important and detailed study of the institutions and practices of banking and monetary control in communist Poland. Although much of the specific detail is, understandably, out of date, it still provides a good basis for comprehending the starting-out framework for post-communist changes.

650 **Foreign capital in Poland.**
Leopold Wellisz. London: Allen & Unwin, 1938. 281p.
Examines the history of the penetration of foreign (mainly West European) capital into the pre-Second World War Polish economy. Heavy industry, including mining, textiles and chemicals, as well as transport and communications were largely owned by French, German, English, Belgian, Swedish and Italian capital. The volume contains useful historical material for post-communist debates about Polish peripheral economic dependency.

651 **One hundred and twenty fifth anniversary of co-operative banking in Poland.** Alicja Wittenberg-Stalewski, translated by Andrzej Porowski. Warsaw: Wydawnictwo Spółdzielcze, 1986. 30p.

A short popular sketch overviewing 125 years of co-operative banking in Poland. It attempts to show the broader historical roots of the financial institutions of the communist period which supported co-operatives such as the 'Społem' food-retailing chain or agricultural circles.

Trade

652   **The economies of Eastern Europe and their foreign economic relations.**
Edited by Philip Joseph.   Brussels: NATO, 1987. 363p.
Publishes the reports presented to a NATO colloquium on the East European
economies and their trading prospects held in April 1986. The Polish contributions are;
Bartolomiej Kamiński on foreign trade, Domenico Nuti on the prospects of economic
reform and Zbigniew Fallenbuchl on internal economic development.

653   **The Poznań International Fair. Historical outline, functions and
economic importance.**
Stefan Kowal, Henryk Wojciechowski, translated by Danuta
Wolfram-Romanowska.   Poznań, Poland: Pospress, 1988. 36p.
An illustrated introduction to the organization, work and influence of the Poznań
International Trade Fair. It is held annually, and has traditionally been the major
occasion of its type in Poland, and one of the major fairs in Europe.

654   **Doing business in Eastern Europe. Poland-Hungary-Czechoslovakia.**
Karen Leibreich.   London: BBC Books, 1991. bibliog.
A guide to doing business in Poland, compiled by a BBC journalist. Contains
background information as well as very useful up to date details on local markets,
etiquette, business frameworks and the most promising sectors. Also Richard J.
Hunter, Leo V. Ryan, 'Uwaga (watch out). Opportunities and pitfalls for an American
doing business in Poland. The political and economic scene', *Polish Review*, vol. 36,
no. 3 (1991), p. 345-62.

655 **Creditworthiness and reform in Poland. Western and Polish perspectives.**
Edited by Paul Marer, Włodzimierz Siwiński.   Bloomington, Indiana: Indiana University Press, 1988. 348p. bibliog.

Contains chapters by Western and Polish specialists on the consequences of Poland's inability to service her huge external debt from 1981 onwards and how this affected her capacity to introduce much needed economic reforms. Major contributors include Brus, Morawski, Brzezinski, Fallenbuchl, Dobroczyński and Bielasiak.

656 **Polish-US industrial co-operation in the 1980s; findings of a joint research project.**
Edited by Paul Marer, Eugeniusz Tabaczyński.   Bloomington, Indiana: Indiana University Press, 1982. 409p.

A very detailed and specialist report of a joint Polish-American study on their trade and industrial co-operation.

657 **The international and the Polish economy in 1989 and 1990.**
Edited by Marian Paszyński, Józef Soldaczuk, Stanisław Fałkowski.
Warsaw: Foreign Trade Research Institute, 1990. 60p.

The second report of the Warsaw Foreign Trade Research Institute on the the Polish economy during 1989-90 and its foreign trade and other external economic relations within the world economy. It contains an assessment of the crucial changes in the economic situation during 1989 and a forecast of developments for 1990.

658 **Transborder data flows and Poland; Polish case-study; a paper prepared by the Foreign Trade Data Centre at the request of the Ministry of Foreign Trade of the Government of Poland.**
New York: United Nations, 1984. 75p.

An official Polish report published by the United Nations which did not lift the veil on information flows so much as demonstrate how open the situation was already.

Industry

659 Structural adjustment policy and the international competitiveness of Polish industry.
Jan W. Bossak, Dariusz Zbylniewski. Warsaw: Foreign Trade Research Institute, 1987. 46p.

A brief discussion by two economists of the extent of rationalization of Polish industry which might be indicated as necessary by international comparisons of technological and performance levels.

660 Controlling top management in large organizations. Poland and the USA.
Barbara Czarniawska-Joerges. Aldershot, England: Gower, 1985. 148p.

A report on a Polish-American cross-cultural study on the psychological motivations of Polish and American industrial managers, mainly carried out in the late 1970s.

661 Industrial co-operation between Poland and the West.
John S. Garland. Ann Arbor, Michigan: UMI Research, 1985. 200p. bibliog. (Research for Business Decisions no. 71).

The report of a collaborative study carried out by specialists from the Warsaw Foreign Trade Research Institute and Indiana University.

662 Industrial reform in socialist countries. From restructuring to revolution.
Edited by Ian Jeffries. Aldershot, England: Edward Elgar, 1992. 294p.

Contains individual chapters on all the countries in Eastern Europe, as well as the USSR and those closely associated with its bloc. George Blazyca concludes his overview of industrial reform in Poland from the mid-1980s onwards by identifying the

153

lack of a coherent industrial policy as the most serious deficiency of the economic policy of the Mazowiecki Government in 1990.

663 The red market. Industrial co-operation and specialization in Comecon.
Vladimir Sobell. Aldershot, England: Gower, 1984. 256p.

A detailed academic monograph, based on Sobell's Oxford doctoral dissertation, which examines Comecon co-operation and specialization in various sectors such as energy, metallurgy, chemicals, the nuclear industry, machine-building and automobile production as well as standardization and research.

664 Coal issues for the 1980s. Management problems arising from technological changes.
Jan Stachowicz. Warsaw: Państwowe Wydawnictwo Naukowe, 1987. 195p. bibliog.

An academic monograph based on the proceedings of an October 1981 seminar on the future of coal mining, as set out in the title. See also Józef Paździora, translated by Mauriel Mierzyńska, Stanisław Bochniak. *Design of underground hard-coal mines* (Warsaw: Państwowe Wydawnictwo Naukowe, 1988. 229p. bibliog.).

665 The socialist corporation and technocratic power. The Polish United Workers' Party, industrial organization and workforce control.
Jean Woodall. Cambridge, England: Cambridge University Press, 1982. 281p. (Soviet and East European Studies series). bibliog.

A detailed examination of the political and other consequences of attempts to introduce economic reforms, and in particular a restructuring of industrial enterprises (the WOGs or Large Production Enterprises) in Gierek's Poland. Woodall argues that excessive industrial integration and concentration in the 1970s was a major contributory factor to Gierek's downfall.

666 Economic reforms in Polish industry.
Janusz G. Zieliński. New York: Oxford University Press, 1973. 333p. maps.

An important study of the economic theory and practice of socialist planning in Poland. Zieliński demonstrated the ineffectiveness of Polish attempts at economic reform and restructuring. He related it to the tendency of socialist enterprises to avoid risk and innovation and the absence of political will for reform.

Agriculture, Forestry and Fishing

667 **Everyday forms of peasant resistance.**
Edited by Forrest D. Colburn. White Plains, New York: M. E. Sharpe, 1990. 288p. bibliog.

The study discusses why peasant rebellions are so rare. It examines the alternative forms of struggle resorted to by peasants in seven countries including Poland.

668 **Agricultural reform in Poland: background and prospects.**
Edward Cook. *Soviet Studies*, vol. 36, no. 3 (1984), p. 406-26.

Examines the historical background to, and the substance of the major reforms of 1980-84 designed to improve the performance of the private peasant farming sector, which at that time ran three quarters of Polish agriculture, as well as the drive to place it on a constitutionally and economically equal footing with socialized agriculture. Cook concluded that the average size of private landholdings had hardly increased since 1970; the directive–quota system of agricultural management still favoured socialized agriculture as the authorities were wary of extending the influence of free market forces which would encourage wider income-differentials and undermine their ideological-power base.

669 **The agriculture revolution in the Soviet Union and Eastern Europe.**
Robert Deutsch. Boulder, Colorado: Westview Press, 1986. 255p. (Westview Special Studies on the Soviet Union and Eastern Europe). bibliog.

Deutsch argues that the communist elites in Eastern Europe had understood that political stability depended upon satisfying consumer demand, especially in food, which inevitably entailed economic reform. His case-studies show these to have been relatively successful in Hungary, Bulgaria and the German Democratic Republic.

Poland, however, faced special political and social problems in its attempts to liberalize existing private ownership and to introduce pricing and marketization reforms.

670 Forests and forest economy in Poland.
Józef Dygasiewicz, translated by Wawrzyniec Dąbrowski. Poznań, Poland: PWRiL, 1988. 110p. maps.

Shows the layout of Polish woodlands and how these resources are husbanded and exploited. As elsewhere a major problem is involved in conserving this valuable, although diminishing, resource.

671 Politics of socialist agriculture in Poland 1945-60.
Andrzej Korboński. New York: Columbia University Press, 1965. 330p. bibliog.

Considers the interplay between politics and agriculture in the first phase of Communist Poland. This saw the defeat of half-hearted attempts at collectivization and the emergence of a dominant privately owned sector co-existing with the state and co-operative ones.

672 The green flag. Polish populist politics 1867-1970.
Olga A. Narkiewicz. London: Croom Helm, 1976. 313p. bibliog.

This remains the authoritative political history of a century of Polish peasant politics from 1867 onwards. The coverage of the peasant parties of the interwar and postwar periods is essential to an understanding of some aspects, including regional differentiation, of the contemporary politics of the Polish countryside and the strategic choices facing it.

673 Family farms in Polish agricultural policy 1945-85.
Jean Charles Szurek. *East European Politics and Societies*, vol. 1, no. 2 (Spring 1987), p. 225-54.

A weighty examination, translated from the French, of the development of communist policy towards the family farm which has been the dominant form of postwar Polish agriculture. Its existence was guaranteed in the constitution in 1983 but the problem of raising its efficiency and of reconciling the free agricultural market with central planning remained.

674 Odra-Świnoujście, 1952-87.
Marian Urbański. Szczecin, Poland: Krajowa Agencja Wydawnicza, 1987. 88p.

A largely historical overview of the development of Poland's maritime fisheries industry based on the mouth of the estuary of the river Oder.

675   **Communist agriculture. Farming in the Soviet Union and Eastern Europe.**
Edited by Karl-Eugen Wadekin, foreword by Gregory Grossman.
London: Routledge, 1990. 331p.

Part Three of this volume, which deals with Eastern Europe contains chapters by Andrzej Korboński on Polish farming after martial law and by Franciszek Tomczak on the need for communist ideological constraints to be abandoned in order to allow for the development of efficient family farms. Coverage of the earlier period is provided by Everett Jacobs & Alec Nove, *The organization of agriculture in the Soviet Union and Eastern Europe.* (Montclair, New Jersey: Allenheld, Osmun, 1980. 500p.).

Transport

676 **Polish aircraft, 1893-1939.**
Jerzy B. Cynk. London: Putnam, 1971. 760p. bibliog.
This illustrated history covers the Polish aircraft industry and all pre-September 1939 aircraft types.

677 **Polish wings.**
Andrzej Glass, translated by Emma Harris. Warsaw: Interpress, 1985. 96p.
Deals exhaustively with military aviation in the 1918-39, 1939-45 and post-1945 periods, Polish Airlines, agricultural and industrial aviation, flying-ambulance services, aviation sports, gliding, ballooning, parachuting and Polish aircraft abroad. The work is lavishly illustrated with glossy photographs of a wide range of aircraft types.

678 **Trans European North-South railway connections.**
Ministry of Transport. Warsaw: Interpress, 1986. 350p.
Poland's centrally placed position in Europe is usually considered from the international security viewpoint but it increasingly has economic significance as well. Independent Poland inherited strongly developed East-West transport connections between Germany and the USSR because of the policy of the partitioning powers. Despite some interwar initiatives connected with the building of the new port of Gdynia the links between the Baltic ports, which now includes Szczecin, and Poland's industrial areas in Silesia were only developed fully through the building of new railway lines and the electrification of old ones from the 1960s onwards. The balancing out and filling-in of the domestic railway network has an important international aspect because of the burgeoning importance of Poland's economic and tourist links with her southern neighbours. This official report thus stresses the growing significance of the Polish Baltic *entrepôt* trade with Czecho-Slovakia and Hungary and of North-South railway connections with Central Europe in general and even with the Balkans.

Employment and Labour

679 **Employment and wage-policies in Poland, Czechoslovakia and Hungary since 1950.**
Jan Adam. London: Macmillan, 1984. 251p. bibliog.
Examines the employment policies practised in a number of different phases between 1950 and and the early 1980s in the countries mentioned in the title. Particular attention is paid to explaining what is meant by 'full employment' and 'labour shortage' in communist economies, and especially to the Polish manipulation of female labour and retirement factors to achieve such goals.

680 **A Polish factory: a case-study of workers' participation in decisions in industry.**
Jiri Thomas Kolaja. Lexington, Kentucky: University of Kentucky Press, 1960. 157p.
A pioneering work, which became something of a classic, on labour-management relations and workers' participation in Poland. The study, based on both printed sources and first-hand observation, produced balanced conclusions about methods of reducing labour–management conflicts in state-socialist societies which are still significant for the theoretical debate on the subject.

681 **Poland's new trade unions.**
David S. Mason. *Soviet Studies*, vol. 39, no. 3 (1987), p. 489-508.
A detailed and fair-minded examination of the banning of Solidarity and other trade unions by the Law of 8 October 1982 and the Polish Government's subsequent launching of new trade unions. These were first organized at the local level building up to the emergence of a national federation, the All-Poland Alliance of Trade Unions (OPZZ), by Autumn 1984. Mason concludes that this represented a moderate success

for the authorities given the conditions of national apathy and withdrawal from political life following martial law. See also Ajit Jain (editor), *Solidarity; the origins and implications of Polish trade unions* (Baton Rouge, Louisiana: Oracle Press, 1983).

682   **The AFL-CIO and Poland's Solidarity.**
   James M. Shevis. *World Affairs*, vol. 144, no. 1 (Summer 1981),
   p. 31-5.
AFL-CIO officials always argued that communist trade unions were fraudulent totalitarian labour-front organizations designed to enforce labour discipline. They considered that the formation of Solidarity vindicated the Federation's longstanding opposition to exchanges between free trade unions and such communist-controlled bodies.

Environment

683 **Pollution in the heart of Europe.**
Jan Marcinkiewicz.   London: Polish Society of Arts and Sciences
Abroad, 1987. 55p.
A London-based academic specialist deals with industrial pollution, its effects on
forests and the pollution of rivers as well as the consequences of industrial emissions on
buildings of historic interest such as the Wawel castle in Kraków. An addendum
considers the effects on Poland of radioactive pollution caused by the Chernobyl
nuclear disaster of April 1986.

684 **Changes in the geochemistry of the natural environment in areas**
affected by industrial emissions.
PAN Komisja Nauk Mineralogicznych w Krakowie.   Wrocław,
Poland: Ossolineum, 1988. 83p.
A report by a specialist committee of the Polish Academy of Sciences on the
environmental consequences of pollution by industrial emissions in Poland. See also
*The economic problems of environmental pollution: an expertise of the Polish team of
experts MAB 13a.* PAN, Polish Committee for the Man and Biosphere Programme
UNESCO – MAB. (Wrocław, Poland: Ossolineum, 1988. 76p.).

Education, Universities and Learning

685 **Education in the Polish People's Republic.**
Czesław Banach, translated by Lech Petrowicz. Warsaw: Interpress, 1987. 94p.

A short and popular introduction to the organization and problems of the Polish educational system.

686 **The flying university in Poland 1978-80.**
Hanna Buczyńska-Garewicz. *Harvard Education Review*, vol. 55, no. 1 (1985), p. 20-33.

Poland has a long and powerful tradition of organizing 'flying universities' to circumvent the censorship of a partitioning or hostile power, such as during the 1883-1905 period in Russian-occupied Poland. This was renewed in 1978-80 with the organization, against the background of the growing discontent which exploded in 1980, of the TKN (Society for Academic Studies). About sixty dissident academics and writers lectured in private flats to audiences of some hundred students on sensitive topics such as the Nazi-Soviet Pact of 1939 which could not be discussed within the official University. A full translation of the TKN's Founding Declaration of January 1978 is included.

687 **Warsaw Medical Academy: history, the present day.**
Jerzy Celma-Panek, translated by Joanna Ciecerska. Warsaw:
Akademia Medyczna, 1983. 119p.

An illustrated history of the Medical Academy established in Warsaw in 1950. It
maintains the traditions and achievements of the Faculties of Medicine and Pharmacy
of the University of Warsaw founded in 1809.

688 **Nicholas Copernicus' complete works.**
Edited by Paweł Czartoryski, translation and commentary by Edward
Rosen, Erna Hilstein. Kraków, Poland; Basingstoke, England:
Państwowe Wydawnictwo Naukowe – Macmillan, 1985.

Volume i in this series (1972) was a facsimile in Copernicus' own hand of his 'On the
Revolutions' while volume ii (1978) was an English translation of this work. Volume iii
Minor Works (380p.) is an English translation, with commentaries, in large format of
everything else written by Copernicus, many of the writings being made available in
English for the first time. Rosen, an Emeritus Professor from the City University of
New York, describes the material as all that is left of Copernicus' literary, epistolatory,
administrative, financial and scientific writings apart from 'On the Revolutions'. See
also Jerzy Dobrzycki (editor), *The reception of Copernicus' heliocentric theory:
proceedings of a symposium organized by the Nicolas Copernicus Committee of the
International Union of the History of Philosophy and Science.* (Dordrecht, Netherlands: D. Reidel, 1972. 368p. bibliog.).

689 **Malinowski between two worlds. The Polish roots of an anthropological
tradition.**
Edited by Roy Ellen (et al). Cambridge, England: Cambridge
University Press, 1988. 261p. bibliog.

Contains eight papers from the international conference, held in September 1984, at
the Jagiellonian University, Kraków, his *alma mater*, to celebrate the centenary of
Malinowski's birth. Introduced by Andrzej Paluch, it contains a significant discussion
by Ernest Gellner. The book also has the most extensive bibliography of Bronisław
Malinowski's writings, it summarizes his Kraków doctorate and reproduces six of his
previously unpublished letters.

690 **Revolution and tradition in People's Poland: education and socialization.**
Joseph R. Fiszman. London: Oxford University Press, 1973. 382p.
bibliog.

This study demonstrates one specific case of how the Polish people, and in particular
the Roman Catholic Church and the intelligentsia, preserved entrenched traditional
national values during the communist period. Polish teachers in the countryside
resolved the dilemma of having to propagate official secular values while living in a
traditional Catholic social *milieu* by compromising on a version of superficial
modernization and support for existing power-structures. Fiszman's extensive fieldwork
in the mid-late 1960s also produced much valuable data and many stimulating
conclusions about a wider range of social hypotheses.

691 **The Polish renaissance in its European context.**
Edited by Samuel Fiszman, foreword by Czesław Miłosz.
Bloomington, Indiana: Indiana University Press, 1988. 478p.

Contains twenty-seven papers from a joint Polish-American conference held at Indiana University in 1982. Eleven contributions are devoted to Jan Kochanowski (1530-84), the Renaissance poet and humanist, who provided the central focus for the proceedings. There is also coverage of the following aspects of Renaissance Poland: historical and social aspects, art, science and learning, religion and law and international significance.

692 **Marie Curie. A life.**
Françoise Giroud, translated from the French by Lydia Davis. New York: Holmes & Meier, 1986. 291p. bibliog.

A personal interpretation by a well-known French writer and political activist of Marie Curie-Skłodowska's life (1867-1934) and achievement.

693 **Universities. Today and tomorrow.**
Edited by Jan Jerschina, Anna Kosiarz. Kraków, Poland: UJ One Europe Foundation Research Press, 1990. 313p. bibliog.

Proceedings of a conference held at the Jagiellonian University on the future of higher education in Poland.

694 **Philosophy and ideology; the development of philosophy and Marxism-Leninism in Poland since the Second World War.**
Zbigniew A. Jordan. Dordrecht, Netherlands: Reidel, 1963. 600p. bibliog.

A profound, if difficult, intellectual study of the interaction between philosophical thought and Marxism-Leninism in the early period of Communist Poland.

695 **Analyzing urban-rural disparities in education in Poland.**
Mikołaj Kozakiewicz. Paris: UNESCO, 1987. 113p.

A sharp report of research findings on the above subject by an academic who played an important role in Polish politics as Sejm Marshal (Speaker) in 1989-91.

696 **Education and youth employment in Poland.**
Barbara Liberska. Berkeley, California: Carnegie Council on Policy Studies in Higher Education, 1979. 83p.

An analysis of the demographic patterns of the 15-24 age-group in Poland during 1960-75 and the education and employment policies adopted for them. See also *Education and work in Poland*, (Warsaw: Państwowe Wydawnictwo Naukowe – UNESCO, 1985. 307p.).

697 **Scientific writings and astronomical tables in Cracow (xivth-xvith centuries).**
Grażyna Rosińska. Wrocław, Poland: Ossolineum, 1984. (Studia Copernicana no. 22). 561p + 44 plates.

The first part lists 2,392 treatises, commentaries and notes dealing mainly with astronomy. mathematics, optics and astrology but with some entries for other scientific fields such as mineralogy, geography and alchemy to a much lesser extent. The second part catalogues 215 astronomical, astrological, arithmetical and trigonometric tables. This work is designed to identify the manuscript basis of the flourishing schools of science and astronomy in Kraków in the fourteenth to sixteenth centuries; as such it includes the works of scholars from Kraków and those that either belonged to or were copied from them.

698 **Renaissance culture in Poland: the rise of Humanism, 1470-1543.**
Harold B. Segel. Ithaca, New York; London: Cornell University Press, 1989. 285p.

An examination of the Neo-Latin writers, both Polish and foreign, who contributed to the early development and spread of Humanism in Poland. The ten chapters discuss such representative figures as Gregory of Sanok, Andrzej Krzycki, Fillippo Buonaccorsi and Nicolaus Hussonarius. The volume includes substantial translated passages of their texts.

699 **The founders of Polish schools and scientific models write about their works.**
Edited by Irena Stasiewicz-Jasiukowa, translated by Ludwik Wiewiórski, Tadeusz Niewęgłowski. Wrocław, Poland: Ossolineum, 1989. 212p.

An interesting contribution to the discussion of what constitutes schools or models in academic life. The volume contains the editor's introduction to the above issue, a conclusion by Wojciech Swiętosławski on the functions of heads of scientific teams and seven contributions by founders of major Polish 'schools'; the latter include Kazimierz Michałowski (Mediterranean archaeology), Kazimierz Kuratowski (mathematics), Wiktor Dego (medical rehabilitation) and Stanisław Lorentz (urban preservation).

700 **Anti-communist student organizations and the Polish renewal.**
Charles Wankel. Basingstoke, England: Macmillan, 1992. 288p. bibliog.

A detailed academic study based on original research and theoretical conceptualization of the Independent Students' Organisation (NSZ) during the Polish crisis of 1980-81. See also Barbara Wejnert, 'The student movement in Poland, 1980-81', *Research in Social Movements, Conflicts and Change*, vol. 10 (1988), p. 173-81.

701 **Education for peace in the Polish educational system.**
Eugenia Anna Wesołowska. Warsaw: Interpress, 1986. 32p.

A short popular brochure discussion of how Poland contributes, through its educational system, to general European and bilateral agreements designed to diminish national hatreds and the risk of war.

702 **The beginning of Cyrillic printing, Cracow 1491, from the Orthodox past in Poland.**
Szczepan K. Zimmer, edited by Ludwik Krzyżanowski, Irena Nagurski. Krystyna M. Olszer. Boulder, Colorado: Social Science Monographs, 1983. 292p. (East European Monographs no. 136).
Discusses the historical background and the technical problems encountered by the establishment of the first Cyrillic printing press in Poland in Kraków in the late fifteenth century by Szwajpolt Fiol and Jan Turzo. It also considers the controversy over whether Fiol was a Russian whose writings were in that language.

Literature

Literary history and criticism

703 **Before the thaw: the beginnings of dissent in postwar Polish literature (the case of Adam Ważyk's a poem for adults).**
Stanisław Barańczak. *East European Politics and Societies*, vol. 3, no. 1 (1989), p. 3-21.
Barańczak discusses what he calls the greatest controversy 'in the entire postwar history of Polish literature' stirred up by the publication of Adam Ważyk's 'A Poem for Adults' in the official literary weekly *Nowa Kultura* of 21 August 1955. It marked the beginnings of the 'Thaw' in intellectual life which preceded the Polish 'October'; Barańczak, understandably in view of his anti-socialist prejudices, is critical of the poem's revisionist character which reflected, as well as moulded, the mood of the time that socialism could be reformed and that Stalinism's crimes and mistakes could be put right.

704 **Breathing under water and other East European essays.**
Stanisław Barańczak. Cambridge, Massachusetts: Harvard University Press, 1990. 258p.
A collection of essays which discuss the crucial role of the cultural intelligentsia in undermining communist rule in Eastern Europe. Barańczak emphasizes the wide range of methods resorted to by intellectuals to get around or fool the censorship, the so-called tactic of 'breathing under water'.

705 **The poetic avant-garde in Poland 1918-39.**
Bogdana Carpenter. Seattle, Washington: University of Washington Press, 1981. 234p. bibliog.
A concise and comprehensive study which fills an important gap in the literature through its innovative coverage of such *avant-garde* writers as Tytus Czyżewski, Bruno Jasieński, Stanisław Młodożeniec, Anatol Stern and Aleksander Wat as well as more secondary figures like Julian Przyboś, Tadeusz Peiper and Jakub Kurek.

706 **The mature laurel. Essays in modern Polish poetry.**
Edited by Adam Czerniawski, preface by Neal Ascherson. Bridgend, Wales: Seren Books, 1991. 323p. bibliog.
An influential collection of eighteen British and Polish essays on Polish poetry from Norwid to Miłosz, grouped in three sections. See also his 'The Polish poet as custodian of the nation's conscience', *Polish Review*. vol. 24, no. 4 (1979), p. 3-25.

707 **Political and social issues in Poland as reflected in the Polish novel 1945-85.**
Anna R. Dadlez. New York: Columbia University Press, 1989. 289p. (East European Monographs no. 269). bibliog.
A revised version of a 1973 Syracuse University doctoral dissertation, this is an interesting and comprehensive overview of how, despite censorship, the Polish novel acted as a sensitive barometer of 'frost' and 'thaw' periods in the political atmosphere over a period of four decades. It reflected, and often went ahead of social trends and discontent. The coverage is both historical and thematic but is inevitably somewhat superficial in places given the scope of the subject.

708 **Introduction to Polish literature and culture. Wprowadzenie do literatury i kultury Polskiej.**
L. R. Krajewski Jasieńczyk (sic). London: Unicorn, 1989. 123p.
A very basic introduction in terms of content although the volume is not intended as a textbook on Polish literature and culture. Rather the parallel English text and Polish translation on facing pages are designed as exercises for first year University courses in Polish Studies.

709 **A history of Polish literature.**
Julian Krzyżanowski. Warsaw: Państwowe Wydawnictwo Naukowe, 1980. 2nd ed. 804p.
An authoritative overview by one of the most respected specialists in the field, containing a particularly comprehensive bibliography, both to general and reference works and to particular studies related to the successive chapters in the book. For a commentary on one of the most important periods see Tymoteusz Karpowicz, 'Fire and Snow; the dichotomies and dichomacies of Polish baroque poetry'. (In A. T. Tymieniecka's *Elements of the human condition*, p. 101-22. Dordrecht: Kluwer, 1988).

710 **Contemporary Polish poetry, 1925-75.**
Madeline G. Levine, edited by Irene Nagurski. Boston,
Massachusetts: Twayne, 1981. 195p.

Individual chapters cover the main themes, ideas and style as well as the careers of ten of Poland's major twentieth century poets: Przyboś, Miłosz, Baczyński, Gajcy, Herbert, Różewicz, Szymborska, Białoszewski, Harasymonowicz and Grochowiak.

711 **Two Warsaws; the literary representation of catastrophe.**
Madeline G. Levine. *East European Politics and Societies*, vol. 1, no. 3 (1987), p. 349-62.

Illustrates the fate of Poland during the Second World War through the literary representation of two separate Warsaws; firstly, the completely destroyed Warsaw after the two months' long uprising in Summer 1944 represents 'the suffering and militant heroism of the entire Polish nation'. Secondly, the Warsaw Ghetto Uprising of April 1943 is taken as the symbol of the total destruction, without any hope, of the Polish Jews. See also her 'Polish literature and the Holocaust' (In *Literature, the Arts and the Holocaust* edited by J. Fischel. Westport, Massachusetts: Greenwood, 1987. p. 189-202).

712 **Cyprian Norwid (1821-83): poet – thinker – craftsman.**
Edited by Bolesław Mazur, George Gömöri. London: Orbis Books, 1988. 208p.

Thirteen specialist papers presented at the centennial conference to mark his death held in London in 1983. An uneven collection which includes contributions by Stanisław Barańczak, Nina Taylor, and Tymoteusz Karpowicz amongst others.

713 **The history of Polish literature.**
Czesław Miłosz. Berkeley, California: University of California Press, 1983. 2nd ed. 583p. bibliog.

A historical overview from medieval to modern times, by the celebrated author and literary critic, which devotes a fifth of the coverage to the the post Second World War period. Miłosz also discusses the Polish literary tradition, its significance in the world context, its peripheral and anachronistic features and its artistic and aesthetic values.

714 **Between anxiety and hope. The poetry and writing of Czesław Miłosz.**
Edited by Edward Możejko. Edmonton, Alberta: University of Alberta Press, 1988. 190p.

A symposium on Miłosz. Most of the contributions were written in 1981 and, therefore, somewhat dated by the time of publication. The chapters by Bogdan Czaykowski on 'the idea of reality' in Miłosz' poetry and Madeline Levine's analysis of the weak points of his only political novel, *The seizure of power*, were most commended by the reviewers.

Individual writers

715 Czesław Miłosz and the insufficiency of lyric.
Donald Davie. Cambridge, England: Cambridge University Press, 1986. 76p. bibliog.

This essay on Miłosz developed out of a series of invited guest-lectures by a British academic at the University of Tennessee in 1984. Davie overviews Miłosz' work stressing his significance as a representative twentieth century *deraciné* intellectual rather than as a lyric poet. He argues the case most strongly in a critical appreciation of *The Issa Valley* where he questions the weight traditionally ascribed to Miłosz' Lithuanian roots in explaining the tangled complexity of his work. Davie's writings on different aspects of Russian and Polish literature were published as *Slavic excursions. Essays on Russian and Polish literature* (Manchester: Carcanet, 1990. 312p). The Polish chapters included pieces on *Pan Tadeusz*, Polish Baroque, Zbigniew Herbert and a comparison of Mickiewicz with Pushkin and Walter Scott.

716 Juliusz Słowacki.
Maria Dernalowicz. Warsaw: Interpress, 1987. 151p.

A popular but well-written and informative biography of Słowacki's life (1809-49), work and significance. One of Poland's greatest Romantic writers, alongside Mickiewicz and Krasiński, he is best remembered for his classic poetical plays notably *Kordian, Balladyna, Beniowski, Lilla Weneda* and *Fantazy*. He died abroad in Montmartre and was only reburied in the Wawel Cathedral in 1929. Another similar type of study is Maria Demolowicz, translated by Halina Filipowicz. *Adam Mickiewicz*. (Warsaw: Wiedza Powszechna, 1985. 430p. [Profile Series]).

717 Hen.
Hanna Gosh, translated by Christina Cenkalska. Warsaw: Author's Agency, 1990. 44p. (Profiles of Contemporary Writers). bibliog.

Józef Hen (born 1923) is a well-known popular writer and publicist who has also produced a number of film-scripts.

718 Herbert.
Andrzej Kaliszewski, translated by Christina Cenkalska. Warsaw: Author's Agency, 1989. 45p. (Profiles of Contemporary Writers). bibliog.

A popular essay on the life and work of the lyrical poet Zbigniew Herbert (born 1924).

719 Jerzy Kosiński.
Norman Lavers. Boston, Massachusetts: Twayne Publishers, 1982. 176p. bibliog.

A rough preliminary attempt at a biography and a literary appreciation of Kosiński's (1933-91) writings. Kosiński lived in America from 1957 onwards; his brutal realism is often attributed to that environment while his fantasies are sometimes held to be a carry-over from his Polish roots.

720 **Stanisław Lem.**
Richard E. Ziegfeld. New York: F. Unger, 1986. 188p.
Lem is a high quality literary writer as well as an innovative force in the field of Science Fiction and deservedly has a world-wide reputation. This is one of the few English language studies devoted to all aspects of his life and career as well as an assessment and overview of his key works and their main themes.

English translations

721 **Poland under black light.**
Janusz Anderman, translated by Nina Taylor, Andrew Short.
London: Reader's International, 1985. 131p.
The author (born 1948) expresses his despair as a literary creator faced by what he considers to be the political and moral hopelessnesss of early 1980s Poland.

722 **Ariadne's thread. Polish women poets.**
Translated and introduced by Susan Bassnett, Piotr Kuhiwczak.
London: Forest Books, 1988. 74p.
Contains fifty-one poems by contemporary Polish poets such as Kazimiera Iłłakowiczówna, Maria Pawlikowska-Jasnorzewska, Anna Swirczyńska, Anna Kamionska, Wisława Szymborska, Halina Poświadomska and Ewa Lipska. A fine and representative selection.

723 **A question of reality. Answers from Poland.**
Kazimierz Brandys, translated from the French by Isabel Barzun.
London: Blond & Briggs, 1981. 180p.
Brandys (born 1916), a well-known writer and publicist, achieved great prominence for his semi-documentary rapportage during his period as an *emigré* oppositionist after 1981. In the above work he uses an imaginary dialogue to illustrate not just the course of his life but also the complexity of the Polish predicament. *A Warsaw diary, 1978-81*, translated by Richard Lourie (London: Chatto & Windus, 1984. New York: Vintage Books, 1985. 260p), is a translation of a selection of passages of Brandys' journal published in full in Poland as *Miesiące 1978-79* and *Miesiące 1980-81*. These are quite interesting reflections on the Polish condition and intellectual and literary currents by a writer who despite, or perhaps because of his complexities, achieved a major international reputation. For a continuation of his obsession with Poland see also his *Paris – New York, 1982-84: a memoir*, translated by Barbara Krzywicki-Herburt (New York: Random House, 1988. 180p). For an introductory appreciation, Włodzimierz Maciąg, translated by Christina Cenkalska, *Kazimierz Brandys* (Warsaw: Author's Agency, 1990. 47p. [Profiles of Contemporary Writers]).

724 **Monumenta Polonica. The first four centuries of Polish poetry. A bilingual anthology.**
Edited by Bogdana Carpenter. Ann Arbor, Michigan: Michigan Slavic Publications, 1989. 567p.

An attractively produced and illustrated anthology of the Polish poetry of the fourteenth to the eighteenth centuries. Original and translated versions are presented on facing pages. The collection is organized into four sections on the Middle Ages, the Renaissance, the Baroque period and the Enlightenment. Latin poetry is excluded.

725 **The Burning Forest.**
Edited and translated by Adam Czerniawski. Newcastle upon Tyne, England: Bloodaxe Books, 1987. 184p.

Contains a selection of poetry by Cyprian Kamil Norwid, Leopold Staff, Tadeusz Różewicz, Tymoteusz Karpowicz, Wisława Szymborska, Zbigniew Herbert, Jan Darowski, Wiktor Woroszylski, Andrzej Bursa, Bogdan Czaykowski and six others. The anthology is one of poets born between the end of the First and the Second World Wars, whose work covers the period from 1945 to the present. Czerniawski argues the case for the translatability of his selected poets in terms of their deep intrinsic meaning. See the review of this influential collection of poetry, which made a highly significant impact on the *emigré* Polish literature of the 1980s in the UK, by Piotr Kuhiwczak, 'Before and after "the burning forest": modern Polish poetry in Britain', *Polish Review*, vol. 34, no. 1 (1989), p. 57-70.

726 **Meetings with the Madonna.**
Jan Dobraczyński, translated by Piotr Goc. Warsaw: Polonia, 1988. 288p.

Uses the literary device of the influence of the icon of the Black Madonna of Częstochowa through the last six centuries of the Polish nation to present the stories of fourteen, mostly eminent, Poles. The subjects range from Queen Jadwiga, Nicholas Copernicus, King Jan Sobieski, to Father Maximilian Kolbe. The book was first published in Polish in 1979 but Primate Wyszyński, who had suggested the idea to Dobraczyński, and Pope John Paul were added to the English-language version. This was a widely publicized and much-read work in Poland, written by a Catholic writer and prominent supporter of the Jaruzelski *regime* who became the chairman of its Patriotic Front for National Rebirth (PRON) in the 1980s.

727 **Introduction to modern Polish literature.**
Adam Gillon, Ludwik Krzyżanowski. New York: Hippocrene Books, 1982. 2nd rev. ed. 513p.

An ambitious and comprehensive anthology of twentieth century Polish prose and verse. The quality of the translations is somewhat uneven and the balance of coverage between major and second rank authors seems to favour the latter. Forty-seven writers were represented in the original edition (New York: Twayne, 1964. 480p.).

728   **Russian and Polish women's fiction.**
Edited by Helena Gościlo.   Knoxville, Tennessee: University of
Tennessee Press, 1985. 343p.

An interesting and useful feminist collection which throws light on the values, ways of
life and social conventions which affected women in Poland and Russia from the
nineteenth century to the present. The main Polish excerpts are from Dąbrowska,
Gojawiczyńska, Kuncewiczowa, Konopnicka, Nałkowska, Orzeszkowa and Zapolska.

729   **Selected poems**
Zbigniew Herbert, translated by Czesław Miłosz, Peter Dale Scott.
London: Carcanet, 1977. Reprint of 1969 Penguin edition.

A selection of the works of this prominent twentieth century poet. See also his other
volumes: *Barbarian in the garden. Essays.* (Translated by J. Anders, M. March.
Manchester: Carcanet, 1985) and *Report from the besieged city and other poems.*
(Translated by Bogdana Carpenter, John Carpenter. New York: 1985. Oxford: Oxford
University Press, 1987).

730   **Seven Polish-Canadian poets.**
Edited by Wacław Iwaniuk, Florian Śmieja.   Toronto, Ontario:
Polish-Canadian Publishing Fund, 1984.

An anthology of the poems of Zofia Bohdanowiczowa, Wacław Iwaniuk, Florian
Śmieja, Danuta Bieńkowska, Janusz Ihanatowicz, Bogdan Czaykowski and Andrzej
Busza with translations by various individuals. Most of the poets are *emigrés* although
some left Poland in their infancy. They represent various poetic schools from
'Skamander' to Contemporary but specialists consider that they all fit easily into the
mainstream of Polish poetry.

731   **The collected letters of Joseph Conrad.**
Edited by Frederick R. Karl, Laurence Davies.   London: Cambridge
University Press, 4 vols, 1983-90.

The authoritative annotated edition of Conrad's correspondence organized on a year
by year basis. The four volumes to appear so far cover the following periods; Volume
I, 1861-1897; Volume II, 1898-1902; Volume III, 1903-1907; Volume IV, 1908-1911.
The writings on Conrad, who spent most of his life in exile and wrote in English, are
not comprehensively included in this volume for the same reasons as the exclusion of
much of the material on Isaac Bashevis Singer, that is because of the tenuous
relationship between their works and Poland. Nevertheless, Zdzisław Najder's *Joseph
Conrad. A chronicle* (Cambridge: Cambridge University Press, 1983. 1,008p.) may be
of some interest.

732   **Polish complex.**
Tadeusz Konwicki, translated by Richard Lourie, Celina Wieniewska,
introduced by Joanna R. Clarke.   Harmondsworth, England: Penguin,
1984. 211p.

The writer (born 1926) usually camouflages his narrative role but comes out into the
open in this work to evoke his own personal and tribal/national memory based mainly
on the Second World War experience. Lourie, in his introduction to the New York:
Farrar, Straus & Giroux, 1982 edition (211p.) describes the Polish complex as the

integrated trinity of Polish-Russian, Polish-Western and Polish relations with itself created by the interaction between Polish history and the afore-mentioned syndrome. But the universal problems of existence and justice and the clash between reality and aspiration all tend to be too much and, understandably, depress Konwicki. Other translations of Konwicki's works during the 1980s were; *A minor apocalypse*, translated by Richard Lourie. (London: Faber & Faber, 1983. 232p.); *Moonrise, moonset*, (translated by Richard Lourie. London: Faber, 1988. 344p.).

733 Between the hammer and the anvil.
Stefan Korbónski, translated by Marta Erdman. New York: Hippocrene Books, 1982. 224p.

A wartime Polish undergound leader presents everyday life under Second World War conditions in the literary form of fifteen short stories.

734 Valedictory
Wiesław S. Kuniczak. Garden City, New York: Doubleday, 1983. 389p.

A novel recounting the experiences and disappointments of Polish airmen in Great Britain during the Second World War, especially when the Soviet takeover frustrated their hopes of a return home. Earlier novels by Kuniczak on similar historical themes were; *The March* (New York: Doubleday, 1979. 840p.); *The thousand hour day* (New York: Dial Press, 1966. 628p.).

735 Poland.
James A. Michener. London: Secker & Warburg; New York: Random House; 1983. 556p.

A historical novel by a highly successful writer in this popular *genre*. It follows the contrasting lives of members of successive generations of three Polish families from the Mongol invasions to after the Second World War.

736 Collected poems 1931-87.
Czesław Miłosz. London: Penguin; Viking, 1988. 511p.

A striking literary and political figure, Miłosz has been admired as a poet, novelist and political writer. His other works include: *Native realism: a search for self-definition*. (Translated by Catherine S. Leach. Harmondsworth: Penguin, 1988. 300p. Reprint, London: Sidgwick & Jackson, 1981); *The Seizure of Power*. (Translated by Celina Wieniewska. London: Abacus, 1985. Reprint of London: Faber, 1955. 1982. 245p.); *The Captive Mind*. (Translated by Jane Zielonko. Harmondsworth: Penguin, 1985. 251p. Reprint, London: Secker & Warburg, 1953); *The Land of Ulro*. (Translated by Louis Iribarne. Manchester: Carcanet, 1985. 287p.); *Bells in winter*. (Translated by Czesław Miłosz, Lillian Vallee. Manchester: Carcanet New Press, 1980. 71p.); *The witness of poetry*. (Cambridge, Massachusetts: Harvard University Press, 1983. (The Charles Eliot Norton Lectures 1981-82). 121p.). *The Issa Valley*. (Translated by Louis Iribarne. London: Abacus, 1984. 2nd ed. 219p. Reprint, London: Sidgwick & Jackson, 1981); *Postwar Polish poetry; an anthology*. (Selected and edited by Czesław Miłosz. Berkeley: University of California Press, 1983. 191p. Reprint, Harmondsworth: Penguin, 1970); *Emperor of the earth; modes of eccentric vision*. (Berkeley: University of California Press, 1977. 253p.). See also *The eternal moment: the poetry of Czesław*

Miłosz. Aleksander Fiut, translated by Theodosia S. Robertson (Berkeley: University of California Press, 1990. 191p. bibliog.).

737 **The palace.**
Wiesław Myśliwski, translated by Ursula Phillips. London; Chester Springs, Pennsylvania: Peter Owen, 1991. 200p.
Much acclaimed as a major contemporary novel on first publication in Poland in 1970, *The palace* is now faithfully and fluently translated into English by Ursula Phillips of the School of Slavonic Studies, University of London. The novel, which has been made into a film, conveys the death-throes of the feudal aspects of Polish society on the eve of the outbreak of the Second World War.

738 **Poezje. Poems.**
Cyprian Kamil Norwid, translated by Adam Czerniawski. Kraków, Poland: Wydawnictwo Literackie, 1986. 127p.
This translation provides parallel English and Polish texts taken from the 1971 edition of Norwid's *Collected Works*.

739 **The canary and other tales of martial law.**
Marek Nowakowski, translated by Krystyna Broniewska. London: Harvill Press, 1983. 144p.
A collection of short stories by a well-known Polish dissident writer (born 1935) which illuminate the reality of martial law, particularly at the lower social margins. Kołakowski's preface describe them as 'snapshots taken in haste' which 'make a very convincing panorama' of the first weeks of the 'war' against society declared on 13 December 1981.

740 **Five centuries of Polish poetry.**
Jerzy Pietrkiewicz, Burns Singer. London: Secker & Warburg, 1960. Philadelphia: Dufour, 1962. 154p. 2nd rev. ed. Oxford: Oxford University Press, 1970. Reprinted Westport, Massachusetts: Greenwood Press, 1979. 138p. (with new poems in collaboration with John Stallworthy).
A beautifully produced volume which includes good examples from the canon of Polish poetry. The translations were produced by a professor of Polish at London University and two English poets.

741 **The axioms of Si-tien.**
Adam Podgórecki. London: Poets and Painters Press, 1986. 44p.
One of a series of twenty-two such little volumes published between 1971-86 by the same author. They are made up of short stories and anecdotes, up to a page in length, allegedly set in Imperial China, but designed to illustrate timeless aspects of the human condition and behaviour. Titles range from the Stories, Anecdotes, Epigrams, Puzzles, Maxims to the Riddles of the alleged Chinese sage and philosopher Si-tien.

742 **Conversation with the Prince and other poems.**
Tadeusz Różewicz translated by Adam Czerniawski. London: Anvil
Press Poetry, 1982. 181p.

Różewicz is a highly political writer who has experimented dramatically with poetic
form. This is a representative selection of 118 poems, the vast bulk of which have
previously been published. Reprinted in revised form as *They came to see a poet.*
Tadeusz Różewicz, introduced and translated by Adam Czerniawski (London: Anvil
Press, 1991. 231p.). A selection of his other works includes: *Unease.* translated by V.
Contoski (St Paul, Minnesota: New Rivers Press, 1980. 156p.); *Green rose.* translated
by Geoffrey Thurley (Darlington, Australia: John Michael Group, 1982. 64p.);
Mariage blanc: and the hungry artist departs, translated by Adam Czerniawski (New
York; London: Boyars, 1983. 211p. (translations of two plays)); *The survivor and other
poets*, translated and introduced by Magnus J. Kryński, Robert Maguire (Princeton:
Princeton University Press, 1977. 160p. (Parallel Polish text and English translation));
and *Selected Poems. Tadeusz Różewicz*, translated and introduced by Adam
Czerniawski (Harmondsworth, England: Penguin, 1976. 140p. [Penguin Modern
Poets]).

743 **The complete fiction of Bruno Schulz.**
Bruno Schulz, afterword by Jerzy Ficowski, translated by Celina
Wieniewska. New York: Walker & Co, 1989. 324p.

Schulz, the son of a Jewish merchant, was shot dead by an SS officer in November 1942
on the streets of his home-town of Drohybycz in Galicia where he had taught art at the
local school during the interwar period. This collection contains the translated texts of
his two prose collections 'The Street of Crocodiles' (originally published as 'Cinnamon
Shops', 1934) and 'Sanatorium under the sign of the hourglass' (1937) as well as twelve
of his previously unpublished drawings. Also appeared as *The fictions of Bruno Schulz*,
translated by Celina Wieniewska (London: Picador, 1988. 303p. Reprint, Harmondsworth: Penguin, 1977). Partial editions were: *The Street of Crocodiles, translated
by Celina Wieniewska* (London: Pan-Picador, 1980. 111p. Reprint, New York: Walker,
1963). *Cinnamon Shops* (London: McGibbon & Kee, 1963). See also Schulz's other
works, *Sanatorium under the sign of the hourglass* (Translated by Celina Wieniewska.
London: Hamish Hamilton, 1979. 178p.); *The booke of idolatry*. Edited & introduced
by Jerzy Ficowski, translated by Bogna Piotrowska (Warsaw: Interpress, 1988. 118p.);
The drawings of Bruno Schulz. Edited and introduced by Jerzy Ficowski, essay by Ewa
Kuryluk (Chicago: Northwestern University Press, 1991); *Myths and realities: seven
essays on Bruno Schulz*, Russell E. Brown (München: Sagner, 1991. 131p. [Slavistische
Beiträge no. 276]. bibliog.).

744 **Polish Romantic drama: three plays in translation. Dziady – Nieboska
Komedia – Fantazy.**
Edited by Harold B. Segel. Ithaca, New York: Cornell University
Press, 1977. 322p.

Explains and presents the plots of the three plays mentioned in the title by Mickiewicz,
Krasiński and Słowacki.

745 **With fire and sword in modern translation.**
Henryk Sienkiewicz, translated by Wiesław S. Kuniczak, foreword by
James S. Michener. New York: Copernicus Society of America –
Hippocrene Books, 1991. 1,135p.

The first volume of a proposed translation of Sienkiewicz' Trilogy (*Potop* and *Pan Wołodyjowski*). Kuniczak's expanded translation, specially adapted for an American-English readership, was criticized for going far beyond translation and for 'co-creating' his own version. See also *In Desert and in Wilderness*, translated by Max Antoni Drezma (Warsaw: Polonia, 1991. 452p.); *Quo Vadis?* translated by C. J. Hogarth (Gloucester, UK: Sutton, 1989. 447p. [Continental Classics series]); and *Charcoal sketches and other tales*, translated by Adam Zamoyski (London: Angel Books, 1990. 211p.).

746 **In my father's court: a memoir.**
Isaac Bashevis Singer, translated from the Yiddish by Channah
Kleinerman-Goldstein, Elaine Gottlieb, Joseph Singer.
Harmondsworth, England: Penguin, 1980. 253p. Reprint, London:
Secker & Warburg, 1967; New York: Farrar, Straus & Giroux, 1966.

Singer's great contributions to Yiddish literature are not included in this volume, except where as in this publication, they have a direct bearing on the Polish condition. Here Singer reminisces on the life and experiences of his father's rabbinical court, during his childhood at number 10 Krochmalna (Starch) Street in Warsaw, before the First World War. These pen-portraits have been heavily praised for their lively and colourful evocation of a long-lost way of life focusing on the Rabbi's role as priest, social counsellor, mediator, personal adviser and scholar within the Jewish community of that time and place. The reader may also be interested in the light parable *The Fools of Chelm* (translated from the Yiddish by Isaac Bashevis Singer, Elizabeth Shub, illustrated by Uri Shulewicz. New York: Farrar, Straus & Giroux, 1973. 57p).

747 **An empty room.**
Leopold Staff, translated by Adam Czerniawski. Newcastle, England:
Bloodaxe Books, 1983. 60p.

Contains a selection of thirty-nine of the postwar poems of Leopold Staff (1878-1957) who is widely considered to be one of the most influential modern Polish poets. These poems have been praised for their powerful simplicity and economy of form. The collection is prefaced by short appreciations of Staff's work by such writers and critics as Czesław Miłosz, Artur Sandauer, Mieczysław Jastrun, Kazimierz Wyka and Ryszard Przybylski.

748 **Bitter harvest: the intellectual revolt behind the Iron Curtain.**
Edited by Edmund Stillman, introduction by François Bondy.
London: Thames & Hudson; New York: Praeger, 1959. 313p.

Contains poems, short stories and essays by East European writers. They express dissent, anger and frustration against the conditions created by the Stalinist bureaucracy. One should also mention here the following one-time classic and more broad-based collection of thirty-seven stories and essays edited by Maria Kuncewiczowa, *The Modern Polish Mind; an anthology of stories and essays by writers living in Poland today* (Boston: Little, Brown, 1962. London: Secker & Warburg, 1963. 440p. bibliog.).

749 **Sounds, feelings, thoughts: seventy poems.**
Wisława Szymborska, translated by Magnus J. Kryński, Robert A. Maguire. Princeton New Jersey: Princeton University Press, 1981. 215p.

A parallel Polish-English text, *Poezje – Poems*, of this anthology of Szymborska's (born 1923) poems was published in Warsaw by Interpress in 1989, 237p. Selected translations of work by modern Polish poets also appear in the following anthologies; D & J. Abse, *Voices in the gallery* (London: 1985); Alan Bold, *Penguin Book of socialist verse* (Harmondsworth: Penguin, 1970); Tom Paulin, *The Faber Book of Political Verse* (London: Faber, 1986. 482p.); George Theiner, *They shoot writers, don't they?* (London: Faber, 1984. 199p.); Charles Tomlinson, *The Oxford Book of verse in English* (Oxford: Oxford University Press, 1983. 608p.).

The Arts

History of art

750 **Baroque in Poland.**
Mariusz Karpowicz, translated by Jerzy A. Bałdyga. Warsaw: Arkady, 1991. 350p. (History of Art in Poland). bibliog.
This volume covers the early and mature Baroque period from 1582 to 1710 in richly illustrated detail, with some colour plates. Also available in the same format is Zygmunt Świechowski's *Romanesque art in Poland*, (translated by Alina Kozińska-Bałdyga, Jerzy Bałdyga. Warsaw: Arkady, 1983. 279p).

751 **Neoclassicism in Poland.**
Stanisław Lorentz, Andrzej Rottermund, translated by Jerzy Bałdyga. Warsaw: Arkady, 1986. 309p.
An attractive large-format work made up of a commentary by Lorentz on the artistic beginnings of the Polish Enlightenment, the style and patronage of the period of Stanisław Augustus, and the architectural landscape and painting of the Age of the Enlightenment, as well as trends in nineteenth century Polish Neoclassicism (p. 6-49). The second section is composed of numerous illustrations of the buildings, paintings and artistic work discussed above. The final section is a catalogue drawn up by Rottermund (1974), organized by sections on works in the fields of architecture, painting, sculpture and artistic handicrafts as well as an index of localities and monuments (p. 237-89).

752 **Polish realities. The arts in Poland 1980-89.**
Edited by Donald Pirie, Jekaterina Young, Christopher Carrel.
Glasgow: Third Eye Centre, 1990. 176p. bibliog.

This glossy anthology stems from a city-wide season, initiated by the Third Eye Centre in Glasgow and presented there in partnership with the Polish Ministry of Culture in late 1988. Various chapters cover the range of contemporary arts including literature, theatre, film, visual arts, music, and architecture.

753 **Poland. Nation and art: a history of a nation's awareness and its expression in art.**
Maria Suchodolski, Bogdan Suchodolski, translated by Magdalena Iwińska, Piotr Paszkiewicz. Warsaw: Arkady, 1989. 477p.

Contains 594 illustrations, some in colour, on attractive glossy paper in large format. The paintings are set out in eight chapters with accompanying commentary by the very distinguished authors as follows: Poland – from the Piasts to the Commonwealth: social integration of the nation; historical consciousness, the Homeland, its landscape and environment; World-View and Man's Destiny; the workday and holidays; the Kingdom of Art as a creative force. The volume presents a complex picture of the changing relationship between Polish national and social consciousness and the development of the country's painting.

754 **Symbolism in Poland: collected essays.**
Detroit: Detroit Institute of Arts, 1984. 63p.

The discussion covers the art and literature of the 'Młoda Polska' (Young Poland) pre-Great War Neo-Romantic period. A supplementary publication to an exhibition of Polish Symbolist Art, 1890-1940, held in Summer 1984.

755 **A history of Poland in painting.**
Janusz Walek, translated by Katarzyna Zawadzka. Warsaw: Interpress, 1988. 174p.

An illustrated colour album demonstrating the historical development of Poland through the medium of fine art.

756 **An outline history of Polish applied art.**
Zdzisław Żygulski, translated by Stanisław Tarnowski. Warsaw: Arkady – PWM, 1987. 263p.

A pictorial history of Polish folk-art and handicrafts by Żygulski, a former Polish Minister of Culture. The commentary is at a very high-quality level and this is undoubtedly the most authoritative and comprehensive work on the subject.

Architecture

757 The royal cathedral at Wawel.
Michał Bożek. Warsaw: Interpress, 1981. 177p.
An illustrated introduction for a popular readership. It provides a clear outline which is quite sufficient for most non-specialist purposes.

758 The Marian altar of Wit Stwosz.
Tadeusz Chrzanowski, translated by Emma Harris Warsaw: Interpress, 1985.
An account of the life and work of Wit Stwosz (1447-1533) who came to Kraków in 1477. He was an outstanding painter and sculptor who produced such masterpieces as the celebrated Gothic altar in St Mary's Church, the largest in Europe. The author provides a detailed discussion of the altar and its history. Lavish illustrations and many colour photographs depict the minutest aspects of this impressive work of art from all angles.

759 Gothic architecture in the reign of Kasimir the Great. Church architecture in Lesser Poland, 1320-80.
Paul Crossley. Kraków, Poland: Ministerstwo Kultury i Sztuki, Zarząd Muzeów i Ochrony Zabytków – Państwowe Zbiory Sztuki na Wawelu, 1985. 492p. (Biblioteka Wawelska no. 7).
Architecture and building flourished during the reign of Kazimierz the Great (1333-70), who proverbially inherited a Poland of wood and left it in stone. This study, based on much original research in Kraków, shows how Poland evolved its unique Gothic style, distinct from German models. Crossley reaches very balanced conclusions about the scope and significance of the achievement.

760 Masters of contemporary art. Poland.
Thomas W. Leavitt. Ithaca, New York: Herbert F. Johnson Museum of Art, 1986. 72p.
An illustrated, but given the confines of space, somewhat eclectic selection of contemporary painting in Poland which pays some attention to architectural settings.

761 Polish art and architecture.
Andrzej K. Olszewski, translated by Stanisław Tarnowski. Warsaw: Interpress, 1989. 184p. bibliog.
An illustrated history covering the main trends and individuals in Polish art and architecture during the last century.

762 **The shrine of the Black Madonna at Częstochowa.**
Janusz Stanisław Pasierb, Jan Samek, translated by Bogna
Piotrowska. Warsaw: Interpress, 1989. 3rd ed. 223p.
Contains a twenty page introduction to the history and significance of the Black
Madonna at Częstochowa. The bulk of the publication is composed of high quality
colour plates illustrating it from various angles and showing its context and associated
decorations in the Częstochowa chapel and monastery.

763 **St. Mary's church in Cracow.**
Jan Samek, translated by Chester Kisiel. Warsaw: Interpress-
AGROS, 1990. 251p. bibliog.
Samek's thirty-one page introduction sets out the background to the history of Saint
Mary's church in Kraków, one of Poland's most famous. The remainder of the book is
made up of very attractive colour plates of the church's magnificent internal
architecture and decorations as well as of its external situation in the Old Town
Square.

764 **Polish painting from the Enlightenment to recent times.**
Tadeusz Dobrowolski, translated by Tadeusz Rykowski. Wrocław,
Poland: Ossolineum, 1982. 339p.
A fine collection of Polish paintings, some in colour, drawn from the last two centuries.
Covers the main schools and the most prominent individuals.

765 **Icons from Poland.**
Janina Kłocińska, translated by Magda Iwińska, Piotr Paszkiewicz.
Warsaw: Arkady, 1989. 19p. bibliog.
Contains attractive photographs, some in colour, as well as discussion of seventy icons;
most of these icons originated from Ukrainian inhabited, and therefore religiously
Orthodox, areas of south-eastern Poland during the fifteenth to the nineteenth
centuries. The editor discusses the style, significance and methods of production of
these icons in her introduction and includes a useful bibliography.

766 **Passion by design; the art and times of Tamara de Lempicka.**
Baronness Kizette de Lempicka-Foxhall as told to Charles Phillips.
Oxford: Phaidon Press, 1989. 2nd ed. 192p.
Tamara de Lempicka (née Górska, 1898-1980) was a notable personality on the
interwar cultural scene in Paris, Hollywood and New York. She was an inventor of the
Art Deco style of painting, long before Warhol or Buffet. Her aristocratic marriages,
social and cultural connections and personal flamboyance (à la Garbo) gained her
considerable acclaim, but she fell into obscurity after the Second World War. Her story
is recounted by her daughter and her work is amply illustrated in its striking colour
along with photographs of herself and her entourage.

767 **Rzepiński, Czesław. Malarstwo (paintings).**
Edited by Ryszard Kumorek, translated by Marianna Abrahomowicz.
Warsaw: Krajowa Agencja Wydawnicza, 1986. 162p.
Parallel Polish-English texts. Some of the reproductions are in colour. Rzepiński (born 1905) was linked with the interwar 'Zwornik' and later 'Colourist' schools. He specialized in countrysides, still-life and figures becoming a professor and Rector of the Fine Arts Academy in Kraków.

768 **Polish painting 15th to 20th century.**
Agnieszka Morawińska. Warsaw: Auriga, 1981. 36p.
An illustrated presentation which attempts a synthetic overview of art in the modern age.

769 **Polish contemporary graphic art. Studio graphics. The poster. Book design. Press design.**
Danuta Wróblewska. Warsaw: Interpress, 1988. 188p.
A richly illustrated historical guide to the topics mentioned in the title. The author also includes biographies of contemporary and recent Polish graphic artists with fine quality illustrations of their work.

Performing Arts

Music

770 **Chopin playing. from the composer to the present day.**
James Methuen Campbell. London: Victor Gollancz, 1981. 289p.
A historical and geographical overview of the changing art of the great Chopin players showing the factors that have formed their interpretative styles.

771 **Polish folk music. Slavonic heritage. Polish tradition. Contemporary trends.**
Anna Czekanowska. Cambridge, England: Cambridge University Press, 1990. 226p. (Cambridge Studies in Ethnomusicology). maps. bibliog.
The Director of the Institute of Musicology of the University of Warsaw discusses Polish folk music in all its varied national, regional and *emigré* forms. She considers Poland's folk music legacy to be made up of three basic strata - the Old Slavonic, the dominant culture of the Commonwealth period and the Romantic nineteenth and twentieth century trends which re-transmitted folklorist elements in new patterns.

772 **Chopin. Pianist and teacher as seen by his pupils.**
Jean-Jacques Eigeldinger, translated from the French by Naomi Shohet, Krysia Osostowicz, edited by Ray Howat. Cambridge, England: Cambridge University Press, 1986. 324p. bibliog.
A detailed academic musicological examination, not so much of the Chopin School or Tradition, which Eigeldinger claims he did not found, as of his moulding of his pupils and their influence on later interpretations of his music. The study argues that Chopin ranks foremost amongst modern pianist-pedagogues and that he should be regarded as Mozart's heir and Debussy's predecessor in terms of individual genius. See also William G. Attwood, *Frederyk Chopin; pianist from Warsaw.* (New York: Columbia University Press, 1987. 305p. bibliog.)

773 **Conversations with Witold Lutosławski.**
Tadeusz Kaczyński, translated by Yolanta May.   London: Chester Music, 1984. 152p.

These conversations allowed Lutosławski to talk in a fairly specialized way about his major works composed during 1963-76 (Trois pièces d'Henri Michaux, Paroles Tissées, the Second Symphony, Livre pour l'Orchestre, Les éspaces du sommeil and Mi-parti). He also presented his general views of the problems of contemporary music and musical criticism.

774 **Composing myself.**
Andrzej Panufnik.   London: Methuen, 1987. 369p.

The lively autobiography of the life, times and music of this celebrated composer (1914-92). Panufnik settled in the United Kingdom after defecting from Poland in 1954 and was eventually knighted in recognition of his musical achievement.

775 **Artur Rubinstein, 1887-1982.**
Edited by Bożena Pietraszczyk.   Łódź, Poland: MHML, 1990. 150p.

A compilation, with parallel Polish-English texts, on the virtuoso pianist Rubinstein, who is best known for his performances of Chopin and Szymanowski during his life abroad (mainly in France and the USA). See also his autobiography *My many years*. (London: Cape, 1980. 626p.).

776 **Grażyna Bacewicz: her life and works.**
Judith Rosen.   Los Angeles: University of Southern California, School of Music, 1984. 74p.

Popularizes the music of Grażyna Bacewicz (1906-1969) a violinist and composer of works for orchestra and string quartets.

777 **Rock around the bloc; history of rock music in Eastern Europe and the Soviet Union.**
Timothy W. Ryback.   New York: Oxford University Press, 1990. 272p. bibliog.

A Harvard University history professor chronicles the penetration of rock music in its various forms, including punk, funk, reggae and heavy metal, into the mass cultures of Eastern Europe. Poland is well-covered throughout and especially in chapter twelve which deals with 'Punk in Poland, 1980-86'.

778 **Chopin studies.**
Edited by Jim Samson.   Cambridge, England: Cambridge University Press, 1988. 258p.

A highly academic work for musicologists which includes chapters by specialists like Jeffrey Kallberg and Jean-Jacques Eigeldinger on aspects of his musical language, his intentions as revealed in autograph sources as well as case-studies of individual works.

779 **The music of Chopin.**
Jim Samson. London: Routledge & Kegan Paul, 1985. 243p. bibliog.

A well-known British academic musicologist from Exeter University produces a critical study of Chopin's music analysing its style and structure in the light of both recent Chopin scholarship and modern analytical methods. Samson includes a comprehensive 'List of Works' (p. 235-38). For more popular introductions see Richard Tames' *Polish piano music. Chopin, Frederic 1810-49.* (London: Watts, 1991. 32p.) and Zofia Jeżewska, *Chopin.* (Warsaw: Interpress, 1986).

780 **Music of Szymanowski.**
Jim Samson. London: Kahn & Averill, 1980; 2nd ed, 1990. 220p. bibliog.

The first major English language evaluation of the life and work of Karol Szymanowski (1882-1937) and of the significance of his music. Samson explains why Szymanowski's reputation outside Poland, which has long been neglected, is becoming more widely recognized, and includes a list of his works (p. 211-13). For a good introduction to Szymanowski's work, see C. Palmer's, *Szymanowski.* (London: BBC Music Guides, 1983. 104p.)

781 **Karol Szymanowski. An anthology.**
Edited by Zdzisław Sierpiński, translated by Emma Harris. Warsaw: Interpress, 1986. 216p. bibliog.

This anthology of writings on Szymanowski contains a list of his compositions (p. 208-13).

782 **Fryderyck Chopin. A diary in images.**
Mieczysław Tomaszewski, Bożena Weber, translated by Rosemary Hunt. Warsaw: Arkady – Polskie Wydawnictwo Muzyczne, 1990. 270p.

A popular chronicle of Chopin's life and work (1810-49), with numerous illustrations, of Chopin, his family, and travels, as well as facsimiles of his letters and musical notations. The lively text also includes fragments of letters, anecdotes and reminiscences. Published in October 1990 for the Chopin Piano Competition in Polish and English versions.

783 **Chopin. A new biography.**
Adam Zamoyski. New York: Doubleday, 1980. London: Collins, 1980: Granada, 1981. 416p.

A perceptive and witty biography which dispels the Romantic aura that surrounds Poland's greatest composer. Without going into much musical criticism it provides a clear exposition of his creative genius and his personal life stressing his lifelong commitment to the Polish national cause. Includes a complete list of Chopin's works arranged by date.

784 **Paderewski. A biography of the pianist and statesman.**
Adam Zamoyski.   London: Collins; New York: Atheneum Press,
1982. 289p. maps. bibliog.
Zamoyski reviews recent new work and material on Paderewski's life and career in this
readable biography. It includes a list of his works and musical *opus*.

Theatre

785 **Twentieth century Polish theatre.**
Edited by Bohdan Drozdowski, translated by Catherine Itzin.
London: J. Calder, 1979. 249p. bibliog.
A collection of plays and essays designed to provide a survey of classic and
contemporary Polish theatre. It highlights its most notable practitioners such as
Grotowski and Kantor, and contains a bibliography of Polish plays in English
translation (p. 233-49).

786 **The theatre of Andrzej Wajda.**
Maciej Karpiński.   Cambridge, England: Cambridge University Press,
1989. 135p. (Directors in Perspective).
A critical and comprehensive evaluation of Wajda's work in the theatre, which is quite
significant and complements his achievements as one of the world's most outstanding
film-directors. Written by a well-known Polish writer and drama critic.

787 **The theatre of Grotowski.**
Jennifer Kumiega.   London: Methuen, 1985. 290p. bibliog.
A detailed and perceptive study of the development of the work of Jerzy Grotowski
(born 1933) and his experimental Polish Laboratory Theatre which was largely based in
Wrocław up until its closure in 1984.

788 **National theatre in Northern and Eastern Europe, 1746-1900**
Edited by Laurence Senelick.   Cambridge, England: Cambridge
University Press, 1991. 480p. bibliog.
The chapter on Poland by Karyna Wierzbicka-Michalska (p. 189-230) covers the
period from the inauguration of the National Theatre in 1765, through its
establishment as what the author calls 'a strong and durable element of Polish cultural
life' up to the 1830-31 insurrection. The chapter contains twenty-three readings made
up of a mixture of major commentaries and original sources of the time on the subject.

Cinema

789 World cinema. Poland.

Frank Bren. London: Flicks, 1986. 2nd ed. 209p. bibliog.

A good interpretative overview carried out by historical periods up to post-martial law. It also contains interviews with Wajda and Zanussi and a chronology of the Polish cinema.

790 The Polish film. Yesterday and today.

Stanisław Janicki. Warsaw: Interpress, 1985. 120p.

A heavily illustrated popular overview of the development of the Polish film during the twentieth century.

791 The modern cinema of Poland.

Bolesław Michałek, Frank Turaj. Bloomington, Indiana: Indiana University Press, 1988. 205p. bibliog.

The introductory chapters overview the development of the postwar film industry in Poland. Subsequent chapters provide separate and excellent coverage of Jerzy Kawalerowicz, Andrzej Munk, Andrzej Wajda and Krzystof Zanussi. Concentrates on how the film has both mirrored and helped to make history in Poland.

792 Politics, art and commitment in the East European cinema.

Edited by David W. Paul. Basingstoke, England: Macmillan, 1983. 314p.

This study shows the gradual but basic shift after 1956 of the East European cinema away from commitment to a Socialist Realist style. Polish films are covered in most of the general discussions, while Bolesław Michałek discusses Andrzej Wajda's work in a separate chapter. The appendices discuss the influence of the 1980-81 events in Poland on its film culture.

793 Poland. The cinema of moral concern.

Frank Turaj. In: *Post new wave cinema in the Soviet Union and Eastern Europe*. Edited by Daniel J. Goulding. Bloomington, Indiana: Indiana University Press, 1989. p. 143-71.

A good overview of the major Polish films of the 1980s, which emphasizes the challenges and the problems posed for the film industry by the strained political situation.

794 Double vision. My life in film.

Andrzej Wajda. London: Faber, 1989. 136p.

Wajda explains the film-making process on the basis of the development of his films. He takes the reader through the various stages from an idea in the director's head, through the written scenario, the shooting and editing phases and the finished product at the premiere.

795 **Roman Polański. A guide to references and resources.**
Virginia Wright-Wexman. Boston, Massachusetts: Twayne
Publishers, 1985. 149p. (Twayne's Filmmakers series). London:
Columbus, 1987. 160p. bibliog.
A fine discussion setting out all the relevant information on Polański's life and work.
Born in 1933 in Paris, of Polish-Jewish origins, his family returned to Poland in 1936.
After surviving the Second World War, he made his earliest films there, but left Poland
after making *Knife in the Water* (1963); his subsequent and best known films such as
Repulsion, Chinatown, Dance of the Vampires, Rosemary's Baby and *Frantic* were
made in the USA and have had little direct Polish influence although he has produced
some work in the Polish theatre. Polański's notorious personal life is the subject of
Thomas Kiernan's *The Roman Polański story* (New York: Grove Press, 1980. 262p).
Barbara Leaming's *Polański. The film-maker as voyeur* (New York: Simon & Schuster,
1982. 220p.) is a critical and well-researched biography. See also the autobiography
Polański (New York: William Morrow, 1981. 461p.; London: PAN – Heinemann,
1985. 456p.).

Ballet

796 **A history of Polish ballet 1518-1945.**
Jan Ciepliński, edited & translated from the Polish by Anna Emma
Lesiecka. London: Veritas Foundation, 1983. 82p.
A knowledgeable historical overview by a celebrated interwar Polish ballet-master and
choreographer (1900-1972) with wide international experience. See also *Polish opera
and ballet of the twentieth century. Operas, ballets, pantomimes, miscellaneous works
and illustrated catalogues*. Adam Neuer (editor), translated by Jerzy Zawadzki
(Kraków: Polskie Wydawnictwo Muzyczne, 1986. 132p.).

Folklore, Cuisine, Folk-art and Customs

Folklore and folk-art

797 **Folk-art in Poland.**
Ewa Fryś-Pietraszkowa, Anna Kunczyńska-Iracka, Marian Pokropek, translated by Jerzy A. Bałdyga. Warsaw: Arkady, 1991. 2nd ed. 351p.

A richly illustrated discussion, with some colour plates, of all aspects of Polish folk-art ranging from architecture, pottery, decorative ironwork, fabrics. costume, sculpture, painting, graphic art, ritual art and customs to contemporary folk-art.

798 **In Kaszuby. Regional folk-arts co-operative in Kartuzy.**
Janusz Gierucki, translated by Lech Petrowicz. Warsaw: Wydawnictwo Spółdzielcze, 1987. 23p.

An illustrated brochure on the folk-arts and handicrafts of the picturesque forest and lake Kaszub region to the west of Gdańsk.

799 **Polish folk costumes.**
Text by Christopher Majka, illustrations by Sheilagh Hunt. Halifax, Nova Scotia: Empty Mirrors Press, 1991. 48p.

A basic introduction to the twenty most important Polish folk costumes; each one is described and illustrated and related to its regional origins.

800 **Guide to folk art and folklore in Poland.**
Marian Pokropek. Warsaw: Arkady, 1980. 269p. maps.
This guide deals mainly with wooden objects, including sculpture and objects in
everyday use. It also covers sacred art, coal, rock salt sculpture, earthenware,
embroidery and kelem rugs. Detailed maps and numerous illustrations are included.

Cuisine

801 **A contemporary Polish cookbook.**
Henryk Dębski, translated by Eliza Lewandowska. Warsaw:
Interpress, 1990. 476p.
A comprehensive guide to the culinary arts in Poland. Menus are grouped under
nineteen chapter headings covering everything from hors d'oeuvres to sauces, soups,
fish, meat and game, eggs, desserts, cakes and beverages. Also appears in Polish and
German editions. A similar, but earlier, work including 1,200 recipes for a wide range
of different types of dishes and needs is Zofia Czerny's, *Polish cookbook* translated by
Christina Cenkalska, May Miller (Warsaw: Państwowe Wydawnictwo Ekonomiczne,
1975. 2nd ed. 495p.).

802 **Old Polish traditions in the kitchen and at the table.**
Maria Lemnis, Henryk Vitry, translated by Eliza Lewandowska.
Warsaw: Interpress, 1981. 304p.
A Polish cookbook, made all the more attractive by beautiful reproductions of ancient
engravings, old Polish recipes, anecdotes and examples of special types of Polish
cuisine including hunters' courses and food for festive occasions. The authors also
explore culinary habits and national customs at various social levels.

803 **The Polish kitchen.**
Mary Pinińska, translated by by Christine Simpson. Basingstoke,
England: Macmillan, 1990. 220p.
A treasury of Polish cooking, ancient and modern, presented in an attractive illustrated
form. The various chapters offer a wide range of menus according to type and season.

804 **Old Warsaw cookbook.**
Rysia. New York: Hippocrene, 1990. 304p.
The provenance of this cookbook and its association with Warsaw is somewhat unclear
but it includes a wide range of recipes from appetizers to American, Chinese and
Japanese dishes. 'Rysia' apparently had a Polish childhood but she does a fine job of
adapting her 850 recipes to the conditions of the American kitchen.

805　The best of Polish cooking. Recipes for entertaining and special
occasions.
Karen West.　New York: Hippocrene Books, 1991. 2nd ed. 219p.
A compilation of traditional Polish fare presented in an easy-to-use menu format.
Arrangement follows the seasonal cycle and the menus and foods are designed to
balance each other in a complementary and harmonious manner.

806　Cooking the Polish-Jewish way.
Eugeniusz Wirkowski, translated by Hilda Rusiecka.　Warsaw:
Interpress, 1988. 108p.
Contains an excellent range of traditional everyday dishes illustrating the rich influence
of the Jewish kitchen on cooking in Poland.

Genealogy and honours

807　Polish and proud. Tracing your Polish ancestry.
Jan & Len Gnaciński.　Indianapolis: Ye Olde Genealogie Shoppe,
1983. 78p.
An introductory guide for Polish-Americans interested in discovering their roots.

808　Polish genealogy and heraldry: an introduction to research.
Janina W. Hoskins.　Washington, DC: Library of Congress –
Hippocrene Books, 1987; 1990. 114p.
An introduction for both historians who employ genealogy and heraldry as research
sources, and for Americans of Polish descent who want to discover their ancestral
lines.

809　Polish parish records of the Roman Catholic Church. Their use and
understanding in genealogical research.
Gerald A. Ortell.　Buffalo Grove, Illinois: Genun Publications, 1984.
86p.
A beginner's guide to ecclesiastical records in Polish Catholic parishes as a source for
genealogical research.

810　Polish coats of arms.
Edited by Mieczysław Paszkiewicz, Jerzy Kulczycki in collaboration
with Teresa Korzeniowska.　London: Orbis Books, 1990. 480p.
Contains an index of 20,000 Gentry (*Szlachta*) family surnames by Korzeniowska, the
largest ever published. The volume is otherwise an enlarged edition of Zbigniew
Leszczyc, *Herby Szlachty Polskiej*. (Poznań, Poland: Antoni Fiedler, 1908). The text is
in the original Polish, the coats of arms are reproduced five to a page while the
introductions are in English and Polish.

811 **Tracing your Polish roots.**
Maralyn Wellover. Milwaukee, Wisconsin: The author, 1985. 87p.
maps.
An introductory brochure to local administrative records and other printed sources for Polish-Americans wishing to investigate their family antecedents.

812 **Polish orders, medals, badges and insignia. Military and civilian decorations 1705-1985.**
Zdzisław P. Wesołowski. Miami, Florida: Printing Services, 1987.
404p.
Includes illustrations, some in colour, as well as descriptions of all the military decorations and insignia issued by Polish authorities from the Commonwealth of 1705 till the Polish People's Republic. Also contains material on civilian decorations produced by social and religious bodies and sporting or paramilitary organizations.

Customs

813 **Polish Christmas carols and their cultural context.**
Jerzy Bartmiński. *Slavic and East European Journal*, vol. 34, no. 1
(Spring 1990), p. 83-98.
Illustrates textually in detail his argument that the carol is a key to understanding Polish culture and customs as well as the Polish mentality itself.

Philately

814 **The handbook of Polish perfins in Great Britain 1980-85.**
W. Z. Nowicki. London: Copernicana, 1987. 5 vols.
A comprehensive work which deals with British postage stamps on Polish topics. See also A. Hall, *Poland locals*. (York, England: Barefoot Investments, 1981. 123p. [European Philately series no. 6]). and Jiri Neuman, *The occupation of the Czechoslovak frontier territories by Beck's Poland from the postal point of view* (London: Czechoslovak Philatelic Society of Great Britain, Britain, 1989. 43p. bibliog.).

Sport

815 **Polish sport.**
Zbigniew Chmielewski, translated by Piotr Goc.   Warsaw: Interpress,
1980. 131p.
A guide to the history of Polish sporting achievements. Contains information and the
addresses and committees of the main Polish sporting organizations.

816 **Poland 86. 13th World Cup.**
Stefan Grzegorczyk (et al), translated by Małgorzata Grzegorczyk-
Gonciarz.   Warsaw: Młodzieżowa Agencja Wydawnicza, 1986. 41p.
A coloured commemorative volume on Poland's disappointing performance in the 13th
World Football Championship in Mexico. The team barely survived the qualifying pool
and was easily eliminated by Brazil in the first knockout round.

Libraries, Archives and Museums

817 **A guide to Polish libraries and archives.**
Richard Casimir Lewański. New York: Columbia University Press, 1974. 209p. bibliog. (East European Monographs no. 6).
Provides information on the location, holdings and history of the approximately 100 main library and archival collections on Poland in the USA.

818 **Eastern Europe and Russia/Soviet Union: a handbook of West European archival and library resources.**
Richard Casimir Lewański. New York: K. G. Saur, 1980. 320p. bibliog.
A guide to archival and library holdings of Slavic and East European interest (including those concerning Poland) outside the Slavic and East European area of Europe. Each entry contains comprehensive bibliographies and lists especially important and rare items. The work is arranged schematically and provides catalogues of Slavic and East European materials in individual European countries.

819 **Guide to the archives of the Polish Institute and Sikorski Museum.**
Edited by Wacław Milewski, Andrzej Suchcitz, Andrzej Gorzycki. London: Orbis Books for the Polish Institute and the Sikorski Museum, vol. 1, 1985. 375p.
This work was intended as the first of four volumes. More than three hundred entries give comprehensive information on the material of the Polish Government-in-Exile and the private and subject collections which are housed in the Polish Institute and the Sikorski Museum. This archive constitutes the largest collection of primary documentation outside Poland on Polish history in the period primarily before, during and just after the Second World War. See Bohdan Wroński & Ryszard Dembiński, 'The Polish

Institute and Sikorski Museum in London', *Polish Review*, vol. 30, no. 2 (1985), p. 171-83.

820   **Open-air museums in Poland.**
       Edited by Henryk Nowacki.   Poznań, Poland: Państwowe
       Wydawnictwo Rolnicze i Leśne, 1981. 346p.

A variety of specialists set out the development, organization and problems of open-air museums and rural parks of the 'Skansen' type in Poland. Part Two contains separate chapter descriptions of the dozen major village-parks of this type. Each chapter contains German-language summaries.

821   **The National Museum in Kraków. A historical outline and selected
       objects.**
       Edited by Franciszek Stolot.   Warsaw: Arkady, 1987. 257p. bibliog.

An attractively illustrated introductory guide to the historical background to the museum and the major attractions amongst its contents. See also Joachim Śliwa's *Egyptian scarabs, scaraboids and plaques from the Cracow collections* (Warsaw: Państwowe Wydawnictwo Naukowe, 1985. 93p. + 24 plates).

Books and Book Trade

822 **Books in Poland: past and present.**
Barbara Bieńkowska, Halina Chamerska, edited and translated by
Wojciech Zalewski, Eleanor R. Payne. Wiesbaden, Germany:
O. Harrassowicz, 1990. 110p. bibliog.
Deals with the history of book-publishing, printing, libraries, and archives throughout
Poland's history. Part one (Bieńkowska) covers the history of book-publication in
Poland up till 1980, part two (Chamerska) the history of bibliography, part three
(Bieńkowska, Chamerska) library-history and part four (Chamerska) archival history.
The volume is an interesting overview but is too short to provide in-depth coverage. It
also neglects some modern aspects such as the post-1976 underground publishing
movement.

823 **Underground publishing in Poland.**
Ted Kamiński. *Orbis*, vol. 31, no. 3 (1987), p. 313-29.
Concentrates on clandestine publishing after the declaration of martial law in 1982
especially the major underground presses such as NOWa, KOS, Krąg and *Tygodnik
Mazowsze*. Estimates that about fifteen per cent of the population read the
underground press regularly; the latter formed a major counter-communist alternative
through its links and collaboration with trade unions and independent study and
cultural groups. This also constituted an important data base for Western observers.

824 **Dealers of Polish and Russian books abroad, active 1918 – present. A contribution to the history of the book trade.**
Andrzej Kłossowski, Wojciech Zalewski.   Warsaw; Stanford, California: The National Library – Stanford University Libraries, 1990. 193p.
Confusingly arranged and with irregular and somewhat unreliable annotations. The directory consists of three main sections on post-1945 general Slavic bookdealers, post-1918 sellers of Polish books and of Russian books.

825 **The Ossolinski's National Institute – the publishing house of the Polish Academy of Sciences.**
Jan Trzynadlowski, translated by Irena Jurzywiec.   Wrocław, Poland: Ossolineum, 1987. 67p.
A short overview of the history and activities of one of Poland's most prestigious publishing houses. It publishes the work of the Polish Academy of Sciences as well as a variety of high-quality academic publications and classical literature. Founded in Lwów in 1817 by Józef Maksymilian Ossoliński (1748-1826) it moved to its present home in in Wrocław in 1947.

826 **Book studies in Poland since 1945.**
Wojciech Zalewski. *Solanus*, vol. 2 (1988), p. 56-68.
Book studies in Communist Poland were a vigorous discipline and much less controlled by political factors than elsewhere in Eastern Europe. Zalewski presents a detailed overview of the publications produced by research centres such as libraries, institutes of the Polish Academy of Sciences, University departments and faculties as well as pedagogical colleges, in the field.

827 **Publishing in Poland after 1945.**
Janet Zmroczek. *Solanus*, vol. 5 (1991), p. 61-81.
Discusses two of the three levels of circulation or *obiegi* current in Poland until the collapse of communism, that is the official-state and the dissident-uncensored. The third, emigré publications, is examined by Hanna Świderska, 'Fortunes and misfortunes of Polish emigré publishing after 1945' in the same issue, p. 84-94. The latter is a follow-up to Świderska's 'Independent publishing in Poland; an outline of its development', *Solanus*, vol. 1 (1987), p. 54-75.

Newspapers and Journals

828 **Dziennik Polski.** (Polish Daily.)
London: 1940- . daily.
The main daily newspaper for the British *Polonia*. Its Saturday edition, the *Tydzień Polski* (Polish Weekly), incorporated the *Dziennik Żołnierza* (Soldier's Daily) which had also been published since the Second World War.

829 **Dziennik Związkowy.** (Alliance Daily.)
Chicago: 1881- . biweekly.
One of the longest established American *Polonia* papers and organ of the Polish National Alliance.

830 **Gazeta Wyborcza.** (Electoral News.)
Warsaw: 1989- . daily.
Having started out as Solidarity's daily, this quickly became Poland's best and most widely read newspaper in the early 1990s, under the very capable editorship of Adam Michnik.

831 **Glob 24. Dziennik Illustrowany.** (Globe 24. Illustrated Daily.)
Warsaw: 1991- . daily.
An illustrated and partly coloured all round news review with plenty of advertisements and photographs. The publishers aimed to fill the gap left by the high-powered *Panorama* of the communist era but did not quite succeed at first. The paper fell into financial difficulties and there had been talk of it becoming a weekly in 1992.

Newspapers and Journals

832 **Nie. Dziennik Cotygodniowy.** (No. Weekly Newspaper.)
Warsaw: 1990- . weekly.

A hard-hitting and sensational weekly newspaper specialising in political *exposés* and cartoons. Intended as a serious organ of the populist left, *Nie* makes use of the less attractive traits of the tabloid press, including pornography and explicit language, to gain publicity. It specializes in exposing political scandals and corruption, and made the most of the opportunities for such exposes in the early years of post-communism. The editor is Jerzy Urban, the ex-official press spokesman for the Jaruzelski *regime* of the mid-late 1980s.

833 **Nowa Europa. Dziennik Niezależny.** (The New Europe. An Independent Daily.)
Warsaw: 1991- . daily.

Nowa Europa is jokingly, if inaccurately referred to as Poland's *Financial Times*, because of the pink paper on which it is printed; this does, however, reflect its ambitions and the type of elite readership which it aimed at. It began with the very high-powered Krzysztof Teodor Toeplitz (known colloquially as KTT), as its first editor.

834 **Nowy Dziennik.** (New Daily.)
New York. 1970- . daily.

The most widely read East Coast American *Polonia* daily paper, catering to all generations of the community. A successor to the long-established *Nowy Świat* (New World – 1922).

835 **Państwo i Prawo.** (State and Law.)
Warsaw: 1945- . monthly.

The main journal for academic lawyers and legal specialists, which publishes high-powered articles and reviews and offers news on the development of jurisprudence. Contains English, French and Russian-language summaries of the main articles.

836 **Polityka.** (Politics.)
Warsaw: 1957- . weekly.

An outstanding weekly, with a European, if not world reputation specializing in contemporary Polish and international affairs. Edited from its foundation until the 1980s, when he became directly involved in politics, by Mieczysław F. Rakowski who stamped his communist-reform line on the journal. Rakowski became the last communist Prime Minister as well as the last leader of the PZPR. *Polityka* has not only survived by maintaining the quality of its standards but in the early 1990s had fought off new competitors to maintain its position as the main journal for the Polish intelligentsia.

837 **Po prostu.** (Straight from the shoulder.)
Warsaw: 1990- . weekly.

Harking back in name to the radical students' newspaper of 1956-57 it aimed to establish itself as a similar news and discussion journal for the critical intelligentsia.

838   **Przegląd Sportowy.** (Sports Review.)
      Warsaw: 1945- . weekly.
A successor to a similar interwar publication which established itself as the main Polish periodical covering the whole range of sporting activities.

839   **Przekrój.** (Cross-section.)
      Warsaw: 1945- . weekly.
A weekly news-journal, originally at a very high-quality intellectual level but now aimed at the interests and hobbies of a more popular readership; it also failed to improve its typographical quality as well as its contents during the 1980s.

840   **Res Publica.** (The Common Good.)
      Warsaw (formerly Poznań): 1979- . monthly.
An influential discussion journal for intellectuals which started off on a semi-dissident basis in the late 1970s. Edited by the well-known writer Marcin Król whose extensive family have also played prominent roles since 1980. Another influential, but less highbrow Poznań-based post-communist weekly is *Wprost*, a sort of Polish *L'Express*.

841   **Rzeczpospolita.** (The Republic.)
      Warsaw: 1982- . daily.
The official Government daily publication, *Rzeczpospolita*, publishes official communiqués, and documents as well as good quality news coverage. In 1992 it followed the fashion of the time by printing an 'Economics and Law' supplement on green paper.

842   **Szpilki.** (The Pins.)
      Warsaw: 1935- . weekly.
A humourous and satirical weekly which has an established place in Polish life as it has managed to adapt to changing circumstances and fashions.

843   **Sztandar Młodych.** (Youth Standard.)
      Warsaw: 1950- . daily.
This newspaper has survived the transition from being the official journal of the communist youth movement to becoming a lively and hard-hitting popular news daily.

844   **Trybuna.** (The Tribune.)
      Warsaw: January 1990- . daily.
Trybuna is the successor to *Trybuna Ludu* (The Tribune of the People), the Polish United Workers' Party official daily 1944-1990. The new paper represents the SdRP (the Social Democracy of the Polish Republic). It contains a wide range of good quality news-coverage and commentary.

845   **Twórczość: Miesięcznik Literacko-Krytyczny.** (Creativity: a Monthly Journal of Literary Criticism.)
      Warsaw: 1945- . monthly
A major literary periodical at a very high intellectual level.

846 **Tygodnik Powszechny: Katolickie Pismo Społeczno-Kulturalne.**
(Universal Weekly: the Catholic Social and Cultural Publication.)
Krakow: 1945- . weekly.

The journal of the hierarchy of the Roman Catholic Church in Poland. It survived the communist period by keeping largely to its devotional and pastoral concerns. It contains some discussion of cultural and social questions linked with gnomic political coverage but the main emphasis is, understandably, on ecclesiastical and Vatican matters.

847 **Tygodnik Solidarność.** (Solidarity Weekly.)
Warsaw: 1980-81, May 1989- . weekly.

The main Solidarity journal in 1980-81, and again in 1989, dealing with contemporary affairs and the movement's internal debates over policy. Michnik was the original editor in 1989 but after his replacement by a Wałęsa nominee the Mazowiecki wing was represented by *Gazeta Wyborcza* during 1990 while the *Tygodnik Solidarność* expressed the views of the Wałęsa camp. When Wałęsa became President, and the Solidarity trade union elected Marian Krzaklewski, an independent, as its chairman, the *Tygodnik Solidarność* adopted a more broad-based standpoint. Its influence on the moderate Right was replaced by the daily *Nowy Świat*. *Obserwator Codzienny* launched in Warsaw in December 1991.

848 **Więź.** (The Link.)
Warsaw (formerly Kraków): 1958- . monthly.

The journal of Social-Catholic intellectuals, originally linked to the *Znak* (the Sign) tendency from 1957-72. Edited by Tadeusz Mazowiecki from 1958-81.

849 **Żołnierz Rzeczypospolitej.** (Soldier of the Republic.)
Warsaw: 1990- . daily.

The successor to *Żołnierz Wolności*, established 1945, which had been the official organ of the Polish Army. The weekly, *Żołnierz Polski*, continued, however.

850 **Życie Gospodarcze.** (Economic Life.)
Warsaw: 1945- . weekly.

The most respected and high quality weekly on economic questions.

851 **Życie Literackie.** (Literary Life.)
Kraków: 1951- . weekly.

The main, and mostly successful, competitor to *Twórczość*, in its time, for the title of Poland's major literary-cultural discussion journal.

852 **Życie Warszawy.** (Warsaw Life.)
Warsaw: 1944- . daily.

A popular daily which had already become lively and wide-ranging during the 1980s. In the post-communist period it became much more commercial, even sensationalist, in its successful attempt to maintain its wide appeal.

Professional
Periodicals

853 **American Slavic and East European Review.**
Philadelphia: 1941- . quarterly.
One of the main academic journals covering the whole field of Slavic studies with a good representative spread of articles and reviews on Polish questions.

854 **Antemurale.** (The Bulwark.)
Rome: Instititum Historicum Polonicum, 1954- . annual.
Contains articles in English, Italian and Latin mainly by Polish scholars abroad. Concentrates on Polish ecclesiastical history, relations with the Vatican and on Polish historiography and archival sources in the West.

855 **Archeologia Polona.** (Polish Archaeology.)
Wrocław: Ossolineum, 1958- . annual.
Articles are mainly in English but various other languages are also published. Based on the Institute of Civilization of the Polish Academy of Sciences, the journal concentrates on research on Polish archaeology and on the civilizations of the Oder-Vistula basins.

856 **British Broadcasting Corporation, Monitoring Service: Part 2 – Eastern Europe.**
Reading, England: British Broadcasting Corporation, 1948- . daily.
Contains daily transcripts of translations of news transmitted by radio and television in Poland as part of a wider monitoring service covering the whole of Eastern Europe. These bulletins constitute an important source of up-to-date material on ongoing events in Poland.

857 **Documents in Communist Affairs.**
Edited by Bogdan Szajkowski. Vols. for 1977 (363p. Polish documents
p. 274-88) and 1979 (571p. Poland p. 461-70) were published by the
University College Press, Cardiff; Vol. for 1980, Macmillan. 387p. Vol.
for 1981, Butterworth. 347p. (Poland p. 142-309); Vol. for 1985,
Wheatsheaf–St. Martin's Press. 340p. Vol. for 1986, Brighton:
Harvester Press, 1986. 339p. (Poland p. 247-71).

An irregular series consisting solely of original documents translated into English
covering all the communist regimes. Poland was well represented because of the
author's interests and background as well as the salience of the Polish Crisis at the
time. See also *Communist Affairs: documents and analysis* (London: Butterworth.), a
quarterly edited by Bogdan Szajkowski which appeared from January 1982 (398p.) to
December 1985.

858 **Geographia Polonica.** (Polish Geography.)
Warsaw: 1964- . irregular. maps.

The journal of the Institute of Geography and Territorial Economy of the Polish
Academy of Sciences. Articles are mainly in English, occasionally in French, and
concentrate on Polish research on geographical, environmental and regional studies.

859 **Journal of Central European Affairs.**
Boulder, Colorado: University of Colorado, 1943- . quarterly.

A high-quality academic journal, whose articles, commentaries and book-reviews
concentrate on history, politics, sociology and economics.

860 **Law in Eastern Europe.**
Leiden, Netherlands: Documentation Office for East European Law,
Leiden University, 1958- .

This series is composed of monographs and translations on East European law,
legislation and official documentation. It is an important and academically respected
source of material in this field.

861 **New Polish publications: a monthly review of Polish books.**
Warsaw: Agpol Press, 1953- . monthly.

This was one of the most useful sources during the communist period for reviews of
new books, announcements of future publications and the plans of Polish publishing
houses as well as essays on Polish writers, cultural events and the literary scene in
general.

862 **Oeconomica Polona.** (Polish Economics.)
Warsaw: Polskie Towarzystwo Ekonomiczne, 1974- . quarterly.

The high-powered specialist journal of the Polish Economic Society and the
Committee of Economic Sciences of the Polish Academy of Sciences.

863 **Poland.**
Warsaw: Interpress, 1954- . quarterly.
A lively review with articles, commentaries, interviews and translations presenting the wide range of pro-official views on postwar Polish reality.

864 **Polin.**
Oxford, England: Basil Blackwell, Institute for Polish-Jewish Studies, 1986- . quarterly.
An academic journal of Polish-Jewish Studies founded by Antony Polonsky and his associates which quickly established itself as the premier journal in the field.

865 **Polish-American Studies.**
New York: Polish-American Historical Association, 1944- . semi-annual.
The journal concentrates on the life, views and activities of the American *Polonia* and on Polish-American relations in general.

866 **Polish Film.**
Warsaw: 1949- . fortnightly.
A bilingual, English-French journal, on the life of the Polish film industry.

867 **Polish Music.**
Warsaw: Authors' Agency, 1966- . quarterly.
Contains articles, commentaries and announcements about current developments and events in the field of Polish music.

868 **Polish Perspectives.**
Warsaw: Polish Institute of International Affairs (PISM), 1958- . monthly.
Concentrates on Poland's foreign relations and external problems within the context of its political and cultural development. It also has some coverage designed to explain Poland's domestic developments to a foreign readership and contains book reviews.

869 **The Polish Review.**
New York: The Polish Institute of Arts and Sciences in America, 1956- quarterly.
The Polish Review became the major academic journal outside of Poland, covering the whole field of Polish Studies (articles, commentaries, book reviews and announcements of events) under the editorial direction of Professor Ludwik Krzyżanowski. After his death in 1986, when Stanisław Barańczak became editor, the quality of the contributions in politics, history and sociology declined while the amount of literary coverage and the general polemical tone increased.

Professional Periodicals

870 **Polish Round Table.**
Wrocław, Poland: Ossolineum, 1967-81. originally irregular, then annual.

This was the interdisciplinary yearbook of the Polish Association of Political Science up till the 1980 crisis by which time ten volumes had appeared. Since then the latter body has published it as the *Polish Political Science Yearbook*. The same format of about a dozen articles, book reviews, a bibliography of works on political subjects published in Poland during the year and a chronicle of the profession's life and activities has been maintained and developed. Most volumes have been about 300 pages in length.

871 **Polish Sociological Bulletin.**
Wrocław, Poland: Ossolineum, 1961- . semi-annual.

Reflecting the interests of its sponsor, the Polish Sociological Association, this journal publishes articles in the field of Polish sociological studies, book-reviews, commentaries as well as announcements on current developments and publications.

872 **Polish Western Affairs.**
Poznań, Poland: Instytut Zachodni, 1960- . semi-annual.

Mainly in English but with some French- and German-language articles, *Polish Western Affairs* reflects the interests of the Western Institute in Poznań in Polish-German relations, the Oder-Neisse frontier and territories and maritime and military affairs.

873 **Polish Yearbook of International Law.**
Wrocław, Poland: Ossolineum, 1970- . annual.

Published in English and French by the relevant committee of the Polish Academy of Sciences. The yearbook contains articles on Polish international law, and the legal regulation of such aspects as foreign trade, as well as commentaries by Polish legal specialists on current problems.

874 **Slavonic and East European Review.**
London: School of Slavonic and East European Studies, University of London, 1922- . quarterly.

One of the two major academic quarterlies in the UK covering the whole range of Slavonic studies but concentrating on history, literature and language. The journal carries authoritative articles and a wide range of book reviews.

875 **Soviet Studies.**
Glasgow: 1948- . quarterly.

Complements the previous item by concentrating on more contemporary aspects of the politics, and especially the economics, of what used to be the communist bloc in the USSR and Eastern Europe. There was considerable coverage of Polish issues during the 1980s because of the salience of the country's development during the decade as well as the increasing pressure of Polish academics to get published in the West. In common with many of the journals in this field a change of name was being contemplated, because of the demise of communism, as this book went to press.

876 **Studies on International Relations.**
Warsaw: Polish Institute of International Affairs (PISM), 1973- . semi-
annual.

PISM also publishes various other serials; *Zbiór Dokumentów – Receueil de Documents*
published as a quarterly since 1988, but a continuation of a much older series, contains
the major documents on Poland's external relations mainly in Polish but with some
English translations. Since 1990 a selection of the articles from its monthly journal
Sprawy Międzynarodowe has been published in English translation in the series
International Affairs Studies.

877 **The Review of the Polish Academy of Sciences.**
Warsaw: 1956- . quarterly.
A calender of events and developments in the world of Polish academe.

878 **The Theatre in Poland.**
Warsaw: Institut International du Théâtre, 1958- . monthly.

An attractively illustrated journal in English and French, giving information on new
performances in Poland and abroad, proposed new productions, news about actors and
directors as well as books and press-reviews on the theatre.

Encyclopaedias and Directories

879 **Encyklopedia popularna PWN.** (The popular PWN encyclopaedia.)
Warsaw: Państwowe Wydawnictwo Naukowe, 1992. 22nd ed. 1,008p.

The first post-communist edition of this general single volume encyclopaedia, like its predecessors, it contains a wealth of information about all aspects of Poland, past and present as well as on the general realm of knowledge. It was rightly praised for its splendid coloured illustrations and maps, 1,000 portraits and the up-to-date and objective information contained in its 80,000 entries, and it became an instant bestseller. The State Publishing House had earlier produced an excellent universal encyclopedia in four volumes which is also of interest: *Encyclopedia Powszechna PWN* (Warsaw: Państwowe Wydawnictwo Naukowe, 1983-88. 2nd ed.).

880 **The Soviet Union and Eastern Europe.**
Edited by George Schopflin. London: Muller, Blond & White, 1986.
2nd rev. ed. 637p. maps. (Handbooks to the Modern World).

An area studies guide which provides a country-by-country survey and analysis of key topics such as ideology, political structure, military affairs, and education.

881 **Informator. Polska 91.**
Waldemar Siwiński (et al). Warsaw: Polska Agencja Prasowa, 1990.
400p.

An information guide giving addresses, office-holders and other relevant information concerning the Parliament, Government, central and local bureaus, political parties, trade-unions, churches, education, culture, mass media, business, banking, law, sports and tourism and diplomatic representation. Also contains a Who's Who of prominent personalities, although there are some notable omissions. An English-language edition, along with the continuation of this series on an annual basis (earlier volumes had covered 1984-85 and 1988-89) have been suggested. This seemed essential in view ɔf the end of publication of the *Rocznik Polityczny i Gospodarczy* (Warsaw: Państwowe Wydawnictwo Ekonomiczne, 1949-88) which had provided an indispensable source of comprehensive official information on the communist period in its thirty-nine annual editions. Other useful Polish-language directories and general encyclopedia guides to the country are: *Polska Ludowa. Słownik encyklopedyczny* (Warsaw: Wiedza Powszechna, 1965. 483p.); *Polska. Zarys Encyklopedyczny* (Warsaw: Państwowe Wydawnictwo Naukowe, 1974. 820p.); *Polska. Informator* (Warsaw: Interpress, 1977. 632p.). The most comprehensive compendium on political and state office-holders for the whole of the postwar period is Tadeusz Mołdawa, *Ludzie Władzy, 1944-91* (Warsaw: PWN, 1991. 484p.).

882 **The Polish biographical dictionary. Profiles of nearly 900 Poles who have made lasting contributions to world civilization.**
Stanley S. Sokol, with Sharon F. M. Kissane. Wauconda, Illinois: Bolchazy-Carducci Publishers, 1992. 477p.

Contains fairly short and basic biographical accounts of nearly 900 prominent Poles, fifty of whom are still alive, who 'have contributed to world culture' in the broadest sense of the word. They are grouped in the index according to pursuits or occupations ranging from politics, the military, royalty to the varied spheres of cultural life. The entries are supplemented with further bibliographic references.

883 **Who's who in the socialist countries.**
Edited by Juliusz Strojnowski. New York: K. G. Saur, 1989. 3 vols. 1,376p.

Revised and much enlarged version of Boris Lewytzkyj and Juliusz Strojnowski's *Who's Who in the Socialist countries* (New York: K. G. Saur, 1978. 736p.). There are numerous Polish entries which give comprehensive biographical detail. For individuals holding positions within the communist elite in the early 1980s, see Central Intelligence Agency, *Directory of officials of the Polish People's Republic. A reference aid* (Washington DC: CIA Directorate of Intelligence, 1983. 217p.).

884 **Who's who in Poland.**
Edited by Joseph Wiśniewski. Toronto, Ontario: Professional Translators and Publishers, 1981. 243p.

Contains biographies of prominent living figures in Poland together with lists of political, social and ecclesiastical office holders.

885 **Who's who in Poland.**
Warsaw: Interpress, 1982. 1,107p.

A biographical directory compromising about 4,000 entries on leading personalities in Poland mainly within what was the official *nomenklatura* but also a wide range of individuals in intellectual, cultural and academic life. This is an English-language version of *Kto jest kim w Polsce. Informator Biograficzny* (Warsaw: Interpress, 1984. 1,175p. rev. 2nd ed, 1989. 1,584p.).

886 **Guide to the American ethnic press, Slavic and East European newspapers and periodicals.**
Lubomyr R. Wynar. Kent State University, Ohio: Center for the Study of Ethnic Publications, School of Library Science, 1986. 280p.

The guide is a directory of newspapers and periodicals published by Slavic and East European associations in the USA from January 1985. Polish is the largest of the ethnic groups represented, with twenty-four native language (circulation 141,223), thirty-three bilingual (circulation 309,570) and thirty-eight English titles (circulation 170,172). The Polish National Alliance's *Zgoda* headed the circulation lists with about 93,000.

Bibliographies

887 **Bibliographic guide to Soviet and East European Studies, 1990**
Boston, Massachusetts: G. K. Hall, 1991. 3 vols. (1,006p, 886p, 838p).
Established as an annual series since 1978, the guide contains the most comprehensive coverage of all publications published during the year in the USSR and Eastern Europe or published elsewhere and dealing with them. The criterion for inclusion is cataloguing by the Library of Congress and the New York Public Library.

888 **Poland, past and present: a select bibliography of works in English.**
Norman Davies. Newtonville, Massachusetts: Oriental Research Partners, 1977. 185p. map.
A selective bibliography of 1,800 books and articles on Polish history and civilization which are categorized under eighteen headings. Some items in languages other than English are included. There are few annotations and the compiler has concentrated on history and politics devoting less space to literature, language, the arts and the economy.

889 **Bibliografia Warszawy. Wydawnictwa ciągłe 1795-1863.**
(A bibliography of Warsaw. Publications between 1795 and 1863.)
Edited by J. Durko. Wrocław, Poland: Ossolineum, 1991. 2,400p.
Part of a series which covers all aspects of Warsaw's history. This volume includes continuous publications of the 1795-1863 period. Individual works are included in volume one.

890 **A bibliography of writings for the history of the English language.**
Jacek Fisiak. Poznań, Poland: Wydawnictwo UAM, 1983. 166p.
A deeply learned bibliography of writings on the English language in various languages but mainly English and German. Edited by a distinguished Poznań University academic and former Minister of National Education (Autumn 1988-Summer 1989).

211

891 **Eastern European national minorities, 1919-80. A handbook.**
Stephan M. Horak.   Littleton, Colorado: Libraries Unlimited, 1985.
353p.

The Polish chapter by Kenneth C. Farmer contains a historical overview of the development of each national minority since Poland regained her independence and a bibliography of the literature in various languages but mainly Polish and English (no. 75-317).

892 **Poland's international affairs, 1919-60: a calender of treaties,**
agreements, references and selections from documents and texts of
treaties.
Stephen Horak.   Bloomington, Indiana: Indiana University Press,
1964. 284p.

This book covers treaties of the Polish Republic (1919-39), the Polish Government-in-Exile (1939-44), the Polish Committee of National Liberation (1944-45) and the first half of the Polish People's Republic. Selected declarations, proclamations, protocols and decrees are also included.

893 **Russia, the USSR and Eastern Europe: a bibliographical guide to**
English language publications, 1964-74.
Stephen M. Horak, edited by Rosemary Neiswender.   New York:
Libraries Unlimited, 1978. 488p.

Containing 1,600 entries, this volume covers the pre-1977 decade of Soviet and East European studies in English speaking countries. All major fields are represented and a critical review of the literature is provided. Also Jan Kowalik, *World index of Polish periodicals published outside of Poland since September 1939.* (San José, California: American-Polish Documentation Centre, 2 vols, 1984. Reissued by Lublin: Wydawnictwo KUL, 1988.)

894 **Russia, the USSR and Eastern Europe. A bibliographic guide to English**
language publications, 1981-85.
Stephan M. Horak.   Littleton, Colorado: Libraries Unlimited, 1987.
273p.

A selective, but annotated, bibliography of 1,035 items grouped mainly under individual countries with numerous sub-headings. This is the last work by one of America's major bibliographers in the Slavic field who died in 1986.

895 **The Soviet Union and Eastern Europe. A bibliographical guide to**
recommended books for small and medium-sized libraries and school
media centers.
Stephan M. Horak.   Littleton, Colorado: Libraries Unlimited, 1985.
373p.

An annotated collection of 1,555 items designed as an aid for non-specialist librarians. Poland appears in the fourth section (items 1,374 to 1,460). The grouping is under subject headings and gives a representative enough selection of the most venerable books in the field published since the 1950s.

896   East Central Europe: a guide to basic publications.
Edited by Paul Lewis Horecky.   Chicago: University of Chicago Press,
1969. 965p.
A guide to selected reference works, major texts, classics of literature and
bibliographies concerning East Central Europe up to the late 1960s with concise
annotations. The Polish chapter (p. 599-788) was compiled by Janina Hoskins
(Wójcicka).

897   Ignacy Jan Paderewski, 1860-1941: a biographical sketch and a selective
list of reading materials.
Edited by Janina W. Hoskins.   Washington, DC: Library of Congress,
1984. 32p.
Has a short biography and a bibliography of his works set out in chronological order.

898   Polish books in English, 1945-71.
Janina Hoskins.   Washington, DC: Library of Congress, 1974. 163p.
Hoskins lists about 1,000 books and other publications which appeared in English
during 1945-71. The work covers both translations from Polish and English-language
publications in Poland and outside.

899   Tadeusz Kościuszko, 1764-1817: A selective list of reading materials in
English.
Edited by Janina W. Hoskins.   Washington, DC: Library of Congress,
1980. 24p. maps.
Contains a short biographical outline of Kościuszko's life and of all the publications in
English concerning him in the Library of Congress.

900   The Jews in Poland and Russia: bibliographical essays.
Gershon David Hundert, Gershon C. Bacon.   Bloomington, Indiana:
Indiana University Press, 1984. 276p. (The Modern Jewish
Experience).
Contains historical overviews and separate bibliographies at the end of the chapters on
each historical period. Also of interest is Lerski's *Jewish-Polish co-existence* (q.v.).

901   Poland. An annotated bibliography of books in English.
August Gerald Kanka.   London: Garland, 1988. 395p.
(Garland Reference Library of the Humanities no. 743).
An extensive annotated bibliography of 1,585 books published in English on Poland
during the twentieth century. A good balance is struck between the pre- and post-
Second World War periods but this, inevitably, makes the latter section less than
comprehensive. The subject grouping is by sections devoted to the main periods of
Poland's history as well as to a wide range of individual aspects.

902 **Poland.**
Richard C. Lewański.   Oxford: Clio Press, 1984. 267p. (World
Bibliographical Series no. 32).

The first edition of this volume included 901 books, articles and other varied types of publication covering the postwar period up till about 1981 on a wide range of topics concerning Poland. A number of Polish-language and general East European works were included. All of the items carry helpful, and often perceptive, annotations.

903 **Russia and Eastern Europe. A bibliographical guide, 1789-1985.**
Edited by Raymond Pearsod.   Manchester, England: Manchester
University Press, 1989. 304p.

Organized under historical periods with sections for individual countries and sub-topics.

904 **Polish dissident publications. An annotated bibliography.**
Edited by Joanna M. Preibisz, Jane Leftwich Curry.   New York:
Praeger, 1982. 382p.

Lists a wide range of unofficial books, journals and documents (those published without the permission of the Censorship Office), produced during the 1976-81 period. The bibliography is fully annotated. See also Henry W. Degenhardt, 'Poland'. In: *Political dissent. An international guide to dissident extra-parliamentary and illegal political movements* (Detroit: Gale Research Co, 1983).

905 **The international relations of Eastern Europe: a guide to information sources.**
Edited by Robin Alison Remington.   New York: Gale, 1978. 273p.
(International Relations Information Guide series no. 8).

This volume lists 1,300 books and periodicals from the eight East European countries dealing with their foreign relations. Short annotations are largely included and Poland is well represented.

906 **East European languages and literatures. A subject and name-index to articles in English language journals, festschriften, conference proceedings and collected papers.**
Compiled by Garth Michael Terry.   Nottingham, England: Astra
Press, 1978-91.

The volumes published so far in the series include copious citations of the Polish materials in this field. The five volumes cover the periods 1900-77, 1978-81, 1982-84, 1985-87, and 1988-90. References are organized under the headings of culture, drama, language, literature, poetry, prose and Polish Studies, as well as by individual writers.

907   The American bibliography of Slavic and East European Studies.
       Stanford, California: [n.p.] 1967- .
An annual ongoing series. It includes English-language publications in the humanities
and social sciences and selected foreign-language materials published in the USA and
Canada concerning the USSR and Eastern Europe. Grouped under geographical and
subject categories.

908   Solidarność. A biblio-historiography of the Gdansk strike and birth of
       the Solidarity movement. Monographic publications.
       W. J. Twierdochlebów.   Menlo Park, California: Centre for the Study
       of Opposition in Poland, 1983. 2nd ed. 72p.
Rightly described by the compiler as 'a highly personal work'. It includes summaries of
the main works on Solidarity and the Polish Crisis, published mainly during 1980-81, as
well as commentaries upon them. For a reliable listing of Polish Solidarity and
underground publications, see *Solidarity and other Polish clandestine publications in the
British Library* (London: British Library, Reference Division, 1985. 30p.).

909   Czesław Miłosz. An international bibliography, 1930-80.
       Edited by Rimma Volyńska-Bogert, Wojciech Zalewski.   Ann Arbor,
       Michigan: University of Michigan, Department of Slavic Languages and
       Literature, 1983. 162p.
A partly annotated reference work to Miłosz's writings which provides a broad
picture of the 1982 Nobel Prize for Literature laureate.

910   Official publications of the Soviet Union and Eastern Europe 1945-80. A
       select and annotated bibliography.
       Edited by Gregory Walker.   London: Mansell, 1982. 620p.
Contains separate chapters by specialist academics and librarians with general
introductions on each of the East European countries including the USSR. A standard
format is adopted to facilitate ease of reference to the official sources which are defined
as including a wide range of communist party and state documents and publications.
Poland is covered by Sanford (p. 187-220).

911   Doctoral dissertations and masters theses regarding Polish subjects 1900-
       85. An annotated bibliography.
       Edited by Bernard Wielewiński.   New York: Columbia University
       Press, 1988. 200p. (East European Monographs no. 235).
A catalogue of scholarly works regarding Polish subjects completed at American
colleges and universities between 1900-85, but also including some (not always correct)
British University references.

912 **Polish National Catholic Church, independent movements, Old Catholic Church and related items. An annotated bibliography.**
Edited by Bernard Wielewiński. New York: Columbia University Press, 1990. 751p. (East European Monographs no. 279).
A massive compilation of primary and secondary material on the Polish National Catholic Church prior to June 1989. Entries consist of author, title, publisher, date of publication and comments on the location, subject and audience.

913 **Bibliography of books on Poland or relating to Poland (published outside Poland since 1 September 1939).**
Vols 1-3 edited by Janina Zabielska, vol. 4 by Zdzisław Jagodziński. London: The Polish Library, 1953-1985.
This is the most complete bibliography of works on Poland published outside Poland since the outbreak of the Second World War. Although not annotated, it is very wideranging. Four volumes have appeared so far, covering the periods 1939-1951, 1952-1957, 1958-63, and 1964-1967; supplements to volumes 1-3 also appeared in 1985.

914 **Polonica Canadiana. A bibliographical list of Canadian-Polish imprints, 1958-70, with cumulative supplement 1948-57.**
Vincent Zołobka, Wiktor Turek. Toronto: Polish Alliance Press, 1978. 414p.
A comprehensive listing of Canadian-Polish publications.

Index

The index is a single alphabetical sequence of authors (personal and corporate), titles of publications and subjects. Index entries refer to both the main items and to other works mentioned in the notes to each item. Title entries are in italics. Numbers refer to bibliographic entries.

A

Abortion 360
Abrahamowicz, M. 767
Abramsky, C. 232
Abse, D. 749
Academy of Sciences
   (Polish) see PAN
Adam, J. 611, 679
Adamczewski, J. 53
Adelson, A. 162
Administration
   local government 451-
      452, 456
   local politics 458
*Administration in People's
   Poland* 448
AFL-CIO 682
Agricultural circles 651
Agriculture
   communist farming in
      USSR/Eastern Europe
      675
   family farms 673
   politics of socialist
      agriculture, 1945-60
      671
   reform 668-669
*Agriculture revolution in
   SU and Eastern
   Europe* 669
Ahmar, M. 588
Aids and human rights 359
Aircraft 676-77
*Airforce memorials of
   Lincolnshire* 284
*Airlift to Poland: the rising
   of 1944* 198
Airlines 677
Ajnenkiel, A. 6
AK *see* Home Army

Albright, M. K. 367
Alcoholism 347
Ali Agca, Mehmet 327
Allardt, E. 352
*Allied wartime diplomacy:
   pattern in Poland* 561
All-Poland Alliance of
   Trade Unions 681
Alma Ata 211
Amber 70
Ambroziewicz, B. 197
*American bibliography of
   Slavic and East
   European Studies* 907
American Civil War 268
*American Slavic and East
   European Review* 853
*America through Polish
   eyes* 267
Amin, Idi 396
Amsterdamska, O. 216
*Analyzing urban-rural
   disparities in education
   in Poland* 695
Anderman, J. 721
Anders, J. 729
*And I am afraid of my
   dreams* 159
*And my children did not
   know me: history of
   the Polish-Americans*
   265
Andrews, N. 459
Andrzej Krauze's Poland
   407
*Annus Mundi. 1,500 days
   in Auschwitz-Birkenau*
   159
Antemurale 854
Anthem, national 6
Anti-communist student

*organizations and
   Polish Renewal* 700
Anti-Zionist campaign 233,
   235
Apiculture 72
Applied art 756
Arad, Y. 147, 163
Arato, A. 460
Archaeology 74-79, 855
   earliest farmers 74
   Kujavian communities
      75
   Mesolithic 76
   Neolithic 77-78
   periodicals 855
   unconventional
      approaches 79
Archeologia Polona 855
Architecture 757-62
   landscape 21
   Gdańsk city centre 51
   Gothic (14th century)
      759
   Marian church and altar
      758, 763
   Royal Cathedral at
      Wawel 757
   Shrine of Black
      Madonna 762
   20th century 761
Archives
   Poland 822
   UK 819
   USA 817
   Western Europe 818
Arciszewski, Tomasz 194
*Ariadne's thread. Polish
   women poets* 722
Arms-limitation 565
Armstrong, J. L. 289
Arnhem operation 202

Art 56
Enlightenment to
present 764
15th to 20th century 768
graphic art 769
histories and criticism
750-756, 764-769
icons 765
Artists
Herman, Josef 283
Lempicka, Tamara de.
766
Rzepiński, Czesław 767
Artur Rubinstein, 1887-1982
775
Ascherson, N. 1, 461, 706
Ash, T. G. 462-463, 530
Aslund, A. 612, 635
*Assist and befriend or
direct and control:
report on probation
services in Poland and
England* 363
Assodobraj-Kula, N. 256
Astrology 697
Astronomy 697
Atlas of the Holocaust 173
*Atlas of plant parasitic
nematodes in Poland*
73
Attman, A. 569
Attwood, W. G. 772
*August 1980. Strikes in
Poland* 502
Auschwitz and the Allies
174
*Auschwitz chronicle, 1939-
45* 167
Auschwitz convent
controversy 306, 316
*Auschwitz. Doctor's eye-
witness account* 159
Auschwitz inferno 159
*Auschwitz. Nazi
extermination camp*
156
Auschwitz seen by the SS
148
Austria 124, 554, 586
Austrian Galicia 253-254
Australia 281-282
Authors (literary)
Anderman, Janusż 721

Baczyński, Krzysztof
Kamil 710
Białoszewski, Miron
710
Bieńkowska, Danuta 730
Brandys, Kazimierz 723
Bursa, Andrzej 725
Busza, Andrzej 730
Conrad, Joseph 281, 731
Czaykowski, Bogdan
714, 725, 730
Czyżewski, Tytus 705
Dąbrowska, Maria 728
Darowski, Jan 725
Dobraczyński, Jan 726
Gajcy, Tadeusz 710
Gojawiczyńska, Pola 728
Grochowiak, Stanisław
710
Harasymonowicz, Jerzy
710
Herbert, Zbigniew 710,
725, 729
Ihanatowicz, Janusz 730
Iwaniuk, Wacław 730
Jasieński, Bruno 705
Karpowicz, Tymoteusz
725
Konopnicka, Maria 728
Konwicki, Tadeusz 732
Kuncewiczowa, Maria
728, 748
Kuniczak, Wiesław 734
Michener, James 735
Miłosz, Czesław 706,
710, 736
Młodożeniec,
Stanisław 705
Myśliwski, Wiesław 737
Nałkowska, Zofia, 728
Norwid, Cyprian Kamil
706, 712, 725, 738
Nowakowski, Marek 739
Orzeszkowa, Eliza 728
Peiper, Tadeusz 705
Podgórecki, Adam 741
Przyboś, Julian 705, 710
Różewicz, Tadeusz 710,
725, 742
Schulz, Bruno 743
Sienkiewicz, Henryk 745
Singer, Isaac Bashevis
746

Śmieja, Florian 730
Staff, Leopold 725, 747
Stern, Anatol 705
Szymborska, Wisława,
710, 725, 749
Wat, Aleksander 705
Ważyk, Adam 703
Woroszylski, Wiktor 725
Zapolska, Gabriela 728
Autobiographies
Rubinstein, Artur 775
Szczypiorski, Andrzej
517
Wałęsa, Lech 524
Autre visage de l'Europe
418
Avery, W. P. 368
Axioms of Si-Tien 741

B

Bacewicz, Grażyna 776
*Background to crisis:
policy and politics in
Gierek's Poland* 220
Bacon, G. C. 900
Badyda, E. 38
Bailey, D. 2
Bakuniak, G. 467
Balawajder, A. 259
Balcerowicz, Leszek 613,
615, 632, 637
Bałdyga, J. 66, 750-51,
797
Balkans 618
Balladyna 716
Ballet 796
Ballooning 677
Baltic states 247, 544, 598
Bałuk-Ulewiczowa, T.
291
Banach, C. 685
Banas, J. 233
Bania, Z. 50
Baptists 338-39
Barańczak, S. 703-704, 869
Barbarian in the garden
729
Barbarski, K. 204, 285
Barbey, B. 11
Bardach, J. 444
Barker, C. 464-465
Baroque 724, 750

Baroque in Poland 750
Bartmiński, J. 813
Bartoszewski, W. 164, 209, 234, 306
Barzun, I. 723
Bassnet, S. 722
Batt, J. 542
Battle for the Marchlands 139
Bauman, J. 165, 235
Beck, Józef 548, 552, 578, 581, 586, 814
Beckett, Thomas à 104
Beekeeping in Poland 72
Beginner's course of Polish 293
Beginning of Cyrillic printing, Cracow 1491 702
Beginnings of communist rule in Poland 219
Beksiak, J. 619
Belgium 650
Bells in Winter 736
Belorussia 31, 206, 210, 598
Belweder 62
Bełżec, Sobibór, Treblinka: the Operation Reinhardt death camps 147
Bem, Józef 116
Benes, V. 90
Berger, J. 641
Berlitz 292
Berman, Jakub 226
Bernard, R. 261
Bernhard, M. 369
Beskid mountains 343
Best of Polish cooking 805
Bethell, N. 141
Bettelheim, B. 177
Between anxiety and hope. Poetry and writings of Czesław Miłosz 714
Between the Hammer and the Anvil 733
Between Poland and the Ukraine. Dilemma of Adam Kysil, 1600-53 255
Between two cultures 287

Bezwińska, J. 148
Białecki, I. 346
Bialer, S. 501, 550
Białowieża Forest 38
Białystok 38
Bibliografia Warszawy 889
Bibliographies
  dissident publications 904
  international affairs 892, 905
  Jewry 900
  Kościuszko, Tadeusz 899
  language and literature 906
  Miłosz, Czesław 909
  National Catholic Church 912
  national minorities 891
  Poland 888, 901-902, 913
  Poles in Canada 914
  Polish books in English 898
  Solidarity 908
  Soviet (Russian) and East European Studies 887, 893-96, 903, 907, 910
  Warsaw 889
Bibliographic guide to Soviet and East European Studies 887
Bibliography of books on Poland 913
Bibliography of writings for the history of the English language 890
Biddle, A. J. D. 549
Biegański, P. 66
Bielasiak, J. 466-467, 490, 523, 655
Bielawski, S. F. 166
Bielecki, Jan Krzysztof 881
Bieńkowska, B. 822
Biernat, C. 227
Billip, K. 299
Biographies
  Constantine Pavlovitch, Grand Duke 125
  Hen, Józef 717
  Herbert, Zbigniew 718
  Kosiński, Jerzy 719

Lem, Stanisław 720
Lempicka, Tamara de. 766
Mickiewicz, Adam 716
Miłosz, Czesław 736
Piłsudski, Józef 133
Słowacki, Juliusz 716
Biographies of Polish statisticians 641
Biondi, K. 468
Birkenau 156
Birth of Solidarity. Gdańsk negotiations 480
Biśko, W. 293
Biskupski, M. 262
Bismarck, Otto von. 117
Bison 71
Bitter harvest: intellectual revolt behind the Iron Curtain 748
Bitter Legacy: Polish-American relations in the wake of World War II 607
Blachnicki, Franciszek 317
Black, J. L. 469
Black Book of Polish censorship 378, 421
Blady-Szwajger, A. 181
Blaim, B. 227
Blanchard, O. 619
Blanke, R. 114
Blank Spots 595-96
Blaustein, O. 178
Blazyca, G. 529, 613-615, 624, 662
Błażyński, G. 214, 324
Blejwas, S. 115, 262
Blitzkrieg 145-146, 580
Bloch, A. 3, 41
Błoński, J. 185
Błuszcz, L. 55
Bóbr-Tylingo, S. 93
Bochniak, S. 664
Bogucka, M. 102
Bogucki, P. 74, 77
Bohdanowicz, A. 136
Bohemia 82, 110
Bold, A. 749
Boleslaus the Bold, called also the Bountiful, and the Bishop Stanislaus 104

Boll, H. 175
Bondy, F. 748
Book of Lech Wałęsa 528
Book of Warsaw palaces 63
Books and publishing 822,
825-27, 861
dissident publishing 823,
827, 904
Polish book trade
abroad 824
Books in Poland 822
*Border of Europe: a study
of Polish Eastern
provinces* 31
Bosgrove, James 573
Bossak, J. 659
Boundaries
Czechoslovak 30
Eastern 31, 574
historical development
35-36
Oder-Neisse Line
(Western) 26-28, 30,
566, 582, 872
Bourne, Cardinal 318
Bowen, M. 325
Boyes, R. 334
Boy in the Gulag 208
Bożek, M. 757
Bożyk, P. 616
Braley, A. 312
Brand, K. 311
Brand, W, 311
Brandys, Kazimierz 723
Braun, J. 4
*Breathing under water and
other East European
essays* 704
Breitkop, M. 646
Bren, F. 789
Breum, M. 359
Brezhnev, Leonid 555, 600
*Britain, Poland and
Eastern Front 1939* 572
*British Broadcasting
Corporation.
Monitoring Service* 856
British Friends of Free
Poland 285
*British policy in relation to
Poland in Second
World War* 575

Broadcasting 403
Brolewicz, W. 470
Bromke, A. 91, 370-371,
471-472
Broniewska, K. 739
Brown, J. F. 80, 531, 554
Brown, R. 743
Brożek, A. 263
Brumberg, A. 473
Brus, W. 625, 627, 655
Brzeski, A. 636
Brzezinski, R. 100
Brzezinski, T. 260
Brzezinski, Zbigniew 133,
372, 501, 550, 655
*Brzozowski (Stanisław)
and Polish beginnings
of 'Western Marxism'*
129
Buczek, D. 264
Buczyńska-Garewicz, H.
686
Budrewicz, O. 5
Budurowycz, B. 589
Buell, R. L. 131
Buffet, Bernard 766
Buhler, P. 26
Bujak, Zbigniew 485
Bukato, W. 38
Bukowczyk, J. 265
Bulas, K. 300
Bulgaria 327, 361, 669
Buonaccorsi, E. 698
Burant, S. 585
*Bureaucratic Leviathan:
study in the sociology
of communism* 398
Burke, P. 110
Burning forest 725
Buszko, J. 156
Bydgoszcz 75
Bydgoszcz crisis 496

C

*Cambridge History of
Poland* 97
Campbell, J. M. 770
Canada 259-60, 279, 730,
907, 914
Canadian Institute of
Ukrainian Studies 605
*Canary and other tales of
martial law* 739
*Candle for Poland: 469
days of Solidarity* 519
Cannistraro, P. 549
Cappellari, G. 164
Captive Mind 420, 736
*Cardinal Wyszyński: a
biography* 311
Cargo 302
Carmelite nuns 306, 316
Carnovale, M. 590
Carpathian mountains 21
Carpenter, B. 705, 724
Carpenter, J. 729
Carr, W. 145
Carrel, C. 752
Carter, F. W. 617-618
Carter, S. 419
Cartoons 407
Castle of Kórnik 52
Castles 41
Castoriadis, C. 373
*Catholic Church in
communist Poland* 313
*Catholicism and politics in
communist societies*
307
*Catholic-Marxist
ideological dialogue in
Poland* 322
Catholic University in
Lublin 305, 317
Cave, J. 374, 474, 485
Ceausescu, Nicolae 478
Cegiala, M. 61
Cękalska, K. 95, 305, 717-
18, 723, 801
Celma-Panek, J. 687
Cenkalska *see* Cękalska
Censorship 378, 421, 704,
904
Central Committee of
Physical Culture and
Tourism 48
*Central and Eastern
Europe. The opening
curtain?* 394
Central Intelligence
Agency 883
Central planning in Poland
634
Centre for Research into

Communist
Economies 619, 636
Chamerska, H. 822
Chanas, R. 67
*Changes in the
geochemistry of the
natural environment in
areas affected by
industrial emissions*
684
Charcoal sketches 745
Charemza, W. 620
Charlton, M. 550
Chęciński, M. 375-376
Chełm 186, 746
Chernobyl 683
Chesterton, G. K. 291
Chicago 276
Children of the Ghetto 165
China 419, 434, 741
Chinese cooking 804
Chirot, D. 81
Chmielewski, Z. 815
Chociłowska, Z. 299
Chopin 65, 779
Chopin. New biography
783
Chopin. Pianist and teacher
772
Chopin playing 770
Chopin studies 778
Christian civilization in
Poland 4, 7, 19, 96
*Christian community of
medieval Poland* 305
Christmas carols 813
*Chronicle of the life,
activities and work of
Janusz Korczak* 177
Chronicle of Łódź Ghetto
171
Chrypiński, V. 307
Chrzanowski, T. 758
Chyliński, Z. 39
Ciecerska, J. 687
Ciechanowski, J. 123, 191,
203, 286
Ciechocińska, M. 477
Cienciała, A. M. 135
Cieplak, T. 377
Ciepliński, J. 796
Cierlińska, H. 6
Cieselski, Z. 602

Cieślak, E. 227
Cieszyn 576
Cinema 789-95, 866
Citino, R. 580
*Civil Code of Polish
Peoples Republic* 447
*Civilian population and the
Warsaw Uprising* 192
Clarke, R. C. 116, 621
*Class structure and social
mobility in Poland* 354
*Class-struggles in classless
Poland* 515
*Class-struggles in Eastern
Europe, 1945-83* 83
Cloning 360
Clowes, F. 266
Coal issues for 1980s 664
Coat of Arms 6
*Code of criminal
procedure of Polish
People's Republic* 457
*Coercion and control in
communist society* 397
Cofta-Broniewska, A. 75
Colburn, F. 667
*Collapse of State Socialism.
Case of Poland* 536
*Collected letters of Joseph
Conrad* 731
Colloquial Polish 295
Colourist school of
painting 767
*Combat motivation of
Polish Armed Forces*
438
Comecon 23, 633
*Commemorative book in
honour of Florian
Znaniecki* 257
Commonwealth 82, 101-
102, 106, 109, 239,
255, 753, 771, 812
*Commonwealth of both
nations (Poland and
Lithuania). The silver
age* 106
*Competitive advantage of
nations* 558
Communism 857 *see also*
Government, Politics,
Roman Catholic
Church, Solidarity,

Jewish 232, 252
*Communist affairs:
documents and
analysis* 857
Communist agriculture 675
*Communist Eastern
Europe* 86
*Communist ideology, law
and crime.
Comparative overview
of the USSR and
Poland* 449
*Communist legislatures in
comparative
perspective* 450
*Communist local
government: a study of
Poland* 451
Communists of Poland 441
*Communist Party of
Poland* 383
*Communist regimes in
Eastern Europe* 429
*Companion guide to the
Royal Castle in
Warsaw* 63
Composing myself 774
Comrade Walter *see*
Świerczewski, Karol
Concentration camp 159
Concentration camps 153
Auschwitz-Birkenau
148, 156-59, 165, 167,
173, 179
Bełżec 147
Budzyń 183
Dachau 156
Majdanek 150, 183
Mauthausen 149
Płaszów 151, 183
Ravensbruck 159, 183
Sobibór 147, 186
Sachsenhausen 183
Stutthoff 160
Treblinka 147
Concise grammar of Polish
298
*Concise statistical
yearbook* 643
Confederation for an
Independent Poland
499
Conference on Security

and Co-operation in
Europe 565
Congress Kingdom 125
Connor, W. D. 532
Conrad, Joseph (Pseud.
Józef Korzeniowski)
281, 731
Conscientious objection
380
Constantine Pavlovitch,
Grand Duke. 125
*Constitutions, elections and
legislatures of Poland*
445
*Constitutions of the
communist party-states*
454
*Constitutions of the
communist world* 454
*Contemporary Polish
cookbook* 801
*Contemporary Polish
poetry, 1925-75* 710
*Continuity and change in
Soviet-East European
relations* 590
Contoski, V. 742
*Controlling top
management in large
organizations* 660
Convent at Auschwitz 306
*Conversations with the
Kremlin* 593
*Conversation with the
Prince* 742
*Conversations with Witold
Lutosławski* 773
Cook, E. 668
*Cooking the Polish-Jewish
way* 806
Co-operative banking 651
Copernicus, Nicolaus 8,
688, 697, 726
Copernicus Society of
America 745
Corbridge-Patkaniowska,
M. 296
Corruption 347, 357
Council for Providing
Assistance to Jews *see*
Żegota
Countdown 216

Country reports 642
Courier from Warsaw 196
Coutouvidis, J. 142, 203,
212
Cracow *see* Kraków
*Cracow – a treasury of
Polish art and culture*
56
*Cracow Cathedral on
Wawel* 57
Craig, M. 159, 475
*Creating a market
economy: case of
Poland* 632
*Creditworthiness and
reform in Eastern
Europe* 655
Crises of communism 415
*Crisis and transition. Polish
society in the 1980s.*
346
*Crisis in East European
economy* 622
Crossley, P. 759
Crouch, M. 453
*Crystal spirit. Lech
Wałęsa and his
Poland* 475
Cuba 434
Cuisine 801-806
*Cup of tears: a diary of the
Warsaw Ghetto* 180
Culture 10, 18-19, 56, 391,
845, 851 *see*
Education &
Learning, Literature,
the Arts
Culture shock 407
Curie (-Skłodowska),
Marie 692
Currency 41, 632
Curry, J. L. 341, 378-79,
904
Cynk, J. 676
Cynkin, T. 551
*Cyprian Norwid: poet –
thinker – craftsman*
712
Cyrillic 702
Czapliński, W. 35, 444
Czapski, J. 212
Czarniawska-Joerges, B.
660

Czartoryski, P. 688
Cząsak, A. 177
Czaykowski, Bogdan 714,
725, 730
Czech, D. 148, 167
Czechoslovakia 30, 40,
197, 247, 312, 361,
419, 530, 555, 559,
576-578, 628, 632, 647,
654, 679, 814
*Czechoslovak-Polish
confederation and
Great Powers* 577
Czechowski, W. 68
Czekanowska, A. 771
Czerni, S. 301
Czerny, Z. 801
Czerniawski, A. 706, 725
Czerwiński, E. 18, 267
Czerwiński, J. 67
*Czesław Miłosz.
Annotated
international
biography* 909
*Czesław Miłosz and the
insufficiency of lyric*
715
Częstochowa
Shrine of Black
Madonna 726, 762

D

Dąbrowski, C. 326
Dąbrowski, W. 670
Dadlez, A. 707
Daily Telegraph 40
Danecki, J. 342
Dark side of the moon 212
Darowska, J. 181
Dastych, H. 69
David, J. 168
Davie, D. 715
Davies, G. 380
Davies, L. 731
Davies, N. 92-93, 132, 170,
189, 286, 550, 888
Davies, R. E. 338
Davis, L. 692
Dawidowicz, L. 169
Dawisha, K. 381
Dawson, A. 32
Deacon, B. 361

222

Dealers of Polish and
  Russian books abroad
  824
Death of the Dark Hero.
  Eastern Europe, 1987-
  90 512
Death in the forest: story of
  the Katyń massacre
  213
Dębicki, Roman 552
Dębicki, Ryszard 301
Dębski, H. 801
Debt and development 637
Debussy, Claude 772
Decentralization and local
  government. Danish-
  Polish comparative
  study 452
Degenhardt, H. 904
Dego, W, 699
Dembiński, H. 101
Dembiński, R. 819
Democracy in a
  Communist Party.
  Polish experience since
  1980 395
Democratization in Poland,
  1988-90. Polish Voices
  543
Demography 22-23, 32
Demolowicz, M. 716
Denmark 452
Deportation into the
  unknown 212
Dernalowicz, M. 716
Design of undergound
  hard-coal mines 664
Detroit 275
Detroit Institute of Arts,
  754
Deutsch, R. 669
Devant la Guerre 373
Devlin, K. 527
Dewar, D. 331
Diaries 320, 723
Dictionaries 299-304
  agrophysics 301
  biographical 882
  computer science 301
  electronics 301
  English-Polish and
  Polish-English 299-
  300, 303-304

legal 301
maritime transport 302
technical 301
Dictionary for tourists 301
Dilthey, Wilhelm 256
Diplomat in Berlin, 1933-
  39. Papers and
  memoirs of Józef
  Lipski 581
Diplomat in Paris, 1936-39:
  papers and memoirs of
  Juliusz Łukasiewicz
  578
Directory of officials of
  Polish People's
  Republic 883
Disarmament 565
Distorted world of Soviet-
  type economies 640
Dixon, J. 365
Długosz, Jan 641
Dmowski, Roman 91, 385,
  389, 567
Dobbs, M. 476
Döblin, A. 236
Dobraczyński, J. 726
Dobroczyński, M. 655
Dobroszycki, L. 162, 171,
  241
Dobrowolski, T. 764
Dobrzycki, J. 688
Doctoral dissertations and
  masters theses
  regarding Polish
  subjects 911
Documents in
  Commmunist Affairs
  857
Documents on the
  Holocaust 163
Documents on Polish-
  Soviet relations,
  1939-45 592
Doing business in Eastern
  Europe 654
Dolczewska, B. 52
Domenach, J. 418
Dorosz, J. 444
Double vision 794
Douglas-Kozlowska, C.
  294
Dream of belonging 235

Drezma, M. 745
Drewnowski, J. 622
Drohybycz 743
Drozdowski, B. 785
Drukier, B. 219
Drygalski, J. 382
Drzycimski, Andrzej 528
Dubet, F. 522
Dulczewski, Z. 257
Dumas, R. 474
Durko, J. 889
Dvornik, F. 82
Dyboski, R. 7
Dygasiewicz, J. 670
Dying we live 193
Dynamics of the
  breakthrough in
  Eastern Europe 546
Dziadosz, E. 150
Dziady 744
Działyński family 52
Dziennik Polski 287, 828
Dziennik Żołnierza 828
Dziennik Związkowy 829
Dzierżanowska, H. 197,
  294
Dziewanowski, M. K. 94,
  383

E

Ecumenical Council 339
Eagle and small birds:
  crisis in the Soviet
  Empire from Yalta to
  Solidarity 550
Early Neolithic settlement
  and society at
  Olszanica 78
Early Neolithic subsistence
  and settlement in the
  Polish Lowlands 77
East-Central Europe see
  Europe, East-Central
East-Central Europe: guide
  to basic publications
  896
East-Central Europe in
  transition from
  fourteenth to
  seventeenth centuries
  110
East European languages
  and literatures 906

Eastcott, J. 24
Eastern Europe, *see*
  Europe, Eastern
Eastern Europe 25
Eastern Europe and
  Communist Rule 80
Eastern Europe, 1968-84 85
Eastern Europe and
  Russia/SU. Handbook
  of West European
  library and archival
  sources 818
Eastern Europe: a
  geography of
  Comecon countries 23
Eastern Europe,
  Gorbachev and
  Reform 381
Eastern Europe in
  aftermath of Solidarity
  471
Eastern Europe in the
  postwar world 87
Eastern Europe in
  transition 557
Eastern Europe on a
  shoestring 45
Eastern Europe. Political
  crisis and legitimation
  409
Eastern European national
  minorities 891
Eastern Territories
  British reactions to
    Soviet occupation,
    1939 574
  Jews in (1939-41) 170
  Shtetl Jews 250
  Soviet occupation,
    1939-41 206, 210
East-West technology
  transfer 623
Economic history 569, 627,
  630-31
  backwardness 81
  foreign capital 650
  periodicals 862
  twentieth century 631
Economic history of
  Eastern Europe 627
Economic problems of
  environmental
  protection 684

Economic reforms in
  Polish industry 666
Economic reforms in SU
  and Eastern Europe
  since 1960s 611
Economic theory of the
  Feudal system 630
Economies of Eastern
  Europe and their
  foreign economic
  relations 652
Economist Intelligence
  Unit 614
Economy 494, 612, 621-
  622, 624-627, 636
  banking 649, 651
  Comecon 663
  consumption 633
  employment and wage-
    policy 679-682
  feudal 630
  industry 656, 659-666
  management 611, 624,
    626, 660
  marketization (post-
    1989) 613-616, 619,
    632, 635, 637, 639,
    646
  and martial law 624
  moves towards EEC 614
  periodicals 875
  planning 620, 629, 634,
    638, 640
  factory case-study 680
  reforms 611, 625, 636,
    666
  remodelling system 514
  socialist corporations
    665
  Soviet command model
    634, 640
  technology transfer 623
Education 685-687, 690
  for peace 701
  Higher Education 687,
    693, 911
  political 686
  student organizations
    700
  urban-rural 695
  youth 696
Education and work in
  Poland 696

Education and youth
  employment in Poland
  696
Education for peace in
  Polish educational
  system 701
Education in People's
  Poland 685
Egyptian scarabs,
  scaraboids and plaques
  from Cracow
  collections 821
Eigeldinger, J-J. 772, 778
Eisenbach, A. 237
Eisner, J. 159
Elbląg 160
Elections
  historical overview 445
  1989 elections 537, 541
  1989 role of Catholic
    Church 308
  May 1990 local 541
  no-choice elections 382
  Sejm elections under
    communism 453
Elective Monarchy 106
Ellen, R. 689
Emancipation of Jews in
  Poland 237
Embroidery 800
Embryo-freezing 360
Emperor of the earth 736
Employment and wage
  policies in Poland,
  Czechoslovakia and
  Hungary since 1950
  679
Empty Room 747
Encyclopaedias and
  Directories 13, 879-
  886
Encyklopedia Popularna
  PWN 879
Encyklopedia Powszechna
  PWN 879
End of Outer Empire.
  Soviet-East European
  relations under
  Gorbachev 595
Endecja *see* National
  Democratic Party
Engel, D. 172
Engels, Friedrich 129

England's Baltic trade in
early seventeenth
century 569
English-Polish concise
technical dictionary
301
English-Polish dictionary
of abbreviations used
in electronics 301
English-Polish dictionary
of computer science
301
English-Polish dictionary
of science and
technology 301
English-Polish and Polish-
English compact
dictionary 299
English-Polish pocket
dictionary 299
Enigma code 568
Enlightenment 113, 724,
751
Enlightenment and the
birth of modern
nationhood 113
Environment 32, 683-684
Equality and inequality
under socialism 345
Erdman, M. 733
Erickson, J. 210
Eroding Empire. Western
relations with Eastern
Europe 554
Escape from Sobibór 186
Escape from socialism. The
Polish route 532
Eternal moment; poetry of
Czesław Miłosz 736
Europe
libraries and archives
818
Polish immigrants
257-258
relations with communist
bloc 394, 590
Europe, East-Central
bibliography 896
EEC statistics on East-
Central Europe 642
14th to 17th centuries
110
postwar history 87

Europe, Eastern
backwardness 81, 89
communist rule 80
geography 23, 25
Gorbachev and reform
381
guide to cheap travel 45
in aftermath of
Solidarity 471
in postwar world 87
in transition 557
languages and literatures
906
library and archival
sources 818
national minorities 891
postwar history 80, 85,
87
Europe, Western
and decomposition of
Soviet bloc 534
and post-communist
Eastern Europe 542
European bison 71
European Communities –
Commission 642
Everyday forms of peasant
resistance 667
Evangelical-Augsburg
Union see Lutherans
Evangelical-Reform church
339
Evolution of blitzkrieg
tactics 580
Evolution of communism
440
Exiled Governments.
Spanish and Polish
402
Experience and Future
discussion group 523
Exploring dimension of
ethnicity 270
Extermination. Killing
Poles in Stalin's Russia
212
Eysmontt, J. 621

F

Faber book of political
verse 749
Facts about Poland 644

Failure of authoritarian
change: reform,
opposition and geo-
politics in Poland in
the 1980s 388
Faith and Fatherland:
Polish Church in
Wisconsin 271
Falkowska, M. 177
Fałkowski, S. 657
Fallenbuchl, Z. M. 623-
624, 652, 655
Fantazy 744
Farmer, K. C. 891
Fate of Poles in USSR 290
Fateful meeting at Elsinore
573
Fauna 68-69, 71-73
Fedorowicz, J. K. 102, 569
Fenelon, F. 159
Festival of the oppressed:
solidarity, reform and
revolution 464
Feudalism 630, 737
Ficowski, J. 231, 743
Fiddick, T. 591
Fighting Auschwitz 143
Filipowicz, H. 716
Final Report: diplomatic
memoirs 548
Fine Arts Academy,
Kraków 767
Finland 84, 352
Fiol, Szwajpolt 702
Fiore, B. 521
First Partition of Poland
107
Fischel, J. 711
Fishing 674
Fisiak, J. 890
Fiszman, J. R. 690
Fiszman, S. 691
Fitzgibbon, C. 148
Fiut, A. 736
Five centuries of Polish
poetry 740
Five months within
Solidarity 520
Flag 6
Flam, H. 496
Flashpoint Poland 214

Flis, A. 384
Flying-ambulance service 677
Flying University 686
Folk-art 797-798, 800
Folk-art in Poland 797
Folk-church 308
Folk costumes 799
Folklore 8, 800
Fools of Chełm 746
Foreign capital in Poland 650
Foreign direct investment in Poland 646
Foreign exchange law of February 15, 1989 645
Foreign policy of Poland 1919-39 552
Foreign relations 559-560
  Britain 569-575
  Czechoslovakia 576-578
  France 578-579
  Germany 580-582, 872
  Haiti 583
  interwar 548-49, 552, 556, 571-572, 578, 580-581, 586-589, 591, 609, 652
  late 1980s transition 557-558, 564-565, 595-596
  Lithuania 585-587
  1980-81 crisis 551, 553, 562, 594, 597-598, 600
  Pakistan 588
  periodicals 876
  Soviet bloc and hegemony 85, 513, 550, 554-555, 561, 563, 566, 575, 590
  Sweden 602-604
  Ukraine 605
  USA 549, 606-610
  USSR 199, 206-213, 589-601
Foreign Trade Research Institute 637, 657, 659, 661
Forests 38, 670, 683
Forests and forest economy in Poland 670
For God, country and Polonia 279
Forgotten Holocaust. Poles

under German occupation, 1939-44 154
Formation of the Polish Community in Great Britain 286
Formation of the Polish state 111
Formative years of the Polish seminary in US 279
For your freedom and ours 14
Founders of Polish schools and scientific models 699
Fountain, A. M. 385
Fragments of Isabella. Memoir of Auschwitz 159
Franaszek, A. 54
France 124, 141, 145, 197, 578-579, 554, 650, 775
France and her Eastern Allies 579
Frankland, M. 531
Frasyniuk, Władysław 474, 485
Frederyk Chopin. Pianist from Warsaw 772
Freedom and Peace (WiP) movement 380
Freedom within. Prison notes of Stefan, Cardinal Wyszyński 320
Freely I served 202
Frentzel-Zagórska, J. 386
Friszke, A. 533
From confidence to disarmament 565
From crisis to crisis. Soviet-Polish relations in 1970s 601
From Potsdam to Poland. American policy towards Eastern Europe 606
From the Steppes to the Savanah 212
From out of the firestorm. Memoir of the Holocaust 188

From Versailles to Locarno 135
Fryderyck Chopin. Diary in images 782
Fryś-Pietraszkowa, E. 797
Fuks, M. 238
Funk music 777
Funnel Beaker age 74
Furtak, R. 387

G

Gajl, N. 623
Galician villagers and Ukrainian national movement 253
Garbo, Greta 766
Garland, J. S. 661
Garland, N. 40
Garlicki, A. 203
Garliński, J. 143
Garrett, S. A. 606
Gąsiorowski, A. 103
Gazeta Wyborcza 830
Gdańsk 47, 51, 227, 230
  Agreement 461, 480, 486, 499, 502-503
  shipyard 480
Gdańsk. City sights 51
Gdańsk. National identity and Polish-German borderlands 230
Gdynia 678
Geller, J. 212
Genealogy 807-811
General-Gouvernement 148, 152
General principles of law of Polish People's Republic 446
General Sikorski Historical Institute 592
General Weygand and battle of Vistula 136
Generation of wrath 159
Generation. Rise and fall of Jewish communists of Poland 252
Genocide *see* Holocaust
Geography
  Comecon countries 23
  Eastern Europe 25
  economic 32

human 22
periodicals 858
political 29
urban 34
Geographica Polonica 858
Geremek, B. 102
German Democratic
  Republic 360, 419,
  530, 559, 612, 669
Germans, Poles and Jews
  117
Germany *see* Foreign
  Relations; History
  border disputes with
  Poland 26, 28, 30
  extermination of Jews
  162-175, 177-190, 232,
  238, 245
  Germans in Poland 229-
  230
  interwar relations with
  Poland 84, 131, 135
  Nazi concentration
  camps/administration
  in Poland 147-161
  Poles in Prussian
  Partition 114, 117,
  119-120, 123-124, 128,
  130, 134
  Polish borderlands 60
  revanchism 26
  Second World War 141-
  143, 145-146, 191-193,
  195
*Germany's eastern
  neighbours* 30
*Germany and Poland.
  From war to peaceful
  relations* 582
Gerrits, A. W. 388, 553
Geve, T. 159
Ghetto diary 177
Gierek, Edward 1, 80, 94,
  214, 217, 220, 259,
  343, 350, 370-371, 410-
  412, 523, 601, 665
Giergielewicz, M. 8
Giertych, J. 389
Gierucki, J. 798
Gieysztor, A. 66, 95, 232
Gilbert, M. 173-74
Gillon, A. 727
Giroud, F. 692

Gitelman, Z. 390
Glasgow 621, 752
Glas-Wiener, S. 165
Glass, A. 677
Głębocki, W. 61
Glenny, M. 534
Gliński, J. 301
*Global challenges and East
  European responses*
  616
Glob 24 831
*Głòwny Urząd
  Statystyczny* 641, 643,
  648
Gnaciński, J. 807
Gnaciński, L. 807
Goc, P. 726, 815
*God's politician. John Paul
  at the Vatican* 329
Goldberg, J. 239
Goldberger, J. 212
Goldfarb, J. C. 391
Goldszmit, Henryk *see*
  Korczak, Janusz
Golonka, J. 50
Gomöri, G. 712
Gomułka, S. 392, 622,
  625-626
Gomułka, Władysław 1,
  94, 215, 223-224, 375,
  377
Górale (mountain-
  dwellers) 24
Góralski, J. 584
Gorbachev, Mikhail 381,
  393, 395, 546, 590, 595
Gordon, L. 554
Gorelick, T. 176
Górski, A. 111
Gorzycki, A. 819
Gościlo, H. 728
Gosh, H. 717
Gothic 758-59
*Gothic architecture in reign
  of Kasimir the Great*
  759
Gothic house in Nowy Sącz
  43
Gottlieb, E. 746
Goulding, D. J. 793
Government 13, 387, 397-
  399, 405, 414, 419,
  427, 429, 437

*Government Commission's
  report on Health for
  All* 362
Government-in-Exile 142-
  144, 172, 200, 203,
  285-286, 402, 566, 592,
  819, 892
*Governments of
  Communist Eastern
  Europe* 427
Graber, H. 236
Grabowska, J. 70
Graczyk, R. 71
Graf, M. 151
Graham, L. S. 477
Grand failure 372
Granville, B. 542
Graphic Art 769, 797
Great Britain 141, 144 *see*
  Foreign Relations
  Polish community
  283-287
  Polish, literature in 706,
  725
  Postwar Government-in-
  Exile 285
  Sikorski Museum and
  Polish Institute 819
  Social welfare in Britain/
  Poland 364
*Great Britain, Soviet Union
  and Polish
  Government-in-Exile*
  144
*Great English-Polish
  dictionary* 304
*Great Powers and Poland
  1919-45* 556
*Great Powers and Polish
  Question, 1941-45* 561
*Great Powers and Vilna
  Question* 587
Greece 84
Greek Catholics 340
Green rose 742
Greene, C. 9
*Green flag. Polish populist
  politics, 1867-1970* 672
Greenwood, N. 209
Gregory of Sanok 698
Griffith, W. E. 394
Griffin, Cardinal Bernard
  318

Gronicki, M. 620
Gross, J. T. 152, 206-207, 210
Grossman, G. 675
Grotowski, Jerzy 785, 787
Growth, innovation and reform in Eastern Europe 625
Grudzińska-Gross, I. 207
Grudziński, T. 104
Grunblat, H. 432
Grunblat, J. 432
Gruszewski, T. 619
Grzegorczyk, S. 816
Grzeloński, B. 267-68
Grzybowski, K. 444
Guide to American ethnic press 886
Guide to archives of Polish Institute and Sikorski Museum 819
Guide to folk art and folklore in Poland 800
Guide to Polish libraries and archives 817
Guide to Warsaw and its environs 65
Gulag 208, 211-12
Gutman. Y. 163, 176, 240
Gypsies in Poland 231

H

Hagen, W. 117
Hahn, W. G. 395
Haifa University 250
Haiman, M. 269
Haiti 583
Halecki, O. 96, 552
Halicz, E. 116
Hall, Aleksander 91, 471, 485
Hamburg 119
Handbook of Polish perfins in GB 814
Handbook of Reconstruction in Eastern Europe 540
Handelsman, M. 97
Hanik, M. 33
Hanley, B. 332
Hann, C. M. 343
Hanson, J. K. 192

Harman, C. 83
Harper, J. 363
Harris, E. 70, 113, 268, 677, 758, 781
Hart, K. 165
Health for all by year 2000 362
Healey, E. 231
Heart of Europe. Short history of Poland 93
Heavy metal music 777
Heimler, E. 159
Heine, M. E. 41
Helsinki 118
Hen 717
Hendricks, A. 359
Henze, P. B. 327
Heraldry 808, 810
Herbert 718
Herbert, Zbigniew, 715, 718, 729
Herby Szlachty Polskiej 810
Heritage and future: essays on Poles in Canada 260
Heritage. Foundations of Polish culture 19
Herman, J. 283
Hertz, A. 241
Heydecker, J. 175
Heydenkorn, B. 260
Hicks, B. 467
Hill, R. F. 270
Hills, D. 396
Hilstein, E. 688
Himka, J-P. 253
Hinsley, Cardinal 318
Hippocrene companion guide to Poland 41
Hippocrene concise dictionary 303
Hippocrene practical dictionary 303
Hirszowicz, L. 232
Hirszowicz, M. 397-398
Hiscocks, R. 215
Historical atlas of Poland 35
Historiography 91, 126
History of Eastern Europe Communist 80, 83, 85-87, 89

general 81-82, 110
interwar 4, 89
History of Gdańsk 227
History of Poland
general overviews 16, 20, 90, 92-93, 95-99, 123
10th to 18th centuries 101-113
19th century 114-130
interwar 131-39
Second World War 141-213
20th century 94, 223
Communist Poland 214-226
religious 305, 318, 321
Polish-British relations 144
Polish-French relations *see* Foreign Relations, France
Polish-German relations *see* Foreign Relations, Germany
Polish-Jewish relations 117, 170, 172, 176, 187
Polish-Prussian relations 114, 117, 119-120, 128
Polish-Russian relations 112, 121-122, 125
Polish-Soviet relations 132, 136, 139, 144
Polish-Ukrainian relations 112
History of Poland 95-96
History of Poland: God's Playground 92
History of Poland in painting 755
History of Poland since 1863 123
History of Polish-Americans in Pittsfield 266
History of Polish ballet 796
History of Polish culture 18
History of Polish literature 709, 713
History of Polish settlers in New Zealand 288

Hitler, Adolf 609
Hobart, Tasmania 282
Hoffman, Z. 238
Hogarth, C. 745
Holland 202
Holmes, L. 399
Holocaust 159, 163, 169, 173, 182, 185, 188, 711
Holocaust and the historians 169
Holocaust in history 182
Holy Father, welcome to your fatherland for the third time 326
Holzer, J. 392
Home Army 191, 196
Honecker, Erich 478
Horak, S. M. 891-895
Horecky, P. L. 896
Horn, M. 238
Horowicz, D. 400
Hoskins, J. W. 808, 896-899
House of ashes 183
Howat, R. 772
How to live and study in this city, Cracow 55
Hrubieszów 183
Human geography in Eastern Europe and Soviet Union 22
Humanism 698
Hundert, G. D. 242, 900
Hungary 40, 110, 247, 312, 345, 361, 390, 419, 530, 628, 632, 654, 669, 679
Hunt, R. 782
Hunt, S. 799
Hunter, R. 626, 654
Husak, Gustaw 478
Hussonarius, N. 698
Hutchings, R. L. 555
Hutton, C. 180
Hyde, G. 227

I

Icons from Poland 765
Idealism 370
Ideology in a socialist state. Poland, 1956-83 433
Ignacy Jan Paderewski 897

Iivonen, J. 118
Illustrated guide to Kraków 53
Imperfect autocrat. Grand Duke Constantine Pavlovitch and the Polish Kingdom 125
In defence of my country 389
Independence or incorporation? 118
Independent Eastern Europe 84
Independent Satellite. Society and politics in Poland since 1945 222
Independent social movements in Poland 499
Independent Students' Organisation 700
In desert and in wilderness 745
Industrial co-operation between Poland and West 661
Industrial reform in socialist countries 662
Industrialization 25, 230
Industry
coal 664
management 660
post-communist structural transformation 659, 662
Informator. Polska 91 881
In the German mills of death, 1941-45 159
Ingham, M. J. 284
Inglehart, R. 401
Inhuman Land 212
In Kaszuby 798
In my father's court 746
In search of Poland 562
In shadow of Auschwitz. Polish Government-in-exile and Jews 172
Insider's guide to Poland 41

Intelligentsia 463, 481, 704, 836
defensive reactions to Stalinism 420
dissent 1981-87 25
teachers and socialization 690
Inter-factory Strike Committee 480
International Beekeeping Congress 72
International Brigade 432
International Monetary Fund (IMF) 613, 615, 646
International and Polish economy in 1989 and 1990 657
International relations of Eastern Europe 905
International Relations Studies in Poland 560
International Socialist 83
Interpress 644
Introduction to modern Polish literature 727
Introduction to Polish 298
In vitro fertilization 360
I remember nothing more. Warsaw children's hospital and the Jewish resistance 181
Iribarne, L. 736
Isaac Deutscher 400
I shall live 183
Issa Valley 736
Italy 179, 554, 650
Itzin, C. 785
Ivan the Terrible 112
Iwaniuk, W. 730
Iwanow, M. 210
Iwańska, A. 402
Iwińska, M. 753, 765

J

Jabłonna Palace 65
Jabłoński, K. 62
Jachimczyk, M. 232
Jacobs, E. 675
Jadwiga, Queen 726
Jagiellonian University, 10, 55, 75, 291, 337, 693

Jagodziński, Z. 913
Jain, I. 681
Jakubowicz, K. 403
Jan III Sobieski, King 726
Janicki, S. 790
Janion, M. 603
Jankowski, M. 455
January Insurrection
(1863) 122
Januszajtis, A. 51
Japan 355, 804
Jaroszewski, T. 63
Jaruzelski, Wojciech 335,
388, 395, 416, 422,
430-431, 462-463, 467,
469, 478, 484, 506,
508, 525, 726, 832
*Jaruzelski, Prime Minister
of Poland* 478
Jasieńczyk, L. R. K. 708
Jasienica, P. 105-106
Jaslan, J. 299, 301
Jasna Góra
*Jasna Góra. A companion
guide* 50
Jastrun, Mieczysław 747
Jedlicki, J. 392, 535
Jedlicki, W. 176
Jędraszczyk, A. 619
Jędruch, J. 445
Jędrzejewicz, W. 133, 570,
578, 581
Jeffries, I. 662
Jerschina, J. 392, 693
Jerzy Kosiński, 719
*Jewish community in
Poland* 244
Jewish Historical Institute
237
Jewish-Polish co-existence
243
*Jewish privileges in Polish
Commonwealth* 239
Jews
bibliographies 243, 900
communists 233, 246,
252, 432
in interwar Eastern
Territories 31, 170,
250
in Poland 232-252
periodicals 864

Polish-Jewish cooking
806
Second World war
ghettoes 151, 162, 164-
165, 168, 171, 175,
177-178, 180
*Jews in Eastern Poland and
USSR, 1939-46* 170
Jews in Poland 232
*Jews in Poland and Russia:
bibliographical essays*
900
Jews in Polish culture 241
*Jews in a Polish private
town* 242
Jews in Warsaw 234
*Jews of East-Central
Europe between the
wars* 247
*Jews of Poland between
Two World Wars* 240
*Jews and Poles in World
War II* 176
Jeżewska, Z. 779
John Paul II, Pope. 310,
322-330, 726
John Paul II in Poland 323
Johnson, R. J. 22
Jordan, A. 41, 105-106
Jordan, Z. A. 694
Joseph Conrad: a chronicle
731
Joseph, P. 652
*Journal of Central
European Affairs* 859
Journalists 341
Journey to Poland 236
*Journey without a ticket.
To England through
Siberia* 212
Józef Piłsudski Institute
570
Juliusz Słowacki 716
Jur *see* Lerski, G
Jurisprudence 835
Jurzywiec, I. 825

K

Kacevitch, G. 144
Kaczyński, T. 773
Kadar, Janos 390
Kaliszewski, A. 718

Kallberg, J. 778
Kamiński, B. 536, 652
Kamiński, Ted, 119, 823
Kampinos Forest 65
Kanet, R. 220
Kanka, A. G. 901
Kant, A. 212
Kant, N. 212
Kantor, Tadeusz 785
Kaplan, H. H. 107
Karl, F. R. 731
Karol, K. S. 476
Karpiński, J. 216
Karpiński, M. 786
Karpowicz, M. 750
Karpowicz, Tymoteusz
709, 712, 725
Karski, J. 556
Kaser, M. 627
Kasprzyczak, J. 64
Kaszuby 798
Katarzyńska, B. 302
Katyń massacre 144, 209,
213, 550, 592, 596, 608
Kaufman, M. 479
Kawalerowicz, Jerzy 791
Kawecka, Z. 212
Kazimierz the Great, King.
759
Keim, P. 339
Kelem rugs 800
Keller, U. 175
Kemp-Welch, A. 480
Kennedy, M. D. 481
Kermisch, J. 187
KGB 327
Kielce 242
Kiepuszewski, R. 33
Kiernan, T. 795
King Matt the First 177
Kielar, W. 159
Kieniewicz, S. 95
*King of children;
biography of Janusz
Korczak* 181
Kisiel, C. 546, 763
Kissane, S. 882
Kleinerman-Goldstein, C.
746
Klimaszewski, B. 10, 55

Kłocińska, J. 765
Kłoczowski, J. 305
Kłossowski, A. 824
Kmiecik, J. 208
Knife in the water 795
Kobelius, S. 50
Kochan, L. 233
Kochanowicz, Jan 81
Kochanowski, Jan 691
Kohn, M. L. 344
Kolaja, J. T. 680
Kołakowska, A. 226
Kołakowski, Leszek 322, 468, 550, 739
Kolankiewicz, G. 348, 404-405, 501
Kolarska-Bobińska, L. 361, 621
Kolasiński story 275
Kolbe, Maximilian 331-333, 726
Kołodko, G. 646
Kołodziejski, Jerzy 528
Kolosi, T. 345
Komarnicki, T. 134-35
Komornicka, M. 57
Konopczyński, W. 97, 444
Konspira. Solidarity Underground 485
Konwicki, T. 732
Koralewicz, J. 346
Korba, I. 309, 487
Korboński, A. 590, 599, 628, 671, 675
Korboński, S. 176, 733
KOR. History of Workers' Defense Committee in Poland 413
Korczak 181
Korczak, Janusz 177, 181
Kordian 716
Kornik 52
Korsadowicz, M. 291
Korzeniowska, T. 810
KOS 823
Kościuszko, Tadeusz 113, 116, 899
Kosela, K. 308
Kosiarz, A. 693
Kosiński, Jerzy 41, 719
Kostecki, W. 557
Kostrowicka, I. 21
Kostrowicki, J. 21

Kot, S. 593
Kotlar, H. 188
Kovaloff, T. 549
Kowal, S. 653
Kowalik, J. 893
Kowalik, Tadeusz 480
Kowalski, S. 541
Kowalski, T. 406
Kozakiewicz, M. 695
Kozielsk concentration camp (Soviet) 209
Kozik, J. 254
Kozińska-Bałdyga, A. 750
Kozlowski, S. K. 76
Krąg 823
Kraków 53-57, 617-618, 683, 757
Marian altar 758
Marian church 763
Kraków Ghetto and Płaszów camp remembered 151
Krakowski, S. 176, 178
Krasiński, Zygmunt 716, 744
Krauze, A. 407
Krauze, J. 88
Krauze, T. 354
Krein, G. 151
Krejci, J. 627, 647
Kresy (Eastern borderlands) 31
Krętkowska, K. 128
Kridl, M. 14
KRN *see* National Council for the Homeland 219
Krok-Paszkowski, J. 11
Król, Marcin 392, 840
Kruk, J. 77
Kruszewski, Z. A. 27
Krycki, J. 342
Kryński, M. 742, 749
Krzaklewski, Marian 847
Krzemiński, I. 487
Krzycki, A. 698
Krzywicki-Herburt, B. 320, 723
Krzyżanowski, J. 709
Krzyżanowski, L. 7, 702, 727, 869
Księżopolski, M. 361
Kto jest kim w Polsce 885
Kubiak, Hieronim 337, 471

Kuczyński, S. 6
Kuhiwczak, P. 722, 725
Kujawy region 75
Kuhn, D. 24
Kuhn, F. 24
Kukiel, M. 97
Kukliński, A. 558, 629
KUL see Catholic University in Lublin
Kula, M. 256
Kula, W. 256, 630
Kulawiec, E. 177
Kulczycki, Jerzy 810
Kulczycki, John J. 92, 120
Kulski, J. 193
Kulski, W. 582
Kultura 241
Kulturkampf in Prussian Poland 128
Kumiega, J. 787
Kumorek, R. 767
Kuncewiczowa, M. 748
Kunczyńska-Iracka, A. 797
Kuniczak, W. S. 734, 745
Kuratowska, Zofia 359
Kuratowski, K. 699
Kuroń, Jacek 408
Kurowski, L. 446
Kuryluk, E. 743
Kutrzeba, S. 444
Kuźniewski, A. 271
Kwaśniewski, J. 347
Kwiatkowski, M. 62

L

Laba, R. 482-483
Labedz, L. 484
Ładogórski, T. 35
Lalik, T. 6
Lane, D. 348
Lane, T. 212
Landau, Z. 631
Land of Ulro 736
Lands of partitioned Poland 130
Language
   beginner's courses 293, 295-296, 298, 708
   bibliographies 906
   collocations 294
   for tourists 292
Lanzmann, C. 183, 463

231

Lapides, R. 162
Laqueur, W. 167
Large Industrial
    Enterprises (WOG)
    665
Laskowski, J. 528
Lasocki, W. A. 71
Last European war,
    September 1939-
    December 1941 145
Last of the Titans 264
Last Jew from Węgrów 166
Latawski, P. 134
Latyńska, M. 489
Lavers, N. 719
Law 446
    civil code 447
    code of criminal
        procedure 457
    criminal code 449
    penal code 457
    periodicals 860
    Supreme Court 455
Law in Eastern Europe 860
Layard, R. 619
Łazienki and Belweder 62
Leach, C. 157, 736
Leadership change in
    communist states 434
Leadership and succession
    in Soviet Union,
    Eastern Europe and
    China 419
Leaming, B. 795
Learning 688-689, 691-692,
    694, 697-699, 702
Leavitt, T. 760
Le Chêne, E. 149
Lech Wałęsa 475
Le Corre, D. 323
Le Grand, J. 364
Leibrich, K. 654
Leitner, I. 159
Lelewel, Joachim 126
Lemnis, M. 802
Lempicka, Tamara de 766
Lempicka-Foxhall, K. de
    766
Lepak, K. J. 217
Lerska, H. T. 243
Lerski, G. J. 194, 243, 468
Les, E. 365
Lesiecka, A. 796

Leslie, R. F. 121-23
Leszczyc, Z. 810
Letters from Prison 489
Łętowska, A. 447
Łętowski, J. 448
Let's go to Poland 42
Let's visit Poland 44
Letulle, C. 153
Levi, P. 179
Levine, M. G. 710-711,
    714
Lewandowska, A. 801-802
Lewandowski, J. 604
Lewański, R. C. 817-818,
    902
Lewin, A. 180
Lewin, I. 244
Lewis, P. 335, 405, 409-
    412, 508, 537
Lewitzkyj, B. 883
Liberation of one 428
Liberska, B. 696
Libraries
    USA 817
    Western Europe 818
Liberty's folly 109
Lifton, B. J. 181
Light and life 317
Lilejko, J. 63
Linear pottery 74, 78
Lineberry, W. P. 12
Linz 149
Lipski, Józef 581
Lipski, Jan Józef 413
Lipton, D. 632
Lis, Bogdan 474, 485
Literary criticism
    General 704-707, 709-
        711, 713, 715
    Individuals 703, 712,
        714-720, 735
Literature 16, 727, 731
    bibliographies 906
    emigre 725, 730
    Polish-Swedish contacts
        603
Literature, the arts and the
    Holocaust 711
Lithuania 101, 106, 715
Little King Matty and the
    desert island 177
Local politics in Poland
    458

Locarno 135, 579
Łódź 162, 171
Łódź Ghetto 162
Loeber, D. 426
Łopiński, M. 485
Lord, R. H. 108
Lorentz, S. 66, 751
Los, M. W. 449
Lourie, R. 171, 177, 211,
    241, 723, 732
L'Ouverture, Toussaint
    583
Lovenduski, J. 414
Low Countries 197
Lower Silesia 67
Lublin 219, 305
    provisional government
        219
Ludwikowski, R. 415
Lukacs, J. 145
Lukas, R. C. 154-55, 607-
    608
Łukasiewicz, Juliusz 578
Lukowski, J. T. 109
Lund University 252
Lutheranism 339
Lutkowski, K. 646
Lutos, G. 323
Luxmore, J. 309
Lwòw 211
Lye, K. 42

M

Macarov, D. 365
Macartney, C. A. 84
McCann, J. M. 591
McCauley, M. 419
Macdonald, O. 486
Macharek, K. 54
McLachlan, G 45
McShane, D. 488
Maciąg, W. 723
Mączak, A. 102, 110
Mad dreams, saving graces
    479
Madej, V. 146
Maguire, R. 742, 749
Main Censorship Board
    421, 378
Main School of Economics
    and Statistics 613
Maisky, Ivan 592

Majdanek 150
Majka, C. 799
Majkowski, W. 349
Mąka, H. 60
Making and breaking of Eastern Europe 89
Makowski, A. 447
Malbork 47
Malcher, G. 416
Malinowski, Bronisław 281, 689
Malinowski between two worlds 689
Man for others. Maximilian Kolbe 333
Man in the middle 201
Manteuffel, T. 111
Maple Leaf and White Eagle. Canadian-Polish relations, 1918-78 259
Maps and atlases 35-37, 64
March, M. 729
March 1939: British guarantee to Poland 571
Marcus, J. 245
Marcinkiewicz, J. 683
Marer, P. 655-56
Margoliot, A. 163
Mariage blanc: and the hungry artist departs 742
Marian altar of Wit Stwosz 758
Marie Curie 692
Marie Walewska 127
Markham, P. 497
Marody, M. 346
Marples, D. 210
Marrus, M. 182
Martyr for the truth. Jerzy Popiełuszko 336
Marx, Karl 129
Marxism-Leninism 694
Mason, D. S. 417, 487, 538, 681
Mass media 272
  BBC monitoring service 856

broadcasting studies 403
censorship 378, 421
press and political change 367
press in 1980s 406
Masters of contemporary art. Poland 760
Masuria 21, 30
Maszczak, M. T. 43
Matejko, A. 350
Mature Laurel 706
Mauthausen 149
Maximilian Kolbe 332
Maxwell, Robert 478
May, Y. 773
Mazowiecki, Tadeusz. 249, 311, 418, 452, 531, 537, 541, 619, 662, 847-848
Mazur, B. 295, 712
Mazurkiewicz, L. 22
Meaning and uses of Polish history 91
Męclewski, E. 28
Medals and distinctions 812
Medvec, S. 576
Meetings with the Madonna 726
Mellor, R. 23
Memoirs of an eminence grise 200
Memoirs of a Jewish revolutionary 246
Memoirs of Polish immigrants in Canada 260
Memory offended. Auschwitz convent controversy 316
Mendel, H. 246
Mendelson, E. 240, 247-248
Mengele, Joseph 156
Mesolithic in Poland 76
Methodists 339
Mexico 390, 635, 816
Mianowicz, T. 310
Micewski, A. 311
Michaels, R. 246
Michałek, B. 791-792
Michalik, K. 148

Michałowski, K. 699
Michel, P. 312
Michener, J. A. 735, 745
Michnik, Adam 474, 489, 830, 847
Michta, A. 218
Mickiewicz, Adam 8, 58, 715-716, 744
Mieczkowski, J. M. 633
Międzymorze (Between the Seas Confederation) 134
Mierzyńska, M. 664
Migala, J. 272
Mikes, G. 407
Miklos, N. 159
Milencki, J. 67
Milewski, Jerzy 468
Milewski, W. 819
Miliband, R. 494
Milisauskas, S. 78
Military
  armies 1569-1689 100
  combat motivation 438
  communist period 218
  expenditure 376
  newspapers 849
  1980-82 crisis 416, 506
  Polish airforce in Lincolnshire 284
  Polish armour 1939-45 204
  politics 1918-85 442
  role within Soviet stratocracy 373
Military Rule in Poland. Rebuilding of communist power, 1981-83 506
Military Council of National Salvation 503
Millard, F. 361, 364
Miller, R. F. 490
Miłosz, Czesław. 11, 211, 420, 489, 691, 706, 713, 715, 729, 736, 909
Miłosz. International bibliography 909
Minc, Julia 226
Mind of John Paul II 330
Ministry of Culture 752
Ministry of Transport 678

Ministry of Transport 678
Minor Apocalypse 732
Mirchuk, P. 159
Misztal, B. 490
Młoda Polska 754
Mocha, F. 468
Moczar, Mieczysław 233, 375
Modelski, T. 195
Modern cinema of Poland 791
Modern Polish mind 748
Modernization and political tension management 423
Modjeska, Helena 267
Modzelewski, K. 408
Mokrzycki, E. 539
Mołdawa, T. 881
Momatiuk, Y. 24
Mongol invasions 735
Montias, J. M. 634
Monticone, R. 313
Monumenta Polonica. First four centuries of Polish poetry 724
Moody, J. 334
Moonrise, moonset 732
Moore, G. 216
Morawińska, A. 768
Morawski, K. 61
Morin-Aguilar, E. 418
Moscow and the Polish crisis 594
Moskit, M. 485
Mostwin, D. 273
Motoring 37
Mozart, Wolfgang Amadeus 752
Możejko, E. 714
Muggeridge, M. 320
Muller, F. 159
Multicultural History Society of Ontario 260
Munk, Andrzej 791
Mur, J. 491
Murdoch, Iris 291
Muscovy 112
Museums 820-821
Musialik, Z. 136
Music
 Bacewicz, Grażyna 776
 Chopin, Fryderyk 65, 770, 772, 778-779, 782-783
 folk music 771
 Lutosławski, Witold 773
 Paderewski, Ignacy 784
 Panufnik, Andrzej 774
 periodicals 867
 rock music 777
 Rubinstein, Artur 775
 Szymanowski, Karol 780-781
Music of Chopin 779
Music of Szymanowski 780
Myant, M. 492, 540, 621
My brother's keeper? Recent Polish debates on the Holocaust 185
My century. Odyssey of a Polish intellectual 211
My brother Lech Wałęsa 470
My many years 775
Myrdal, G. 436
Myśliwski, W. 737

N

Nagurski, I. 702
Nahon, M. 156
Najder, Z. 501, 731
Napoleon I, Emperor of France. 124, 127, 583
Napoleon's campaign in Poland, 1806-1807 124
Narkiewicz, O. A. 85, 672
Nathan, L. 211
National Council for the Homeland 219
National Democratic Party 385, 389
National Geographic 24, 33, 249
National income and outlay in Czechoslovakia, Poland and Yugoslavia 647
National Museum in Kraków 821
National theatre in Northern and Eastern Europe 788
NATO 438
Negotiated Revolution 543
Neiswender, R. 893
Nelson, D. N. 450, 538
Nelson, H. 13
Neoclassicism in Poland 751
Neolithic settlement of Southern Poland 77
Neuer, A. 796
Neugroschel, J. 236
Neuman, J. 814
New Eastern Europe 80
New Eastern Europe. Social policy, past, present and future 361
New Eastern Europe. Western responses 542
Newman, S. K. 571
New Polish Publications 861
New political parties of Eastern Europe and Soviet Union 544
New regime: structure of power in Eastern Europe 437
Newspapers (Polish language)
 in Poland 830-833, 836-844, 846-852
 abroad 828-829, 834
New Zealand 288
Next to God. . .Poland 319
Nice promises 511
Nicholas Copernicus' Complete Works 688
Niczów, A. 421
Nie 832
Nieboska Komedia 744
Niedzielska, K. 351
Niemcewicz, Julian Ursyn 267
Niewęgłowski, T. 699
Niezabitowska, M. 249
Nightmare memoir 153
Nilsonn, N. 603
1980-81 crisis 12, 17, 85, 220, 371
Nissenbaum Foundation 251
NKVD 209

Nobility 102-103
Noel-Baker, P. 565
Norwid, Cyprian Kamil 706, 712, 738
Notes from a Welsh diary 283
Notes on ships, ports and cargo 302
Nothing but honour. Story of the Warsaw Uprising 205
No time-limit for these crimes! 158
Nove, A. 675
Novels 707, 728, 732-37, 745
November 1918 140
NOWa publishers 823
Nowacki, H. 820
Nowa Europa 833
Nowa Huta 231
Nowa Kultura 703
Nowak, J. 196, 550
Nowak, K. 467
Nowakowski, Marek 359, 739
Nowicki, W. Z. 814
Nowy Dziennik 834
Nowy Sącz 43
Nowy Świat 834
Nowy Świat. Obserwator Codzienny 847
Nuti, D. M. 493-494, 622, 652

O

Oasis movement 317
Obidinski, E. 274
Ochab, Edward 226
October 1956 224, 550
Oder-Neisse boundary and Poland's modernization 27
Oder-Neisse line: reappraisal under international law 26
Odra-Świnoujscie 674
Oeconomica Polona 862
Official publications of SU and Eastern Europe 910
Okęcki, S. 197

Oklahoma 261
Okrasa, W. 364
Old Polish traditions in kitchen and at table 802
Old Slavonic 771
Old Town and Royal Castle in Warsaw 66
Old Warsaw cookbook 804
Olson, D. M. 450
Olszanica 78
Olszer, K. 14, 702
Olszewski, A. K. 761
O'Mahony, P. 360
On the border of war and peace: Polish intelligence and diplomacy in 1937-39 and origins of the Ultra secret 568
On cultural freedom. Exploration of public life in Poland and America 391
One hundred and twenty fifth anniversary of co-operative banking in Poland 651
One hundred years young. History of Polish Falcons of America 277
Oni. Stalin's Polish puppets 226
Ontario 260
On trial in Gdańsk 474
Open-air museums in Poland 820
Open Letter to the Party 408
Operation Reinhardt 147
Optics 697
Orenstein, H. 183
Organic Work 115
Organization of agriculture in SU and Eastern Europe 675
Organizational structure of Polish-Canadian community 260
Origins of backwardness in Eastern Europe 81
Orpen, N. 198

Ortell, G. 809
Orthodox church 255, 340
Orton, L. 254, 275
Osa, M. 314
Osostowicz, K. 772
Ossolinski, Józef M. 825
Ossolinski's National Institute 825
Ost, D. 422, 495
Ostach, H. 72
Other Europe 504
Otok, S. 29
Out of the inferno. Poles remember the Holocaust 155
Outline history of Poland 98
Outline history of Polish applied art 756
Outline history of Polish culture 10
Oxford book of verse in English 749
Ozinga, J. R. 559

P

Pachoński, J. 583
Paderewski, Ignacy 267, 784, 897
Paderewski. Biography of pianist and statesman 784
Pajestka, J. 477
Palace 737
Palmer, A. W. 84
Palmer, C. 780
Paluch, A. 689
PAN (Polish Academy of Sciences)
Committee of Economic Sciences 862
Committee for Spatial Economy and Regional Planning 629
Institute of Civilization 855
Institute of State and Law 301, 448, 457
Institute of Zoology 68
Komisja Nauk Mineralogicznych 684
Komitet Nauk

Historycznych
(Committee for the
Historical Sciences)
103, 444
Polish Committee for
Man and Biosphere
Programme 684
Panel services for offenders
366
Panorama 831
Panorama of Polish history
6, 20
Państwo i Prawo 835
Pan Tadeusz 715
Panufnik, A. 774
Pan Wołodyjowski 745
Papal Nuncios 321
Parachuting 41
Paris-New York, 1982-84
723
Parliament 444, 450
Parot, J. 276
Partisan faction 158, 233,
375
*Partisan warfare in 19th
century Poland* 116
Partitions 107-109, 130,
321
*Party Statutes of the
Communist World* 426
Pasierb, J. 762
Passion by design 766
Pastor of the Poles 262
Pastusiak, L. 560
Paszkiewicz, M. 810
Paszkiewicz, P. 753, 765
Paszkowski, L. 281
Paszyński, M. 657
Patriotic Front for
National Rebirth 726
Patriot's revolution 531
Paul, D. W. 792
Pawełczyńska, A. 157
Pawłowski, Zbigniew 641
PAX 322
Payne, E. 822
Paździora, J. 664
Pearson, R. 903
Peasants 667, 673
Immigrants in Europe
and America 257-258
populist politics, 1867-
1970 672

rebellions 667
rituals 8
Pease, N. 609
Pelc, J. 297
Pełczyński, Z. 123, 541
Peleg, M. 184
Peleg-Mariańska, M. 184
*Penal Code of the Polish
People's Republic* 457
*Penguin book of socialist
verse* 749
*People's Poland. Patterns
of social inequality and
conflict* 349
*Perestroika. New thinking
for our country and
the world* 393
Periodicals 853-878
American press 886
archaeology 855
economics 862
geography 24, 858
Jewish affairs 864
literary criticism 845
Polish affairs 863, 868-
869, 872
Slavic and East
European Studies 853,
859, 874-875
Persky, S. 496
*Persistence of freedom:
sociological
implications of Polish
student theatre* 391
Peter the Great, Czar 112
Petlura, Semeon 132, 605
Petre, F. L. 124
Petrowicz, L. 28, 72, 150,
156, 238, 251, 584,
685, 798
Petterson-Hórko, S. 287
Pfeiffer, C. 15
Philately 814
Philippines 639
Phillips, Ursula 737
Philosophy and ideology
694
*Philosophy and romantic
nationalism* 129
Photographs
aircraft types 677
gypsies 231
Warsaw ghetto 175

Piast dynasty 104-105, 111,
753
Piast Poland 105
Piątkowski, J. 447
Piekalkiewicz, J. 451
Pienkos, A. 125
Pienkos, D. 277-278
Piesakowski, T. 290
Pietraszczyk, B. 775
Pietrkiewicz, J. 740
Pilichowski, C. 158
Piłsudska, W. 133
Piłsudski, Marshal Józef
132-134, 137, 248, 370,
548, 567, 586
*Piłsudski. A life for
Poland* 133
Pinchuk, C-B. 250
Pinińska, M. 803
Pinkus, O. 183
Piotrowska, B. 50, 53, 238,
743, 762
Pirages, D. C. 423
Pirie, D. 752
Pisarski, B. 68
Piszczek, R. 251
Pittsburgh 270
*Planned economies of
Eastern Europe* 638
Planning
Soviet command model
629, 634
spatial economic
planning 32, 342
*Planning in Eastern
Europe* 32
*Plans and disequilibria in
centrally planned
economies* 620
Playing for time 159
Płock 369
Ploss, S. 594
Płoszajski, P. 532
Plot to kill the Pope 327
*PNA. Centennial history of
the Polish National
Alliance of USA* 278
Pobòg-Jaworowski, J. 288
Podbielski, L. 641
Podolski, T. 649
Podgórecki, A. 741
Poem for adults 703
Poetry 710, 722, 724-725,

729-730, 738, 740, 742.
747-749
*Poetic avant-garde in
Poland* 705
Pogonowski, I. C. 36, 303
Pokropek, M. 797, 800
Polak, J. 52
Poland 9, 12, 41, 46, 90,
735, 863, 902
Poland after Solidarity 490
*Poland. Annotated
bibliography of books
in English* 901
*Poland between the
Hammer and the Anvil*
223
*Poland between the
Superpowers* 563
Poland between the wars
138
*Poland. Bridge for the
abyss* 215
*Poland challenges a divided
world* 564
*Poland and coming of
Second World War* 549
*Poland, Communism,
Nationalism, Anti-
semiticism* 375
Poland. Country study 13
Poland. Crisis for socialism
492
Poland. Economy in 1980s
621
Poland 86 816
Poland for beginner's 5
*Poland. Genesis of a
revolution* 473
Poland. Historical atlas 36
*Poland in British
Parliament* 570
*Poland in Christian
Civilization* 4
Poland – India 584
Poland in 1980s 490
Poland in perspective 223
*Poland in perspective of
global change* 558
*Poland in Second World
War* 143
Poland in twentieth century
94
Poland into the 1990s 613

Poland invites you 39
Poland in world civilization
7
Poland: key to Europe 131
*Poland. Land of freedom
fighters* 15
*Poland. Landscape and
architecture* 21
Poland. Nation and Art
753
*Poland 1981. Towards
Socialist Renewal* 500
*Poland, 1980-81. Solidarity
versus Party* 459
*Poland, 1944-62.
Sovietization of a
captive people* 221
*Poland 1990. Statistical
data* 648
Poland, past and present
888
*Poland. Politics,
Economics and Society*
405
Poland. Protracted Crisis
371
*Poland. Role of press in
political change* 367
Poland. Rough guide 45
Poland since 1956 377
Poland's Caribbean tragedy
583
*Poland. Socialist state,
rebellious nation* 225
*Poland, stagnation.
collapse or growth* 636
Poland, 1939-47 142
*Poland's international
affairs* 892
*Poland's journalists:
professionalism and
politics* 341
*Poland's next five years:
dash for capitalism* 613
Poland's place in Europe
566
Poland's politicised army.
Communists in
uniform 416
*Poland's politics: idealism
versus realism* 370
Poland's secret envoy 194
Poland's self-limiting
revolution 514

*Poland's Solidarity
movement* 468
*Poland, Solidarity,
Wałęsa* 476
Poland. State of Nation
523
Poland to the 1990s 614
Poland to Pearl Harbour
145
Poland. Tourist guidebook
48
Poland and Ukraine 605
Poland under black light
721
Poland under Jaruzelski
484
*Poland, US and
stabilization of Europe*
609
Polański, Roman 795
Polański 795
*Polański. Film-maker as
voyeur* 795
Poles 17
Poles abroad
Australia 281-282
Brazil 256
Canada 259-260, 279,
914
Chicago 276
Detroit 275
Europe 257
general 258
Great Britain 283-287
Massachusetts 264, 266
Oklahoma 261
Pittsburgh 270
USA 256-257, 261-280,
606, 865, 886
Wisconsin 271
*Poles in Australia and
Oceania* 281
Poles in Oklahoma 261
Poles in USA, 1776-1865
268
*Policy and politics in
contemporary Poland*
529
Polin 234, 864
Polish aircraft 676
*Polish airforce in
Lincolnshire* 284
Polish amber 70

237

Polish-American Congress 606
Polish-Americans, 1854-1939 263
Polish-American's guide to Poland 49
Polish-American Studies 865
Polish arguments. Poland on the Odra, Lusatian Nysa and Baltic 28
Polish armies, 1569-1696 100
Polish armour, 1939-45 204
Polish army, 1939-45 204
Polish art and architecture 761
Polish August. Documents from the beginnings of the Polish workers' rebellion 486
Polish August. What has happened in Poland 461
Polish Baptist Union *see* Baptists
Polish biographical dictionary 882
Polish-Black encounters: history of Polish and Black relations in America since 1609 280
Polish books in English 898
Polish campaign 1939 146
Polish Catholics in Chicago, 1850-1920 276
Polish challenge 503
Polish children during the Second World War 161
Polish cities 47
Polish civilization 8
Polish coats of arms 810
Polish Committee of National Liberation 892
Polish Communism in crisis 507
Polish complex 732
Polish contemporary graphic art 769

Polish contribution to ultimate Allied victory in Second World War 195
Polish cookbook 802
Polish Detroit and the Kolasiński Affair 275
Polish dilemma. Views from within 477
Polish diplomacy, 1914-45 567
Polish dissident publications 904
Polish drama, 1980-82 527
Polish economy in twentieth century 631
Polish-English and English-Polish dictionary (Kościuszko) 300 (Stanisławski) 304
Polish-English dictionary of legal terms 301
Polish-English and English-Polish dictionary of agrophysics 301
Polish factory 680
Polish Film 866
Polish film. Yesterday and today 790
Polish folk costumes 799
Polish folk music 771
Polish folkways in America 274
Polish for travellers 292
Polish genealogy and heraldry 808
Polish grammar in dialogues 295
Polish Institute of International Affairs 557-558, 560, 868
Polish-Jewish relations *see* Jews
Anti-Zionism in communist politics 233, 375, 432
Auschwitz convent controversy 306, 316
bibliographies 243, 900
Jews in Poland 232-252

Second World War 154-155, 164, 169-170, 176, 178, 182, 184-185, 187, 189-190
Polish-Jewish relations during Second World War 187
Polish Jewry. History and culture 238
Polish kitchen 803
Polish Music 867
Polish National Alliance 278, 829, 886
Polish National Catholic Church 337, 912
Polish national liberation struggles and genesis of modern nation 116
Polish nobility in Middle ages 103
Polish opera and ballet 796
Polish ordeal 517
Polish orders, medals, badges and insignia 812
Polish painting, 15th to 20th century 768
Polish painting from Enlightenment to recent times 764
Polish paradox. Communism and self-renewal 510
Polish paradoxes 392
Polish parish records of the Roman Catholic Church 809
Polish Parliament at the summit of its development 444
Polish past in America 269
Polish peasant in Europe and America 257
Polish people and culture in Australia 282
Polish Perspectives 868
Polish piano music. Chopin 779
Polish politics. Edge of the abyss 466
Polish politics and revolution of November 1830 121

Polish presence in Canada and America 279
Polish and proud 807
Polish publicists and Prussian politics 119
Polish radio broadcasting in the US 272
Polish realities. Arts in Poland 752
Polish Renaissance in its European context 691
Polish Resistance movement in Poland and abroad, 1939-45 197
Polish Review 869
Polish Revolution. Solidarity, 1980-82 462
Polish road to capitalism 615
Polish Romantic drama 744
Polish Round Table 870
Polish Socialist Party (PPS) 413
Polish Society 356
Polish society under German occupation 152
Polish Sociological Bulletin 871
Polish-Soviet relations, 1932-39 589
Polish-Soviet relations, 1918-39 592
Polish-Soviet War 1920 132, 136, 139, 589, 591-592
Polish sport 815
Polish Studies Centre, Indiana University 138
Polish-Swedish literary contacts 603
Polish Transformation: programme and progress 619
Polish United Workers Party (PZPR) 222, 224, 836
  and consumption 633
  elite-recruitment 439
  extraordinary ninth congress 507-508
  ideology 433, 435, 449
  internal democracy 395, 507
  leadership and martial law 508
  leadership and succession 419, 434
  local officials 374
  newspaper 844
  nomenklatura capitalism 546
  party secretaries 411-412
  political histories 383, 441
  and the socialist corporation 665
  statutes 426
Polish University Abroad 285
Polish-US industrial co-operation 656
Polish way. Thousand year history of the Poles and their culture 99
Polish Western Affairs 872
Polish white book: official documents concerning Polish-German and Polish-Soviet relations, 1933-39 199
Polish wings 677
Polish yearbook of international law 873
Politics 671-672 see Polish United Workers' Party, post-communism, Solidarity
  censorship and cultural freedom 378, 391, 703-704
  civil-military relations 218, 376, 416, 438, 442, 849
  civil society 386, 460
  communist period 216, 225, 349-50, 370, 440
  communist political rituals 384
  constitutions 445, 454
  crisis-management 423, 435-437, 536
  decomposition of communism 372, 379, 381, 388, 390, 392-393, 401, 404, 409, 415, 422, 436, 443, 463, 479, 495, 504, 512, 518, 546
  elections 308, 382, 445, 453, 537, 541
  establishment of communist rule 142, 219, 221
  Gierek regime 214, 217, 220, 369, 371, 411, 523
  Gomułka regime 215, 222, 224, 375, 377, 703
  international aspects 388, 394, 471, 501, 513
  Jaruzelski regime 346, 368, 388, 392, 395, 411, 422, 443, 474, 477-478, 484, 489, 506, 508, 525, 726
  and Jewish factor 232-33, 235, 249, 252, 432
  legal codes 447, 457
  martial law 430-31, 469, 485, 489, 491, 508, 511, 739
  nationalism 385, 389
  opposition 408, 413, 420, 424, 489, 499
  press 403, 406
  public opinion 417
  religious minorities 338-40
  Roman Catholic Church 307-310, 312-315, 318-319, 322, 334-336
  rural 343, 672
  social and professional groups 341, 348, 403, 425, 700
  Solidarity and 1980-81 crisis 367, 371, 373, 410, 417, 425, 428, 459, 461-462, 464-468, 492-498, 500-503, 505, 507, 509-510, 514, 519-522, 526-529
  Stalinist period 215, 221-222, 226, 320
Political authority and Party secretaries in Poland, 1975-86 411

239

Political geography 29
Political ideas in
contemporary Poland
443
Political opposition in
Poland, 1954-77 424
Political and social issues in
Poland as reflected in
Polish novel 707
Political systems of socialist
states 387
Political trials in Poland,
1981-86 430
Politics, art and
commitment in East
European cinema 792
Politics of socialist
agriculture in Poland
671
Politics in the communist
world 399
Politics in Independent
Poland 137
Politics and religion in
Eastern Europe 312
Politics and society in
Eastern Europe 414
Polityka 836
Pollution in heart of
Europe 683
Polmart 1989 623
Polonia Restituta 285
Polonica Canadiana 914
Polonsky, A. 96, 123, 137,
170, 180, 185, 203,
219, 232, 234, 237,
392, 561
Półtawska, W. 159
Pomerania 30
Pomian, J. 200
Pomian-Szrednicki, M. 315
Pope from Poland 325
Pope John Paul II. His
travels and mission 328
Pope John Paul II. Man
from Kraków 324
Popescu, J. 44
Popiełuszko, Jerzy 334-
336
Po Prostu 837
Porajska, B. 212
Porter, B. 527
Porter, M. 558

Ports 302
Porowski, A. 651
Portrait of Poland 11
Positivism 115
Post-communism
apathy and
demobilization 538
capitalist threat to
democracy 535
collapse of state-
socialism and
command economy
536
democratization, 1988-90
543
dynamics of 1989
revolution 546
guide to new Eastern
Europe 547
nationality conflicts 534
1989 revolutions in
Eastern Europe 530-
531
Polish moves away from
communism 392, 518,
532
political scene in 1989
533
regional overview of first
18 months 540
socialist structural
constraints on reform
539
Post new wave cinema in
SU and Eastern
Europe 793
Potel, J. Y. 497
Potichnyj, P. J. 605
Potop 745
Potsdam Agreement 607
Potter, W. 590
Pottery 797
Pounds, N. J. 25, 90
Poznań 58-59, 119, 653
Poznań. Guide to amenities
58
Poznań International Fair
653
Practical English-Polish
dictionary 299
Pravda, A. 498, 595
Prazmowska, A. 572
Prehistoric contacts of

Kujavian communities
with other European
peoples 75
Preibisz, J. M. 904
Prelude to Solidarity.
Poland and the politics
of the Gierek regime
217
Preserving traces of Jewish
culture in Poland for
the living and the dead
251
Pressure groups 341
Priest who had to die.
Tragedy of Father
Jerzy Popiełuszko
334
Printing 702
Prisoner of martial law 491
Private enterprise in
Eastern Europe 612
Private Poland 357
Private war. Surviving in
Poland on false
papers, 1941-45 189
Proceedings of the third
April conference of
university teachers 291
Professionals, power and
Solidarity in Poland
481
Prout, T. 184
Provisional Government
219
Prussian Poland in
German Empire 114
Przegląd Sportowy 838
Przekrój 839
Public opinion and
political change in
Poland, 1980-82 417
Punk music 777
PUNO see Polish
University Abroad
Pushkin, A. 715
Puzyrewski, P. 623

Q

Question of life: its
beginning and
transmission 360
Question of reality 723

Quo Vadis? 745

R

Rachwald, A. R. 562-563
Radice, E. 627
Radio-active pollution 683
Radio Free Europe 502
Radio in USA 272
Radom 369, 413
Rady, M. 112
Railways 678
Raina, P. 424, 499-500
Rakowski, Mieczysław F. 836
Rambouillet Agreement 578
Ramet, P. 307
Ramsey, P. 570
Ranki, G. 627
Rapacki plan 559
Rapacki, R. 613, 615
Raschke, R. 186
Realism 20, 115, 319, 370
Realism in Polish politics 115
Real Poland: anthology of self-perception 3
Real Socialism 616
Rebirth of History 534
Rebirth of Polish Republic 134
Reception of Copernicus' heliocentric theory 688
Reconstruction of Poland, 1914-23 134
Red Army 206
Reddaway, W. F. 97, 133
Red Eagle. Army in politics 1944-88 218
Red market Industrial co-operation and specializaion in Comecon 663
Reform and insurrection in Russian Poland, 1859-65 122
Reforms of legal and financial system of enterprises in Poland and other socialist countries 623
Reggae 777

Regional studies in Poland 629
Regulski, J. 452
Reinharz, J. 240
Reiquam, S. 501
Reitz, E. 463
Relations between Poland and Sweden over the centuries 602
Religion 305, 338-339 *see* Roman Catholic Church
Baptists 339
Greek Catholics/ Orthodox 340, 343
Polish National Catholic Church 337, 912
Politics 312, 314, 319, 335
Protestants 339
secularization 307, 315
Religious change in contempory Poland 315
Remington, R. A. 425, 905
Remnants. Last Jews of Poland 249
Renaisance 691, 698, 724
Renaissance culture in Poland 698
Renkiewicz, F. 279
Rensenbrink, J. C. 564
Report from the besieged city and other poems 729
Republic of nobles 102
Resistance movements 197, 201
Res Publica 840
Retinger, J. 200
Return to Auschwitz 165
Return to diversity. Political history of East Central Europe since World War II 86
Return to Poland 396
Review of the Polish Academy of Sciences 877
Revolution and tradition in People's Poland 690
Revolution from abroad. Soviet conquest of

Poland's Western Ukraine and Western Belorussia 206
Reykowski, J. 477
Reynolds, J. 142
Riga Treaty 592
Ringleblum, E. 187
Rise of Solidarity 526
Rittner, C. A. 316
Rivers, D. 207
Rivers
Oder 79, 674, 855
Vistula 79, 136, 855
Warta 58
Road atlas of Poland 37
Road to Gdańsk. Poland and USSR 513
Road to Katyń 209
Roberts, Frank 203
Robertson, T. 736
Robinson, W. F. 502
Rock around the bloc 777
Rocznik Polityczny i Gospodarczy 881
Rocznik Statystyczny 643
Rodzińska-Chojnowska, A. 103
Rollo, J. 542
Roman Catholic Church 307, 313-314, 319
Auschwitz convent controversy 306, 316
communist takeover 381
ecclesiastical affairs 846, 848, 854
ideological dialogue with marxism 322
Jerzy Popiełuszko 334-336
Martial Law 309
Maximilian Kolbe 331-33
1989 election 308
Papal visits to Poland 323, 326, 328
Pope John Paul II 310, 323-330
Stefan Wyszynski 311, 320
Vatican 321
Roman Dmowski: party, tactics and ideology, 1895-1907 385
Roman Polański story 795

Romanesque art in Poland
750
Romania 247, 548
Romano, E. 159
Romantic Nationalism 126,
129
*Romantic nationalism and
liberalism* 126
Ronowicz, D. 56, 62
Roos, J. P. 352
Roosevelt, Franklyn D.
608
Roots of Solidarity 482
Rosen, E. 688
Rosen, J. 776
Rosen, M. 407
Rosińska, G. 697
Rostowski, J. 625-626, 635-
636
Rostworowski, E. 95
Roszkowski, W. 631
Rotfeld, A. 565
Roth, J. K. 316
Rothert, E. 5
Rothschild, J. 86
Rottermund, A. 751
Round Table 388, 512
Royal Castle 63, 66
Royal Cathedral at Wawel
757
Royal Way 63
Rozek, E. 561
Rożek, M. 56-57
Rozenbaum, W. 170
Różewicz, Tadeusz 742
Rozwadowski, Tadeusz
136
Ruane, K. 503
Rubinstein, Artur 775
Rubinstein, E. F. 188
*Rule by the people. Study
of local councils* 456
Rupnik, J. 504
Rusiecka, H. 806
Russell-Hodgson, C. 529
Russia 40, 98, 112 *see*
Foreign Relations,
History
interwar relations with
Poland 84, 589
Russian Partition of
Poland 116, 118, 121-
123, 125, 130

*Russia and Eastern
Europe.
Bibliographical guide*
903
*Russian and Polish
women's fiction* 728
*Russia's retreat from
Poland, 1920* 591
*Russia, USSR and Eastern
Europe* 893-94
Ruthenia 255
Rutkowska, J. 65
Rutkowski, H. 6
Ryan, L. 654
Ryback, T. 777
Rychard, A. 346, 361
Rykowski, T. 764
Rysia, 804
Rzeczpospolita 841
Rzepiński, C. 767

S

Sabbat, K. 285
Sachs, J. 632, 637
Sadowski, C. 505, 558
Sagajłło, W. 201
Saga of an European bison
71
*Saint of Auschwitz. Story
of Maximilian Kolbe*
331
St. John-Stevas, N. 328
*St. Mary's Church in
Cracow* 763
Sakwa, G. 95, 453, 578,
586
Salt 33
Salter, M. 45
Samek, J. 762-763
Samplawski, K. 64
Samson, J. 778-780
Samsonowicz, H. 102, 110
*Sanatorium under the sign
of the hourglass* 743
Sandauer, Artur 747
Sanford, G. 419, 426, 506-
509, 529, 540, 543-544,
595, 910
Sas-Skowronski, M. 285
Savile, J. 494
Sawicka, L. 297
Scandinavia 197

*Scapegoats: exodus of
remnants of Polish
Jewry* 233
Schatz, J. 252
Schaufele, W. E. 510
Schild, R. 79
*School strikes in Prussian
Poland* 120
Schopflin, G. 529, 880
Science fiction 720
Scott, P. 729
Scott, Sir Walter 715
Schulz, B. 743
*Scientific writings and
astronomical tables in
Cracow* 697
Sculpture 797, 800
Sebastian, T. 511
Second Partition of Poland
108
Segel, H. B. 698, 744
Sejm *see* Parliament
Sęk, J. 140
Selbourne, D. 512
*Selected English
collocations* 294
Semiotics in Poland 297
Senelick, L. 788
Senn, A. E. 587
September 1939 campaign
141, 145-146
Seven days in Cracow 55
*Seven Polish-Canadian
poets* 730
Sharman, T. 46, 526
Shattered dream 432
Shatyn, B. 189
Shelton, R. 229
Shevis, J. 682
Ships 302
Shmeruk, C. 240
Shohet, N. 772
Shopping 41
Short, A. 721
*Shrine of Black Madonna
at Częstochowa* 762
*Shtetl Jews under Soviet
rule* 250
Shub, E. 746
Shulewicz, U. 746
Siciński, A. 352
Siemaszko, Z. 210
Siemieńska, R. 353, 401

Sienkiewicz, Henryk 267, 745
Sierpiński, Z. 781
Sikorska, G. 317, 336
Sikorski, J. 323
Sikorski, Władysław 194, 203, 284, 566, 592-593
Sikorski Museum 819
Sikorski. Soldier and Statesman 203
Silesia 30
Simmonds, J. 363
Simpson, C. 803
Simon, M. D. 220, 450, 466
Simons, T. W. 87
Simons, W. B. 454
Simons, W. E. 426
Singer, B. 740
Singer, D. 400, 513
Singer, Isaac Bashevis 731, 746
Singer, J. 746
Sisyphus and martial law 469
Si-tien 741
Siwiński, Waldemar, 881
Siwiński, Włodzimierz 655
Skamander 730
Skansens 820
Skendel, E. 275
Skilling, H. G. 427
Skoniecki, Alphonse A. 264
Skowronek, J. 6
Skrzyński, M. 301
Skrzypiński, W. 455
Skurnowicz, J. 126
Skutnik, T. 160
Skwarczyński, P. 97, 573
Slavic excursions. Essays on Russian and Polish literature 715
Slavonic and East European Review 874
Slavs in European history and civilization 82
Slavs, their early history and civilization 82
Śliwa, J. 821
Słomczyński, K. M. 344, 354-355

Słowacki, Juliusz 716, 744
Slowes, S. 209
Śmieja, F. 730
Smith, A. H. 638
Sobell, V. 663
Sobótka, M. 323
Socha, M. 621
Social Democracy of the Polish Republic 560, 844
Social background of Sir Paul Strzelecki and Joseph Conrad 281
Social circles 358
Social forecasting 342
Social policy and ethical issues 361
Aids 359
beginnings and transmission of life 360
Social policy in New Eastern Europe 361
Social and political history of Jews in Poland 245
Social welfare 364-365
health 362
probation services 363, 366
Social welfare in Britain and Poland 364
Social welfare in socialist countries 365
Socialism see Polish United Workers' Party, Politics, Solidarity
Isaac Deutscher 400
Jewish 246
Rise in Poland 115, 129
Russian 118
Soviet 118
Society 356-358
1980s crisis 346
social deviance 347
social groups 341, 348, 351, 353
social mobility and change 342-343
social stratification 344-345, 349-350, 354-55

sociology periodicals 871
urban life-styles 352
Social change and stratification in Eastern Europe 350
Social groups in Polish society 348
Social stratification in Poland 354
Social structure and change. Finland and Poland 352
Social structure and mobility. Poland, Japan and USA 352
Social structure and self-direction 344
Socialist banking and monetary control 649
Socialist corporation and technocratic power 665
Socialist regimes of East-Central Europe, 1944-67 88
Socialist Register 1981 494
Society and deviance in Communist Poland 347
Society for Academic Studies (TKN) 686
Sokol, S. S. 882
Sokolewicz, W. 454, 477
Sokołowska, M. 361
Soldaczuk, J. 657
Soldier and the Nation 442
Soldiers and peasants 258
Solidarity
bibliographies 908
birth 461, 480, 486, 497-498, 502, 520
Civic Committee 308
civic committees 541
congress 1981 509
development, 1980-81 514, 520, 522
during 1980s 477, 479, 495
Fundamentalists 464
influence on Soviet workers 597-598
internal life and organization 467-468,

481-483, 488, 496, 505,
509
international aspects
472, 501, 513
martial law and
underground period
469, 485, 489, 491,
493, 506, 511, 519
obsolescence of 514
political role 1980-81
459, 462, 464-466, 472-
473, 476, 492, 500,
507, 510, 514-516, 519,
526-527, 529
Pragmatists 464
registration dispute 486
relations with Catholic
Church 313
Rural 343
social movement 487,
490, 499, 522
social newtworks 505
values and Christian
ethos 487, 490, 521
Wałęsa, 470, 475-476,
524, 528
War at the Top 541
working-class politics
425
*Solidarity. Analysis of a
social movement* 522
*Solidarity Congress 1981.
Great Debate* 509
*Solidarity: origins and
implications of Polish
trade unions* 681
*Solidarity and other Polish
clandestine
publications* 908
Solidarity and Poland 501
*Solidarity. Poland in
season of its passion*
526
*Solidarity. Poland's
independent trade
union* 488
Solidarity source book 496
*Solidarity and politics of
anti-politics* 495
*Solidarity and the Soviet
worker* 598
*Solidarność. Biblio-
historiography* 908

*Solidarność. From Gdańsk
to military repression*
465
*Some crucial aspects of
IMF adjustment
programs* 646
Soroka, W. 573
Sorokowski, A. 340
Sosabowski, S. 202
Sounds, Feelings, Thoughts
749
South Africa 198
*Soviet-East European
relations.
Consolidation and
conflict, 1968-80* 555
*Soviet policy in Eastern
Europe* 599
Soviet Studies 875
*Soviet takeover of Polish
eastern provinces* 210
*Soviet Union and Eastern
Europe* 880, 895
*Soviet and United States
signalling in Polish
crisis* 551
Spain 402, 432
Spasowski, R. 428
Spirit of Solidarity 521
Spokesman for Civil Rights
447
Sport 815-16
Sprawy Międzynarodowe
876
*Spring in October. Story of
the Polish revolution,
1956* 224
Sproule, A. 2
Square of sky 168
Staar, R. F. 221, 429
*Stabilization policy in
Poland* 646
Stachowicz, J. 664
Staff, Leopold 747
Stalin, Joseph 210, 212,
566
Stalinism 1, 83, 86, 94,
221-222, 226, 420, 611,
634, 703, 748
Stalin's little guest 212
Stallworthy, J. 740
Stanisław Augustus,
King. 751

Stanisław, bishop of
Kraków. 104
Stanisław Lem 720
Stanisławski, J. 299, 301,
304
Staniszkis, J. 346, 392, 514,
545-546
Stankiewicz, W. J. 16
Stanley, D. 45
Starski, S. 515
Stasiewicz-Jasiukowa, I.
699
Staszewski, Stefan 226
Statistics 641-645, 647-648
Stehle, H-J. 222
Stephenson, J. 41
Steven, S. 17
Stevens, H. 593
Stillman, E. 748
Stok, D. 181
Stolot, F. 821
Stomma, S. 91
Stone, G. 298
*Strange Allies. US and
Poland, 1941-45* 608
Street of crocodiles 743
Strikes 369, 502
Strojnowski, J. 883
Strom, R. 207
Strong, J. W. 469
*Structural adjustment
policy* 659
*Structure of fauna of
Warsaw and urban
pressure on animal
communities* 68
Struggle for Baltic markets
569
Struggles for Poland 1
Student organizations 700
newspaper 837
*Studies on International
Relations* 876
Stutthof 160
Strzebielinek internment
camp 491
Strzelecki, J. 522
Strzelecki, Sir Paul
Edmund 281-282
Strzembosz, T. 210
Stwosz, Wit 758
Suchcitz, A. 819
Suchodolski, B. 18, 753

Suchodolski, M. 753
Sudetan mountains 21
Summer before the frost 497
Sunday Times team 325
Supreme Court of Polish People's Republic 455
Surge to Freedom 531
Survey 484
Survival in Auschwitz and the re-awakening 179
Survivor 159
Survivor in us all 188
Sussex, R. 282
Sutherland, C. 127
Swan, O. 189, 298
Swastek, J. 279
Sweden 252, 602-605, 616, 650 *see* Foreign Relations
Swedish contribution to Polish Resistance Movement 604
Świaniewicz, S. 550
Świderska, H. 827
Świdlicki, A. 430-431
Swięchowski, Z. 750
Świerczewski, Karol 432
Świętosławski, W. 699
Sword, K. 203, 210, 286, 318, 547, 574
Symbolism in Poland 754
Syrop, K. 223-224
Sysyn, F. 255
Szafar, T. 233, 375, 516
Szajkowski, B. 319, 490, 544
Szajna, T. 596
Szalai, J. 361
Szczecin 60, 678
Szczecin agreement 461, 499, 502
Szczepański, J. 91, 356, 558
Szczygiel, A. 73
Szczypiorski, A. 517
Szelenyi, J. 546
Szkutnik, L. 295
Szlarski, M. 538
Szpilki 842
Sztandar Mlodych 843
Szulc, T. 24, 518
Szurek, A. 432

Szurek, J. C. 673
Szymanowski, Karol 780-781
Szymański, L. 519
Szymborska, Wisława 722, 725, 749

T

Tabaczyński, E. 656
Taborski, B. 528
Tadeusz Kościuszko 899
Tames, R. 779
Taras, R. 225, 433-435
Tarczyński, Stanisław 281
Tardigrada of Poland 69
Tarkowski, J. 436
Tarniewski, M. 437
Tarnowski, S. 63, 448, 756, 761
Taylor, I. M. 156
Taylor, J. 520
Taylor, Nina 712, 721
Tazbir, J. 95, 102
Teachers 690
Teach yourself Polish 296
Teague, E. 597-598
Tec, N. 190
Teczarowska, D. 212
Terlecki, Marian 881
Terlecki, R. 170
Terry, G. M. 906
Terry, S. M. 566, 599
Theatre 391, 785-788, 878
Theatre in Poland 878
Theatre of Andrzej Wajda 786
Theatre of Grotowski 787
Theiner, G. 749
They shoot writers don't they? 749
Third Eye Centre 752
Thomas, W. I. 257
Thousand hour day 734
Through darkness to dawn 212
Thurley, G. 742
Tighe, C. 230
Times Guide to Eastern Europe 547
Tischner, J. 521
Toeplitz, Krzysztof Teodor 833

Tokarz, Z. 161
To lose a war: memories of a Polish girl 229
Tomaszczyk, J. 197
Tomaszewski, J. 88, 238, 631
Tomaszewski, M. 782
Tomczak, F. 675
Tomiak, J. 529
Tomlinson, C. 749
To New York, Chicago and San Francisco 268
Topolski, J. 6, 98, 102
Torańska, T. 226
Toronto 260
Touch of earth. Wartime childhood 168
Touraine, A. 522
Toruń 335
Towards Poland 2000 342
Tracing your Polish roots 811
Trade 652-58, 661
Trade unions 472, 482-483, 498, 681-682, *see also* Solidarity
Tradition of Polish ideals 16
Tranda, B. 339
Transborder data flows and Poland 658
Trans European North-South railway connections 678
Transplanted family 273
Traugutt, Romuald 116
Travel guides
cheap travel 45
for Polish-Americans 49
for the young 44
national 39, 41-42, 45-48
Travels with my sketchbook 40
Treece, P. 333
Trevisan, D. 476
Triska, J. F. 454
Trotskyism 246
Trudnowski, W. 58
Trybuna 844
Trybuna Ludu 844
Trzeciakowski, L. 128
Trzynadlowski, J. 825

245

Tsars, Russia, Poland and Ukraine 112
Tukhachevsky, Mikhail 132
Turaj, F. 791, 793
Turek, W. 914
Turkey 605, 618
Turzo, Jan 702
Twain, Mark 291
Twentieth century Polish theatre 785
Twenty One Demands 497, 526
Twierdochlebów, W. 908
Twilight of French Eastern Alliances 579
Twórczość 845
Tydzień Polski 828
Tygodnik Mazowsze 823
Tygodnik Powszechny 322, 846
Tygodnik Solidarność 847
Tymieniecka, A. 709

U

Uganda, 396
Ukraine
influence of 1980-81 Poland 598
nationalism in 19th century Galicia 253-254
relations with Poland 112, 605
Soviet occupation of West Ukraine, 1939-41 206
Ukrainians in Poland 31, 253-255, 765
Ukrainian national movement in Galicia 254
Unconventional archaeology 79
Unequal Victims. Poles and Jews during the Second World War 176
Unierżyński, J. 59
Union of Lublin in the Golden Age 101
Union of Soviet Socialist Republics see Foreign Relations

agriculture 675
attempted assassination of John Paul II 327
bibliographies 887, 893-895, 903, 907, 910
border disputes with Poland 31
Comecon links 663
economic reforms 611
geography 22-23
Gorbachev and collapse of Soviet power 372, 381, 393
handbook 880
moral and social issues 360-361
Polish community in 289-290
relations with Poland
interwar 84, 131-132, 135-136, 139, 199
postwar 86-89, 98, 134
Second World War 141-144, 146, 170, 191-192, 198, 203, 205-213, 250
Russian books abroad 824
Soviet-type economies 640
Woman's fiction 728
United Evangelical Church 339
United Nations 658
United Nations University 616
United States *see* Foreign Relations
cooking 804
dissertations on Polish subjects 911
industrial co-operation with Poland 656, 661
libraries and archives 817
newspapers and journals 823-24, 834, 865, 869, 886
Polański's career in USA 795
Polish-American tourists 49

Polish community in 256-257, 261-280, 337, 775
Sienkiewicz for Americans 745
social & cultural comparisons with Poland 344, 355, 391
United States and Poland 610
Universities, today and tomorrow 693
University Teachers of English 291
Unplanned society. Poland during and after communism 358
Upper Silesia 229
Uprisings
November 1830 121, 125
1863 122
Warsaw 1944 16, 191-192, 198, 205, 284
Urban ecology in planning 34
Urban, Jerzy 832
Urbański, M. 674
Ursus tractor plant 369
Uses of Adversity 463
USSR 360-61, 449

V

Vale, M. 523
Valedictory 734
Valkenier, E. 596
Vallee, L. 491, 736
Values and violence in Auschwitz 157
Van Duren, P. 285
Vasa dynasty 106
Vatican 321, 846, 854
Vatican and Poland in age of Partitions 321
Verb valency in contemporary Poland 297
Versailles Peace Conference 134-135, 609
Vietnam 434
Village without Solidarity 343

Vischer, M. 456
Vitry, H. 802
Voices in the gallery 749
Volyńska-Bogert, R. 909

W

Wadekin, K-E. 675
Wajda, Andrzej 181, 528,
786, 789, 791-792, 794
Walek, J. 755
Walendowski, E. 438
Wales 283
Wałęsa, Lech 464, 470,
475-476, 524, 528, 541,
847
Walicki, A. 91, 113, 129,
392, 525
Walker, G. 910
Wallace, W. 621
Walshaw, R. 188
Walshaw, S. 188
Wałtos, S. 457
Wandycz, P. S. 130, 567,
577, 579, 610
Wankel, C. 700
Wapiński, R. 203
Ward, P. 47
*War Hitler won: fall of
Poland, September
1939* 141
Warhol, Andy 766
*War of the doomed: Jewish
armed resistance in
Poland, 1942-44* 178
*War through children's
eyes. Soviet occupation
of Poland and the
deportations, 1939-41*
207
Warmia 30
Warnock Committee 360
Warsaw 47, 711
bibliographies 889
fauna 68
guides 61-66
interwar 228
Jews in 234
medical academy 687
Old Town 66
Royal castle 63, 66
University 29, 75, 363,
535, 621, 687, 771

uprising 16, 191-192,
198, 205
Warsaw as it was 64
*Warsaw between World
Wars* 228
*Warsaw children's hospital
and Jewish resistance*
181
Warsaw. A concise guide
61
Warsaw diary, 1978-81 723
*Warsaw Ghetto; a
Christian's testimony*
164
*Warsaw Ghetto in
photographs* 175
*Warsaw Ghetto:
photographic record*
175
Warsaw Medical Academy
687
Warsaw Pact 438, 540, 555
Warsaw Rising of 1944 191
Wasilewski, J. 439
Wat, A. 211, 705
Watson, J. 287
Watson, M. 346-347
Wawel 54, 57, 617, 683,
757
Wawel Castle 54
Wawrocki, R. 48
Way of Hope 524
*Ways of life in Finland and
Poland* 352
Ważyk, Adam 703
Weber, B. 782
Weber, K. 465
Weber, Max 256
Wedel, J. 357-358
Węgierski, J. 210
Weitz, R. 600
Wejnert, B. 700
Welfe, W. 639
We lived in a grave 188
We live in Poland 2
Wellisz, L. 650
Wellover, M. 811
Wereszycki, H. 95
Werfel, Roman 226
Weschler, L. 485, 526
Wesołowska, E. 701
Wesołowski, W. 352
Wesołowski, Z. P. 812

West, K. 805
Western Institute 872
Western Territories 26-28,
30
Westfal, S. 298
Westoby, A. 440
We the people 530
Weydenthal, J. B. de. 441,
527
Weygand, Maxime 136
*When light pierced the
darkness* 190
*White Eagle, Red Star.
Polish-Soviet war,
1919-20* 132
White, P. 24
White, S. 426, 450, 540
Whitefield, F. J. 300
Who's Who in Poland 884-
85
*Who's Who in the socialist
countries* 883
Why learn Polish? 298
Wiatr, J. J. 442, 458, 477
Wielewiński, B. 911-12
*Wieliczka. Seven centuries
of Polish salt* 33
Wieniewska, C. 517, 528,
732, 736, 743
Wierzbicka-Michalska, K.
788
Wieviorka, M. 522
Wiewiórski, L. 699
Więź (The Link) 311, 322,
418, 848
Wigura, S. 676
Wilczek, M. 48
Wiles, T. 138
Wilk, M. 485
Willey, D. 329
Williams, G. H. 330
Wilno 587
Wilson, R. K. 583
Wilson, T. 363, 366
Wine trade (medieval) 618
Winiecki, J. 619, 640
*Winter in the morning.
Young girl's life in the
Warsaw Ghetto and
beyond* 165
Wirkowski, E. 806
Wisconsin 271
Wiskemann, E. 30

Wisłok 343
Wiśniewski, J. 884
With Fire and Sword in modern translation 745
With the skin. Selected poems (Wat) 211
Witness. Life in occupied Kraków 184
Witness of poetry 736
Wittenberg-Stalewski, A. 651
Włocławek 75
Wnuk-Lipiński, E. 345-346
Wodarski, John P. 262
Wojciechowski, H. 653
Wojciechowski, S. 60
Wojnowski, T. 49
Wojtasiewicz, O. 98
Wojtowicz, J. 295
Wojtyła, Karol *see* John Paul II
Wolff, L. 321
Wolfram, K. 38
Wolfram-Romanowska, D. 653
Women
fiction 728
in contemporary Poland 351
poetry 722
social movements 353
Women and social movements in Poland 353
Women in contemporary Poland 351
Woodall, J. 414, 529, 665
Woolf, S. 179
Workers' Defense Committee 413, 443, 483, 489, 499
Workers' participation 680
Working Group of Experts 480
World cinema. Poland 789

World index of Polish periodicals published outside of Poland since September 1939 893
Worstynowicz, W. 33, 263
Woytak, R. 568
Wozniuk, V. 601
Wprost 840
Wright-Wexman, V. 795
Writing home 256
Wróblewska, D. 769
Wrocław 67, 787
Wrocław, Lower Silesia, Poland 67
Wroński, B. 819
Wynar, L. R. 886
Wynot, E. 228, 549
Wyszyński, Cardinal and Primate Stefan 310-311, 320, 726
Wytrwal, J. A. 280

Y

Yalta 203, 550, 607
Year 1990 639
Year of martial law. Cartoons by Andrzej Krauze 407
Young, J. 752
Youth hostels 41
Youth in chains 159
Ystradganlais 283
Yugoslavia 395, 647

Z

Zabielska, J. 913
Zaborska, M. 19
Zachwatowicz, J. 66
Zajdlerowa, Z. 212
Zaleski, Auguste 552
Zaleski, M. B. 521
Zalewski, W. 824, 826, 909
Zaloga, S. 146, 204

Zamoyski, A. 99, 139, 745, 783-784
Zamoyski, Count Władysław 52
Zand, H. S. 274
Zanussi, Krzysztof 789, 791
Zaremba, P. 34
Żarnowski, J. 20, 140
Zawadzki, J. 796
Zawodny, J. K. 205, 213
Zbylniewski, D. 659
Żegota 184
Żelazowa Wola 65
Żeligowski, Lucjan 132, 587
Zeman, Z. 89
Zgoda 886
Zięba, W. 320
Ziegfeld, R. 720
Zieliński, J. 666
Zielonka, J. 443
Zielonko, J. 420, 737
Ziemska, M. 363
Zimmer, S. 702
Zionism 180, 246, 248
Zionism in Poland 248
Zmijewski, N. 322
Zmroczek, J. 827
Znak (The Sign) 311, 322
Znaniecki, Florian 256-257
Zochowski, S. 575
Żołnierz Rzeczypospolitej 849
Zolobka, V. 914
Żółtowski, A. 31
Zubrzycki, J. 258, 282
Żuzowski, R. 413
Żwirko, F. 676
Zwornik school of painting 767
Życie Gospodarcze 850
Życie Literackie 851
Życie Warszawy 852
Żygulski, Z. 756

English equivalents of Polish place and geographical names.

Cassubia	Kaszuby
Cracow	Kraków
Cuyavia	Kujawy
Greater Poland	Wielkopolska
Lesser Poland	Małopolska
Lower Silesia	Dolny Sląsk
Masuria	Mazury
Mazovia	Mazowsze
Neisse	Nyssa
Oder	Odra
Podlachia	Podlasie
Pomerania	Pomorze
Upper Silesia	Gorny Sląsk
Vistula	Wisła
Warsaw	Warszawa

Map of Poland

This map shows the more important towns and other features.

es